Screening the Operatic Stage

EXPLORATIONS IN HISTORY, TECHNOLOGY,
AND PERFORMANCE

A series edited by David J. Levin and Mary Ann Smart

ADVISORY BOARD

Carolyn Abbate
Gundula Kreuzer
Emanuele Senici
Benjamin Walton
Emily Wilbourne

ALSO PUBLISHED IN THE SERIES

Music in the Present Tense: Rossini's Italian Operas in Their Time
Emanuele Senici

*Singing Sappho: Improvisation and Authority in
Nineteenth-Century Italian Opera*
Melina Esse

Networking Operatic Italy
Francesca Vella

"Don Giovanni" Captured: Performance, Media, Myth
Richard Will

New Orleans and the Creation of Transatlantic Opera, 1819–1859
Charlotte Bentley

Screening the Operatic Stage

TELEVISION AND BEYOND

Christopher Morris

THE UNIVERSITY OF CHICAGO PRESS
CHICAGO AND LONDON

The University of Chicago Press, Chicago 60637
The University of Chicago Press, Ltd., London
© 2024 by The University of Chicago
All rights reserved. No part of this book may be used or reproduced in any manner
whatsoever without written permission, except in the case of brief quotations in
critical articles and reviews. For more information, contact the University of Chicago
Press, 1427 E. 60th St., Chicago, IL 60637.
Published 2024
Printed in the United States of America

33 32 31 30 29 28 27 26 25 24   1 2 3 4 5

ISBN-13: 978-0-226-83127-5 (cloth)
ISBN-13: 978-0-226-83129-9 (paper)
ISBN-13: 978-0-226-83128-2 (e-book)
DOI: https://doi.org/10.7208/chicago/9780226831282.001.0001

This book has been supported by the General Fund of the American Musicological
Society, supported in part by the National Endowment for the Humanities
and the Andrew W. Mellon Foundation.

Library of Congress Cataloging-in-Publication Data

Names: Morris, Christopher, 1966– author.
Title: Screening the operatic stage : television and beyond / Christopher Morris.
Description: Chicago : The University of Chicago Press, 2024. | Series: Opera
   lab: explorations in history, technology, and performance | Includes
   bibliographical references and index.
Identifiers: LCCN 2023029703 | ISBN 9780226831275 (cloth) |
   ISBN 9780226831299 (paperback) | ISBN 9780226831282 (ebook)
Subjects: LCSH: Simulcasting of opera. | Operas—Film adaptations—History
   and criticism. | Operas—Television adaptations—History and criticism.
Classification: LCC ML1700 .M78 2024 | DDC 782.1/154—dc23/eng/20230626
LC record available at https://lccn.loc.gov/2023029703

♾ This paper meets the requirements of ANSI/NISO Z39.48-1992
(Permanence of Paper).

To the memory of my mother,
Vivienne Christine Foster

Contents

List of Figures ix

INTRODUCTION 1

PART 1

1: SCREENING THE STAGE/STAGING THE SCREEN 25

2: SPLIT LOYALTIES 57

PART 2

3: WHAT TIME IS IT IN NEW YORK? 91

4: YOU ARE HERE 109

5: YOU ARE MORE THAN HERE 125

6: YOU ARE NOT HERE 137

PART 3

7: HOSTS AND GHOSTS 161

CONCLUSION 185

Acknowledgments 193
Notes 195
Bibliography 231
Videography 249
Index 251

Figures

Figure 1 PBS advertisement in the *Philadelphia Inquirer*, April 12, 1980. 2

Figure 2 Marketing image, OperaVision.eu. 3

Figure 3 Web page, OperaVision.eu. 5

Figure 1.1 *Das Rheingold*, director, Frank Castorf, 2016 (original production, 2013). 33

Figure 1.2 *Das Rheingold*, director, Frank Castorf, 2016 (original production, 2013). 33

Figure 1.3 *Siegfried*, director, Frank Castorf, 2016 (original production, 2013). 34

Figure 1.4 *Tannhäuser*, director, Tobias Kratzer, 2019. 36

Figure 1.5 *Tannhäuser*, director, Tobias Kratzer, 2019. 37

Figure 1.6 Catherine Malfitano and Maria Callas, "Vissi d'arte." *Tosca*, director, Christophe Honoré, 2019. 41

Figure 1.7 *Das Rheingold*, director, Frank Castorf, 2016 (original production, 2013). 42

Figure 1.8 *Das Rheingold*, director, Frank Castorf, 2016 (original production, 2013). 42

Figure 1.9 Froh (Tansel Akzeybek). *Das Rheingold*, director, Frank Castorf, 2016 (original production, 2013). 43

Figure 1.10 *Das Rheingold*, director, Frank Castorf, 2016 (original production, 2013). 44

Figure 1.11 *Das Rheingold*, director, Frank Castorf, 2016 (original production, 2013). 44

Figure 1.12 Tannhäuser (Stephen Gould). *Tannhäuser*, director, Tobias Kratzer, 2019. 46

Figure 1.13 Tannhäuser (Stephen Gould). *Tannhäuser*, director, Tobias Kratzer, 2019. 47

x | FIGURES

Figure 1.14 Isolde (Anja Kampe). *Tristan und Isolde*, director, Dmitri Tcherniakov, 2018. 47

Figure 1.15 Tannhäuser (Stephen Gould) and the Young Shepherd (Katharina Konradi). *Tannhäuser*, director, Tobias Kratzer, 2019. 48

Figure 1.16 *Tannhäuser*, director, Tobias Kratzer, 2019. 50

Figure 1.17 *Die Walküre*, director, Frank Castorf, 2016 (original production, 2013). 51

Figure 2.1 *Written on Skin*, director, Katie Mitchell, Royal Opera House, 2013. 63

Figure 2.2 *Written on Skin*, director, Katie Mitchell, Festival d'Aix-en-Provence, 2012. 64

Figure 2.3 Angel 1/the Boy (Bejun Mehta). *Written on Skin*, director, Katie Mitchell, Royal Opera House, 2013. 66

Figure 2.4 The Protector (Christopher Purves) and Angel 1/the Boy (Bejun Mehta). *Written on Skin*, director, Katie Mitchell, Royal Opera House, 2013. 73

Figure 2.5 *Judith*, director, Katie Mitchell, Bayerische Staatsoper, 2020. 75

Figure 2.6 *Judith*, director, Katie Mitchell, Bayerische Staatsoper, 2020. 76

Figure 2.7 Bluebeard (John Lundgren) and Judith (Nina Stemme). *Judith*, director, Katie Mitchell, Bayerische Staatsoper, 2020. 76

Figure 6.1 Lucia (Anna Netrebko). *Lucia di Lammermoor*, director, Mary Zimmerman, 2009. 148

Figure 6.2 Lucia (Anna Netrebko). *Lucia di Lammermoor*, director, Mary Zimmerman, 2009. 148

Figure 7.1 Rigoletto (Plácido Domingo) and Marullo (Giorgio Caoduro). *Rigoletto in Mantua*, director, Marco Bellocchio, 2010. 168

Figure 7.2 *Rigoletto in Mantua*, director, Marco Bellocchio, 2010. 168

Figure 7.3 Rigoletto (Plácido Domingo). *Rigoletto in Mantua*, director, Marco Bellocchio, 2010. 169

Figure 7.4 Rigoletto (Plácido Domingo). *Rigoletto in Mantua*, director, Marco Bellocchio, 2010. 170

Figure 7.5 *La bohème im Hochhaus*, director, Anja Horst, 2009. 173

Figure 7.6 *La bohème im Hochhaus*, director, Anja Horst, 2009. 173

Figure 7.7 *La bohème im Hochhaus*, director, Anja Horst, 2009. 178

Figure 7.8 *La bohème im Hochhaus*, director, Anja Horst, 2009. 179

FIGURES | XI

Figure 7.9   Rodolfo (Saimir Pirgu) and Mimì (Maya Boog). *La bohème im Hochhaus*, director, Anja Horst, 2009. 181

Figure 7.10 Rodolfo (Saimir Pirgu) and Mimì (Maya Boog). *La bohème im Hochhaus*, director, Anja Horst, 2009. 181

Figure 7.11 Musetta (Eva Liebau) and Marcello (Robin Adams). *La bohème im Hochhaus*, director, Anja Horst, 2009. 182

Introduction

"Pull up an easy chair," reads the copy of a 1980 newspaper advertisement for PBS, "because this week you can see San Francisco Opera's 'La Gioconda' starring Renata Scotto and Luciano Pavarotti in the comfort of your own home" (see fig. 1). On offer, the banner text promises, is nothing less than "the best seats in the house," a sketched illustration of which occupies the center of the advertisement: two armchairs, both facing forward, flank a table with a lamp. Their occupants will not be facing each other, it seems. Instead, they will look at something implied but unseen in front of them. It is of course a television set, the event in question a telecast of a performance (together with "making of" documentary) taped in September 1979 and now presented, one act per night, on PBS. The advertisement caught the attention of Peter Conrad, who reads it as indicative of something about the two media forms it promotes. "One of television's favours to us," he writes, "is to make everything as easy as watching television." That includes something as apparently difficult to produce as *La gioconda* (the copy refers to the insight the telecast will offer into the "agonies of rehearsals") and as forbidding and alien as opera ("you don't have to be an opera buff"). Instead, as Conrad puts it, all that spectacle and noise will be packaged neatly in a box and will unfold in a "flatteringly" depicted domestic space: "That room, the box's auditorium, is now the measure of the event it temporarily contains."[1]

Fast-forward (or drag the playback cursor) some forty years, and note how much and how little has changed. A banner image welcomes visitors to the website of OperaVision, the EU-funded streaming platform developed by Opera Europa. Shared on social media as part of a promotional campaign, the image is a richly composed photograph depicting an über-chic domestic interior with bookshelves, a contemporary fireplace, and a designer chair. In front of the chair a book rests on a footstool, beside it an unopened bottle of red wine. On one side of the image a text insert

FIGURE 1. PBS advertisement in the *Philadelphia Inquirer*, April 12, 1980.

FIGURE 2. Marketing image, OperaVision.eu. © Opera Europa. Used by permission.

reads "Your opera house" (see fig. 2). The contrast is stark. Viewed next to the sketched late twentieth-century interior of the 1980 advertisement, the OperaVision image suggests a historical gap far greater than a few decades. And that gap is widened by the realization that the device for watching and listening, missing from the image just as it was in 1980, is no longer a single apparatus but a range of possibilities, none of them explicitly pictured. Leaping from the analog telecast era of the PBS advertisement to OperaVision's digital ecosystem, we encounter the living room as host for a range of screen devices on which the chair's occupant will summon a production on demand via a wireless signal. "Maybe you are casting on a TV," reads the post accompanying the image on Facebook, "or tapping on a tablet, or typing on your laptop."[2] The device, that is, might be the flat-screen descendent of Conrad's box, but only in its "smart-TV" guise as another streaming device. Between the two living rooms and bypassed completely is a whole generation of physical media and their associated devices—VHS, laser disc, DVD—that were, for a while, the mainstay of remediated opera but are now consigned, the OperaVision promotion suggests, to the media museum (together with the print media that hosted the PBS advertisement). Finally, not to be overlooked, two seats have given way to one: the image of the television set as proxy fireplace in a familial/shared domestic setting gives way to the solitary monitoring of screen media, very possibly in tandem with glances at other images and devices. The duet in front of the screen becomes the dual-screening individual.

Still, awareness of these disparities—of this shock of the new—needs to be tempered by acknowledgment of continuity. Evident in both promotions is what Conrad calls *flattery* and what the marketing profession might term *lifestyle advertising*. If the earlier advertisement offers a mainstream, even retro/nostalgic representation of a living room that taps into something middle-class, suburban, and prosperous in a tellingly PBS manner, the second appeals to a target viewer as hip, urban apartment dweller with an eye for design (the same design chic that will adorn the stages of many of the productions featured by the platform). The pitch, that is, is different, and that pitch may magnify the apparent historical gulf between the two, but the advertisements share a strategy of imagining a domestic space that is the reader's space or the space to which the reader aspires. And, thanks to technology, that space enters into a magical, commodified exchange with the auditorium of the opera house. In a temporary transformation—cued by the bottle of wine, one wants to say transubstantiation—your living room becomes your opera house.

This book is about that transformation: as imagination, desire, technology, rhetoric. It is about how spaces other than the opera house *become* the opera house, how screens and speakers both contain and channel opera's sights and sounds, presenting them with an apparent immediacy that nourishes a pleasurable fantasy of virtual presence, sometimes "not quite" and sometimes "more than" the real thing it models. It is a transformation delicately poised, an invitation with reservations attached. For it is almost exclusively the companies devoted to the staging of opera in opera houses that issue this invitation, and they typically do so as a means of enhancing their primary mission of performing opera in the theater. This is not to say that opera companies are uninterested in the generation of content specifically for screen media (OperaVision, e.g., hosts commissioned video shorts) or in the potential for generating revenue from video productions (the productions I consider are overwhelmingly available commercially). Yet, as the OperaVision project manager Luke O'Shaughnessy puts it, the platform is a "promotional tool" for the art form developed with the goal of encouraging audiences to attend opera.[3] As a *New York Times* feature on the *La gioconda* telecasts points out, much the same strategy informed that project. The project, the host Tony Randall is quoted as saying, is "a blatant attempt to seduce you to the pleasures of opera, to initiate the opera-shy step by step."[4]

YOUR OPERA HOUSE

Part of this initiation, if the imagery in the advertisement is anything to go by, is the comforting emphasis on the familiar opera house in the living room rather than the one in San Francisco, just as OperaVision emphasizes ownership: "your opera house." Conrad observes that the "gaudy trinketry of the opera house" is nowhere to be seen in the PBS advertisement.[5] But this is hardly representative of the promotion and packaging of opera telecasts more generally. Understood as a form of "initiation," as Randall puts it, telecasts interface between the home and that other opera house. In fact, the marketing and promotion of opera on screen media cannot get enough of the gaudy trinketry. Advertising copy framed by theatrical curtains and elaborate proscenium arch outlines is a recurring theme in the print promotion of opera on television, and the packaging of physical media has often connoted ornamentation and luxury.[6] The telecasts themselves have for decades insisted on framing the performance with establishing shots of the grand exterior of the house followed by a selection of angles of the audience assembling in their ornate—and, at the very least, plush—surroundings.

As for streaming, witness the banner image from the "about us" page of the OperaVision website (see fig. 3). It is a panoramic shot of the upper balcony of the Hungarian State Opera showing its golden classical columns, spectacular chandelier, and frescoed ceiling. Welcome, it seems

FIGURE 3. Web page, OperaVision.eu. Photograph by Atilla Nagy © Opera Europa. Used by permission.

to say, to *the* opera house. As primary domesticate space for leisure, the living room has occupied center stage in this exchange between locales. Having once afforded pride of place to the television set, the living room now accommodates engagement with other screens and devices. But the mobility of those devices undermines the privileged role of the living room as site of engagement, instead offering invitations to a night or day or moment at the opera from wherever we happen to be. Two additional images in OperaVision's "your opera house" promotion map out these forms and spaces of access explicitly: one depicts a laptop sitting on a desk, the other a young woman viewing her phone in a café.[7] And now the movie theater, once the privileged site of a screen apart, dresses up as an opera house for live transmissions.

This slippage or mutability between opera houses imagined and real is one of the issues I address in this book, particularly in part 2. To do so means confronting a term that comes with considerable theoretical baggage: *presence*. From the *bodily copresence* summoned by the theater scholar Erika Fischer-Lichte as definitional of performance to the post-structuralist critique of the *metaphysics of presence*, and from the remote operation of physical objects dubbed by Marvin Minsky *telepresence* to the *presence effects* that, according to Hans-Ulrich Gumbrecht, precede meaning, this is a term that gets around.[8] How the rhetoric around—and the grammar and conventions of—opera telecasts, DVDs, and streams discursively negotiates presence is revealing of the cultural, even ideological territory they articulate, occupy, and reinforce.

Whether understood in the classic formulation of the impression of "being there" or in that of the corollary of a "there" that comes "here," presence emerges in the economy of opera and screen media as at once what is lacking and a problem overcome, at once what is contested and contestable. When Matthew Lombard and Theresa Ditton define *presence* as the "illusion of nonmediation," they touch on one of the problems this book must confront.[9] For the spatial imaginary I have described plays out against, perhaps triggers, a tension between the very possibility of presence and the foregrounding of the mediation that produces it. This tension is what the theory of *remediation* articulated by Jay David Bolter and Richard Grusin helps identify. Remediation, the incorporation of one medium into another, is characterized neither solely, Bolter and Grusin insist, by an immediacy that renders the process transparent nor by an opacity that foregrounds media and reveals the process at work. Rather, they argue, the two tendencies oscillate in dialectical tension with one another. The claim to immediacy implies an authenticity, even superiority, that draws attention to the new medium *as medium*, while what they call *hypermediacy* asserts

INTRODUCTION | 7

its own reality (its own mediality) but does so with a sensory surplus—
Bolter and Grusin write of a "satiety of experience"—conducive to a mode
of engagement that is direct, authentic, and immediate.[10]

Conrad marvels at the assertive pitch of the PBS advertisement and what
he identifies as its claim to improve on the original by retaining opera's
signature features—spectacle, song, raw emotion—without the discomfort and expense. "With superb effrontery," he writes "television doesn't
apologize for its denaturing of the object but contends that the offending
article . . . has been bettered in the process." Television, in his reading,
occupies a privileged place in the wider media economy, and it shows
in the confidence with which it bends source material to its remediat-
ing will. Like television sports coverage, opera on television becomes, in
this view, no apologetic or submissive—let alone transparent—copy of
a preferred original; rather, it refashions in its own terms and in a way
that makes a spectacle of its own means. I offer sports as a comparison
here because its coverage shares with opera telecasts the apparatus of
live multicamera production and the medial grammar developed by and
through that apparatus: the multiple simultaneous perspectives—from
above, from afar, close-ups, zooms—presented via an edited sequence of
cuts. We should not—and this book cannot—overlook this grammar *as*
an intervention, a hypermediate transformation of the original. Television
and its streaming descendants have a way of picturing opera, just as they
do sports, and I want to address its syntax and assumptions to understand whether and how this intervention might be understood, in Conrad's terms, as a distortion or a greedy colonization. As we shall see, other
critics, less troubled by screen remediation, wonder whether television's
confidence is justified. This is the point made by Steve Wurtzler when he
observes that attending sports in person—no replays, no close-ups, save
for those provided by giant screens on site—becomes "a degraded version
of the event's televisual representation."[11] Could it be, as some critics have
suggested, that the screen copy of opera does indeed offer a form of presence that is somehow "more than" its original? That the original might
come to seem disappointing or lacking?

SELF-OBLITERATION

But what if the almost manic hypermediacy of multicamera production—
and here is the twist articulated by Bolter and Grusin—authenticates its
own reality, becomes *immediate*? How, they ask, is hypermediacy affected
by familiarity, which allows viewers to "look through" media conventions.[12] In this case the "effrontery" identified by Conrad becomes its op-

posite: the televisual appropriates and colonizes not by asserting its power to intervene but precisely by donning the cloak of transparency, by naturalizing itself. The grammar of multicamera television has not remained static historically, but its conventions have evolved only slowly, and it has endured and proliferated over decades and across multiple genres: not only sports and theater but also current affairs, talk shows, sitcoms, and soap operas. In opera, this grammar, introduced by television and preserved and redisseminated on physical media, has survived the transition to streaming and to live screening in cinemas, both of which still mobilize the same production apparatus and the editing techniques associated with it. Not only do they inherit and recall the historically developed grammar of multicamera television; they also share its personnel. Gary Halvorson, the director of ninety-nine transmissions in the *Met: Live in HD* series at the time of writing, is also an experienced director of award ceremony telecasts and sitcoms (including fifty-five episodes of *Friends* and sixty-one episodes of *Everybody Loves Raymond*).[13] This overlap is not unique to this series or to the Met: the history of telecasts of opera on stage is a history of multicamera direction.[14] The same "outside broadcast" units that park outside sports stadiums park outside opera houses. (*Outside broadcast* is the term applied to all nonstudio productions.) Lining the walls of these mobile units and linked to cameras and microphones in the venue are the same monitors and mixers, operated by some of the same personnel.

This is not to say that the production of opera on screen has not developed its own grammar or identity, or that directorial practice has not modified over time, or even that individual directors or production teams do not impose a certain authorial stamp. But the coherence of this grammar—its availability to meaning—depends on a degree of familiarity and an appeal to convention: the perspectives implied by camera position, the number and range of shot types, the cutting rate. Questioned about the impact of new technologies and resources (high-definition images, cranes, remotely operated cameras), the multicamera director Brian Large dismissed what he called "toys" and stressed the historical continuity of the "grammar" and "technique" of shooting staged opera with a multicamera setup.[15] If his claim that much has remained unchanged since the era of black and white risks flattening out some important developments over time (not least the ability of cameras to function without customized stage lighting), his insistence on a televisual continuity is nevertheless persuasive.

And although Large does not reference multicamera television production outside of opera, the familiarity of models, from sports telecasts to sitcoms shot in front of audiences to breakfast television and talk shows, only reinforces the point that this is a form readable because familiar. It is a form predicated on investment in the televisual capacity to bear witness with apparent immediacy, preserving intact the event it captures despite splitting it into discrete, synchronically fed perspectives and reassembling them diachronically in a live editing process. As John Ellis argues, this quality of multicamera production defines televisual practice: "The use of several cameras and the possibility of alternation between them produces a style of shooting that is specific to TV: the fragmentation of events that keeps strictly to the continuity of their performance."[16]

But there is more than convention and familiarity at work in this transparency. Contrast Conrad's view with what Stanley Cavell had to say about opera and screen media. Impressed with how staged performances are handled by television, Cavell wonders whether, quite unlike the "boredom" he associates with opera films, his positive response stems from a sense that television honors the "foreign conventionality" of the theater and is willing, in effect, to get out of the way?[17] This is precisely the attitude evident in the rhetoric of the practitioners involved in these productions. Multicamera directors, for example, demonstrate acute awareness of the ways in which the form of what is unfolding on stage determines how they direct. Jonathan Haswell, who has directed multiple productions for the Royal Opera House's *Live Cinema Season*, draws attention to the differences between the grammar for shooting opera and that for shooting ballet. If opera invites tightly framed shots with occasional cuts to wider angles to provide context, ballet demands quite the reverse: here it is the "medium-wide angle" that predominates, with close-ups possible only when dancers are "in repose."[18] But, above all, what comes to the fore in the rhetoric multicamera directors use to describe what they do is a belief that a measure of success is for their work to go unnoticed. Here is "transparent immediacy" not merely as the outcome of familiarization with a visual grammar but as a conscious strategy of concealment. Speaking on a panel in an event devoted to the *Met: Live in HD* series, Large defined his practice in polite, collegial, almost deferential terms: "You have to say to yourself 'I need to respect, first of all, the music; I need to respect the librettist; I must respect the performer—performers—the conductor, the production, and the audience.'"[19] This is language that arguably undervalues the sometimes powerfully mediated intervention in the work of this most prolific of multicamera directors of opera telecasts (including six productions of *The Met: Live in HD*), but it may tellingly reflect the compact at work in remediated opera in two ways.

First, the attitude adopted by multicamera directors in opera needs to be situated within a wider televisual discourse. In a classic text that has stood as one of the manuals of television production, Desmond Davis wrote: "The best technique highlights that which is important, eliminates that which is unimportant and obliterates itself by its own perfection."[20] This ideal of "self-obliteration" has been highlighted recently, for example, by the success of live transmissions of spoken theater in cinemas, a development that has confronted practitioners, critics, and scholars alike with newly urgent questions about what these transmissions do.[21] "Our aim is to film your performance, not shape your performance for film," the video director Tim van Someren assures the cast of the National Theatre's *This House* in rehearsal for an *NT Live* transmission.[22] His colleague John Wyver, the director of the *RSC Live* series, articulates his approach to stage directors in similar terms: "It's terribly important from my point of view that the stage director always feels that what I'm doing is collaborating with him and trying to get in my terms what he would want if he was directing the cameras."[23] And Nick Sabel, the former head of digital at the United Kingdom's National Theatre, cites the National Theatre artistic director, Nicholas Hytner, in his account of the role of the video production: "Nick says it's like filming a sports match; you take the audience's eye to where the ball goes. If we've done our job, you should feel you saw a piece of theatre, not a film, even though there were probably lots of close ups where the director was choosing what you see."[24]

If these seem like new issues for spoken theater (which has historically been subsumed in the form of television drama and not telecast live from the stage), they have a longer pedigree in opera. Yet here too the emergence of transmissions to cinemas has focused attention on the work of multi-camera direction, and here too there is a rhetoric of self-obliteration. As Halvorson puts it: "Precisely because I have directed a lot myself, including all those sitcoms, I have respect for what the opera director does. . . . The production is separate from me; it is done for the stage. Period."[25] Haswell acknowledges the potential contradiction of an intervention that conceals itself but nonetheless maintains a self-effacing stance: "I see my job as to generate engagement and to attempt—and I know this is naïve of me—but to attempt to do that in a way that appears as though there is no mediation. So, I want to become totally invisible, so that the viewer's attention, their emotional focus, is entirely on the performers."[26] This desire for invisibility is not without consequences: as André Gaudréault and Philippe Marion argue, multicamera directors can find their work consigned to a supplemental space, their role robbed of agency. What these directors are associated with, they conclude, "is neither more nor less than a plastic interpretation of So-and-So's opera, directed by Someone Else."[27]

This leads me to a second observation about the compact at work in remediated opera. Multicamera directors may express a desire for invisibility—they may seem, that is, to assume willingly a role marked by service to others—but it also the case that the nature of the agreement between broadcasters and opera companies dictates the status of their work. Outlining what he regards as the Met's "cautious" approach to video production, Martin Barker observes that, with the exception of backstage interviews and features, *The Met: Live in HD* "almost consciously avoids adding much."[28] Barker is not alone in observing that something carefully contained is being presented here. If television—and now computer screens and cinemas—has offered the platform on which staged opera is remediated and disseminated, it relies for its content on the cooperation and willing participation of the producers of opera: no opera on stage, no content. This partnership has amounted to a form of permission granted by the host: set up the cameras and microphones as unobtrusively as possible, and record a live event that will take place whether this apparatus is present or not.[29] True, accommodating cameras in early telecasts involved compromise—the television director Kenneth A. Wright recalled having to install "six great floodlights . . . that turned night into day"—but the default value has always been discreet surveillance, a mode of production further facilitated in recent years by the introduction of remotely operated cameras. These are the terms of engagement, if *engagement* is even the right word for what is an afterthought to an already-completed stage production. That is, the attitude of respect that Large and others articulate may represent a willing acceptance, but it is equally a necessity, perhaps a choice born of necessity. Either way, the result is the same: a modesty of ambition supported by a rhetoric of deference and fidelity. Could it be, however, that this modesty is what has allowed remediated opera to proliferate, to endure, and to amass, thanks to physical media, a back catalog of three thousand commercial titles, not to mention an ever-expanding (mostly pirated) archive on YouTube?[30] Is it, picking up on the dialectic articulated by Bolter and Grusin, precisely the transparency of this compact that licenses remediated opera to become a medium in its own right? The question of this medial identity is one of the core concerns of *Screening the Operatic Stage*.

TELEVISION/TELEVISUAL

When Large stresses the enduring nature of the techniques and grammar of his craft, he identifies a historical continuity with its roots in an era dominated by broadcast television. Though always niche, the live and delayed telecast of complete staged performances of opera from major houses formed, together with telecasts of orchestral performances and ballet, what was once termed *cultural* programming. Beginning in the 1950s, but peaking in the last two decades of the twentieth century, broadcasters—especially state-funded entities like the BBC (the United Kingdom), NHK (Japan), RAI (Italy), and ZDF (Germany) but also commercial operators like NBC (the United States)—built on the model of live radio broadcasts to offer a televisual alternative, often in parallel (simulcast) with radio transmissions of the same performance.[31] The last two decades of the twentieth century represent a high-water mark for this kind of programming: if hardly a regular feature, opera was no stranger to the television schedule either. But this was not to last. Prompted in part by new conceptions of their role (especially the need to diversify their audience), of the kind of programming that serves that role, and of what counts as culture, broadcasters revisited their mandates. Opera, in effect, lost its privilege(s) with state and mainstream broadcasters and found itself increasingly represented by specialty and subscription channels, backed up by regular releases of commercially available DVD titles based on those telecasts.

Something else began to happen then too. In a development scholars have dubbed *postbroadcast television* or even *posttelevision*, the monopoly of signal-based transmission (first analog, then digital) was broken by streaming technologies (both live and on demand) based on Internet technologies and protocols.[32] There was now a new way to disseminate and access content, and there were new devices—laptops, phones—on which to view and hear that content. True, as the OperaVision promotion implicitly acknowledges, the television set has fought back in the form of the smart TV (and streaming devices that plug in or cast to the TV), effectively transforming itself into a digital hub that combines the function of television set and computer.[33] But in the postmillennial media ecology this kind of convergence is accompanied by fragmentation: audiences can choose from multiple platforms and devices to view and hear programing once available only as broadcasts, and broadcasters are already preparing to replace signal transmission with streams. The device that once screened the telecasts of opera no longer occupies center stage in the home; indeed, we no longer need to be at home. Yet, as Large rightly observes, the forms and conventions established by the telecasts endure in these new forms of dissemination. Television as a specific apparatus is fading, but the *televisual*—a term that connotes the extension of characteristics, values, and aesthetics beyond the confines of specific technologies or media—will be an important focus for *Screening the Operatic Stage*.[34]

Outside the book's remit is the history of new operas commissioned for television and their digital-era successors in work commissioned for online dissemination.[35] This is a history and a repertoire that have already been considered in the scholarly literature, and, although worthy of further investigation, they raise issues—how the media characteristics of television/video predetermine the gestational process, how librettists and composers collaborate with screen-media producers—that are distinct from those that concern me here. Nor is *Screening the Operatic Stage* a history of televised opera. Although it considers some historical practices and precedents, it does not seek, for example, to chronicle the emergence of live television broadcasts of staged opera or trace the development of a market for opera on home video. This is not to question the value of or need for historical investigation of this kind—far from it. While a substantial body of literature has attended to opera in filmic form (i.e., operas produced and shot as films) and to opera's historical encounters with cinema more broadly, the history of the television broadcast and video recording of staged opera is only beginning to receive the attention it deserves.[36] This historical project, in other words, still requires much work, but it is a task I leave to others for now. My interest here lies in more conceptual territory: in definitions of media and creative roles in the context of opera's encounter with the televisual, in the rhetoric of presence and liveness that accompanies opera on screen, in the conventions of camerawork and sound, and in the sites and circumstances of engagement with screens and speakers.

It is a project much aided by some of the richly cross-disciplinary scholarship devoted to the visual and sonic syntax of televised opera. Informed by scholarship on media, television, and theater, and supported by close readings of some of the productions that now form a substantial archive on DVD and online, this body of work has begun to articulate a vocabulary and a critical framework to attend to conventions, their development, and their subversion.[37] One of the themes that emerges from these studies is the value of attentiveness to a reflexive media economy in which stage productions reflect or anticipate their own remediation. Aware, that is, of the kind of oscillations highlighted by Bolter and Grusin and of stage practices increasingly saturated (for better or worse) by screens, scholarship on remediated opera has drawn attention to a playful exchange and self-awareness between stage and screen. This relationship is something I will foreground in *Screening the Operatic Stage*, in part because of its prevalence, and in part because it illustrates explicitly a wider and sometimes less evident reflexivity.[38]

Spending time watching video remediations of the operatic stage—and I have perhaps done more of this than anyone really should—has made me aware, too, of the need to think carefully about the practices and practitioners associated not only with multicamera production but also with the technologies and environments that form part of the screening of that stage. True, this is not an ethnography of spectatorship. I do not, for example, engage at length with participant observation (although I try to explain how my experience has shaped my thinking about remediated opera); nor do I mobilize empirical research to map or document spectatorial experience.[39] I am interested, rather, in the extent to which screens and speakers, projections and headphones, and the images and sounds of playback extend, amplify, or undermine the production values and assumptions of production and recording.

When I refer to these environments as part of the *apparatus* of remediated opera, I do not mean to suggest a technological determinism in which forms of spectatorship are shaped by the environment and technology of the encounter in a one-way process, still less by the classic "apparatus" theory associated with film studies, which presented the submissive spectator as a subject passively enmeshed in an ideologically driven "machinerie de rêves" (machinery of dreams), as Jean-Louis Comolli put it.[40] I am, however, interested in the extraordinary diversification of modes and environments of spectatorship that has accompanied the remediation of opera, especially in the last twenty years. The apparatus theory articulated in the *Cahiers du cinéma* in the 1960s paid comparatively scant attention to television, but, when it did so, it presented the medium as a reinforcement of all that was troubling, ideologically, about the cinematic apparatus.[41] An earlier and rather different view in the journal is to be found in Comolli's 1966 essay "Notes sur le nouveau spectateur," which ponders the effects of the movie theater's darkened auditorium. Is there not critical resistance, he asks, in the fact that television is typically viewed in an illuminated environment?[42] I cite this observation in part because it has a bearing on the question of the televisual apparatus of remediated opera. Just as cinema has found new homes outside the darkened auditorium, so the video recording of the opera stage has relocated from its original home on the television set to screens much larger and smaller. And, just as the attentive spectatorship promoted by the movie-theater environment has given way to what Francesco Casetti calls the *logic of the display*, so remediated opera finds itself windowed on a computer desktop and streamed in bite-size chunks to any number of mobile devices.[43] This is something OperaVision understands when it promotes an anywhere-anytime vision of opera. The productions I consider are viewed on screens from the largest scale (outdoor relays to public plazas) to the smallest (a window in the operating system of a phone), through tiny earbuds or through arrays of speakers, and in environments from the most public to the most private.

What, this book asks, are we to make of this new plurality of environments, its diverse scales and forms of interface? In what ways, I ask, might this diversity encourage us to rethink image composition (e.g., close-ups) and audio mix (stereo or surround sound, matched to visual perspective or independent of it)?

A STRANGE HOMECOMING

The question of cinematic relocation—of film's departure from the auditorium—has a corollary in the live transmission of opera to cinemas. Here is a development indebted, as I have suggested, to the televisual apparatus of remediated opera but one that relocates the televisual screen to, of all places, the darkened environment of the movie theater. Unpacking the implications of *this* relocation—was the stage screened in the movie theater not filmed in a darkened opera house?—is one of the priorities of *Screening the Operatic Stage*. Now into their second decade, but still without an agreed-on name, live opera transmissions to cinemas—what I will call *cinecasts*—continue to occupy a strangely liminal space in our media economy. They cut an odd figure among the typical fare of the multiplexes that host them. I was reminded of this when, during a *Met: Live in HD* cinecast, I felt a vibration beneath my feet. It was the subwoofer of an adjacent cinema signaling an on-screen explosion or the approach of some immense spaceship and a reminder that the audiences in the theaters around me were immersed in sensory and narrative experiences that belong, in more ways than one, to other worlds. If I needed any confirmation of this outsider status, it came when I was interviewed by a journalist looking for input from an academic for an article he was writing on the cinecast phenomenon for a national newspaper. Although he had never attended a cinecast, he volunteered that he and his friends had seen a number of trailers in the movie theater and found them "hilarious." It did not occur to me at the time to ask what, in particular, he found so amusing, but I admit that seeing cinecasts in the movie theater and seeing their trailers in the context of movie trailers is jarring. Is it something about the televisual quality of the image? The close-ups of opera singers at full throttle? The theatricality—and, in the case of the Met, a dated, cheesy theatricality? Or is the journalist seeing something that I, habituated as I am to opera, have lost the ability to see?

Hilarious or not, opera cinecasts have attracted a small but thought-provoking body of scholarship.[44] Opera, however, has no monopoly on cinecasts. If live broadcasts of spoken theater historically failed to gain traction on television in the way opera did, the same cannot be said of cinecasts. The Metropolitan Opera may have been a pioneer in live transmission to cinema, but theater has developed a considerable profile and now commands some of the most impressive attendance figures, at least for certain individual performances, if not necessarily cumulatively.[45] Perhaps unsurprisingly, the success and unexpected endurance of this new form (or is it a medium?) have attracted considerable interest among theater and performance studies scholars, who bring with them a range of perspectives and methodologies, not least the well-developed scholarly discourse on liveness, presence, and the evental quality of theater.[46] One of the questions this body of work poses for *Screening the Operatic Stage* is its relevance to opera. Is there, in other words, something specific— beyond their obvious differences as genres—about the way theater and opera are remediated for cinecasts? And what do they share?

OPERA HEARS ITSELF

We can try to articulate a phenomenology of film sound, Steven Connor argues, but it will not be *of* the film because sound will always belong somewhere other than the *à voir* of film, somewhere belated and other to film's domain of seeing.[47] A possible exception to this otherness, Connor concedes, might be found in music, which at times "allows the film to hear itself, allows hearing itself to rise into self-consciousness." Yet even here, he retorts, we must contend with a disjunction: "Music does not come from cinema's mouth, from the mouth of the screen, from the speaking lips."[48] The video remediation of staged opera seems to complicate and reconfigure Connor's claims in at least two ways. First, video, unlike film, is a properly *audiovisual* medium rooted in the electromagnetic media of radio and telephony, not in photochemical process. Second, in remediated opera, music indeed comes, as it were, from the mouth of the screen, from the *singing* lips. If these observations are true, is it not then the case that video (telecast, on tape) properly honors and accommodates opera as sound and vison? Is it not a properly operatic medium?

Not so fast, say the critics. In a piece for *The Atlantic* in 1983, Lloyd Schwartz identified what he considered television's weakness as a medium for opera. Sound quality, he observed, "is the reason a lot of opera lovers refuse to watch opera on television."[49] In the same year, *New Scientist* ran a feature on attempts by the consumer electronics industry to address the "poor sound" on home videocassettes and players with the introduction of "Hi-Fi" standards.[50] In the crosshairs here is not the medium of video per se but its commercial implementation via technologies of transmission, storage, and playback. That these concerns were still circulating (and still without immediate resolution) when the compact disc had already been introduced and after decades of high-fidelity refinement associated with the long-playing record suggests a significant gap between the sound quality of video/television and that of audio-only technologies. Introduced in the immediate postwar period, the LP had a decisive impact on the availability of complete recordings of opera. Here at last, at thirty-three rpm and thirty minutes a side, was a medium capable of accommodating operatic time spans in a practical way. Labels embarked on a series of recording projects, and a substantial catalog of opera recordings emerged. And all this was in parallel with broadcasts of complete performances of opera on radio. Despite the niche appeal and the monopolization of three hours of programing, live broadcasts of opera were already a well-established feature on radio by the mid-1930s. By the 1980s, radio had also considerably refined the audio quality of the broadcasts. No surprise, then, that Schwartz points to radio simulcasts as the only way to tolerate opera on television.

LPs and radio seemed to offer, in what Senici calls the era of the "medial 'musicalization' of opera," a viable alternative or substitute for opera in the theater.[51] In short, they refashioned opera as music. What matter if they came at the cost of seeing opera when seeing was such a compromise? Samuel Chotzinoff, the head of NBC's music division, wrote in 1946: "The limitation of radio in the matter of sight proved actually to be an asset. . . . Who ever said that opera was ridiculous? It certainly was not over the radio."[52] Now, the distractions of staging could be replaced by the imagination, the irritations of poor seats and fellow spectators by visceral, concentrated engagement. "Listening to these records," Andrew Porter wrote in 1959 of the famous Culshaw-produced *Ring*, "is not just like going to the opera house without looking at the stage. In some mysterious way they seem to catch you up in the work—not in a particular set of performers—more intimately than that."[53] That the televising of concerts had generated language like this seems less surprising. Writing in the same volume as Chotzinoff, Herbert Graf, the director of the NBC Opera at the time, anticipated an ongoing concern when he worried that producing a telecast of an orchestral performance generated a conflict between the televisual need for something "visually sufficient" and the risk of distracting from the predominantly sonic appeal of concerts. Are close-ups of laboring musicians not, he asks, in fact "disconcerting"?[54] Drawing a clear distinction between concerts and what he calls *visual* forms, Graf concludes that televising opera and ballet raises no such issues. Yet the musicalization of opera via sound recording and radio, with its promise of a purity of experience, suggests that even here the perceived compatibility with seeing, with visual media, is no given. Against this backdrop, opera on television and video could be read as a double compromise: both sound quality and purity of experience were tarnished.

The arrival of the DVD format in the 1990s and the improvement of sound technologies in television (including the introduction of stereo and digital transmission) would address the issue of quality and fidelity. Does the DVD not represent a kind of digital *Gesamtkunstwerk* capable of accommodating the treasured sonic fidelity of the LP and CD but now combined with the stage image, itself much improved? Yet, as I will show, this ideal union of music and image raises questions of its own. Sound may seem to come from the lips on screen, to return to Connor's imagery, but the synchronization of sound and image in production is a complex process, its artificiality exposed when a continuity of sonic perspective contradicts varied and contrasting visual perspectives. And consider the sound mixes offered on DVD, a format developed not only with the home viewing of feature films in mind but also as a means of bringing cinematic listening into the home. What, I will ask, are the implications for opera on DVD of the almost default availability of a surround-sound mix, something that it inherited from those feature films and that it now shares with opera cinecasts?

OPERA SEES ITSELF

I want, as well, to consider an inversion of Connor's argument, to ask whether video might raise *vision* in opera to self-consciousness—whether, that is, remediation might allow opera to see itself or at least to see itself anew. I add this last qualification in anticipation of an obvious objection: that opera has long seen itself. A medium in which spectacle has played such a central role—in the case of baroque opera or grand opera, self-consciously so—is not blind to its specular elements and effects. Accounts by critics and other spectators have borne witness, throughout opera's history, to the pleasures of seeing. They have also highlighted the perils of seeing: we need only summon the history of calls for operatic reform—calls often predicated on perceptions of spectacular excess—to encounter evidence of a medium aware of how it looks and unhappy with what it sees (the musicalization of opera to which I referred above is arguably one extension of this critique). And what of the history of visual representation of opera: of set designs and maquettes, of *livrets de mise en scène* and *disposizioni sceniche*, of costume sketches and publicity photographs of singers in costume? In short, if opera has always been seeing itself—

representing and scrutinizing itself visually—what is new about the self-awareness made possible by video?

One possible answer is that the substantial market and audience for opera on video (at least by operatic standards) has made possible a circulation of imagery that has significantly affected opera's visual economy. Video's role in the production of opera is in part a functional one: video recordings represent important in-house documentation to facilitate future remountings, while closed-circuit transmission as part of the production process facilitates visual communication, for example, between conductor and singers or stage manager and stage. But *Screening the Operatic Stage* concerns itself with a more public circulation of video. It asks what commercial video—on tape, on disc, broadcast, and streamed—has done to foreground opera as a visual medium and what form that visuality has assumed. It takes the view that, unlike the still images and ekphrastic accounts that have constituted the visual record historically, this video-based visual economy has raised the stakes of visual awareness by recording and circulating movement, gesture, unfolding—in short, the temporality of spectacle.

Video production, that is, processes and mediates opera's unfolding as performance, as a playing out of theater and music. It can suspend the event, prolong a moment, and accelerate a duration. It also edits, frames, refocuses, and rescales bodies and scenography, often in ways that elide its own intervention. It is at once bound by the constraints of what it represents (camera positioning, e.g., tends to be discreet in order to avoid disrupting a live performance) and free to reconfigure it (takes can be spliced together from performances on different nights). Technological limitations, convention, and commercial imperative restrict what is possible or at least what is done in the production process. In playback, these restrictions can elicit pleasure (a close-up unavailable to the live audience) and frustration (an angle that excludes something apparently important from the frame) in equal measure. And playback introduces freedoms and constraints of its own: of the possibilities and limitations of specific environments and technologies, of engagement and distraction in the absence of the commitment that the seat in the auditorium seems to demand, of attachment to an event brought into intimate focus and detachment from an event made remote, of things concealed and unveiled. As image resolutions improve, the stakes are raised even higher: now video can relay the stage in forensic detail, a capacity that can equally enthrall or sweep any remnants of illusion away, that can motivate or (as we shall see) terrify performers. Video, in other words, tantalizingly offers too much and too little; it supplements and detracts; it reveals all, only to reveal its own limitations. What video shows and what it conceals or reframes matters in the (trans)formation of operatic vision.

Part 1 of this book addresses this question of how opera sees itself in video by focusing on two types of reflexive encounter between stage and video production. In chapter 1, I confront the proliferation of video projection on stage in recent productions, unpacking the implications of the mobilization and configuration of the moving image. But I do so by attending to the ways in which these onstage screens are themselves remediated for screen when the productions are broadcast or streamed. The mise-en-scène of these stage productions, I argue, assigns a certain theatrical agency to projected video, effectively casting it in roles associated with contemporary image gathering (surveillance, documentary, narrative), modes of engagement (attentiveness, monitoring, distraction), and the materiality of screens (scale, texture). But how, I ask, does the video remediation *of* this stage register video *on* the stage? Does it see itself in these videos? Or are we encouraged merely to look *through* one screen in order to look *at* another?

Chapter 2 considers what has become a recurrent theme or concept in contemporary opera staging: grids of compartments or boxes, each representing a different space (and, in some cases, a different time). Here, the video director is confronted with a problem: this multiplicity of spaces forms a spatial montage that seems to demand simultaneous visibility of all its parts. But this is a demand that the video production can fulfill only at the expense of its own grammar. The stage seems to ask, that is, for a static wide shot, when multicamera production is predicated on a sequence of cuts between shots of various angles and proximities—on a temporal montage. But the video director is also confronted with something familiar. Is the grid of compartments, with its multiplicity of perspectives and spaces, not a likeness of the bank of monitors in front of which she practices her craft?

I have remarked on the strangely liminal cultural and conceptual space occupied by the cinecasts, the focus of part 2. What to make, for example, of the special trappings of the cinecasts (ushers showing patrons to their seats, printed programs, provisions for intermissions)? Perhaps this in-betweenness has something to do not just with movie theaters and multiplexes but with some of the other locations cinecasts temporarily occupy. I am thinking of how *The Met: Live in HD* is screened in performing-arts venues that at other times host in-the-flesh opera productions, as though these venues served as conduits or sites of exchange in a proper Bolter-and-Grusin-style dialectic of remediation. And what are the implications of the experience of *The Met: Live in HD* when US West Coast audiences attend a morning at the opera? Focusing on the much-promoted liveness of the cinecasts, chapter 3 addresses the concept of distant simultaneity: that the now of New York in one of the *Met: Live in HD* transmissions is imagined to be my now in Dublin even though I am near the end of the day and New York is still in the middle. This international now—it is not quite global because the hour will be an unsocial one in many parts of the world—is one of the tricks the cinecasts learned from satellite television broadcast, which is effectively what they are, despite the cinematic pretense. Less televisual and, I argue, still strikingly odd is the cinecast network of theaters: literally and figuratively satellite audiences. Struck by this juxtaposition of the familiar and the strange in the cinecasts, I investigate this networked now as articulated in Metropolitan Opera transmissions of a much-traveled and much-repeated production of *La traviata*.

The remainder of part 2 considers various states or intensities of presence implied and signaled by the cinecasts. Taking their bearing from a phrase designed to provide locational bearing on a map, chapters 4–6 ask how the cinecasts, at once keen to signal their capacity to bridge distance and to preserve the aura of the "actual" experience, solicit and limit the experience of presence. Chapter 4 reads the presentational rhetoric, camerawork, and sound as invocations of the message "You are here." But the commitment to immediacy and impact, evident above all in the work of close-ups, takes on a particular quality and intensity given the scale of the image, just as the sonic resources of the movie theater are mobilized as an immersive imaginary. This impression of immediacy, I will argue in chapter 5, is put into the service of the message that you are in fact *more than* here. Finally, what if this presencing needs to be contained or simply fails? What if the mediated space of the cinecasts is punctured by awareness of the place the spectator occupies, of a locale, a movie theater, that is not anonymous and transparent but asserts its own immediacy? And what if the collective sense of audience emerges not from the globalized network but from the bodies occupying seats right here. The message that you may in fact *not* be here is the topic of chapter 6.

If cinecasts encourage the viewer of remediated opera to get out of the house, site-specific productions allow opera to get out of its house. Fashionable but problematic, site-specific production provokes criticism of the superficiality of the choice of location and definition of concept. It has also exposed the producers of opera to charges of exploitation and elitism and in terms often more fraught than the barbs typically hurled at opera when it remains in its native space. Part 3 examines how screen media have been mobilized in two trilogies of site-specific operas conceived for television. With the resources of multicamera production and multimicrophone recording at their disposal, these productions are liberated to go where they please—even to the actual locations imagined in the libretto—and redefine opera's spatial imaginary. But camerawork and recording, image and soundscape, have a familiar ring, as though the site in question turned out to be none other than the opera house—or, rather, the opera house as remediated and imagined in countless telecasts, as archived on tape and DVD, and now enjoying a third life in streamed form on the web. The screens that offer to set opera free from the opera house also bring it back there, as though affirming the lure of opera's home.

Part 1

CHAPTER ONE

Screening the Stage/ Staging the Screen

Interviewed for a promotional feature presented on the Bayreuth Festival's online platform, the video artist Manuel Braun reflected on his role in the 2019 production of *Tannhäuser*, directed by Tobias Kratzer. His task, he suggests, is to convince skeptics who will inevitably dread hearing about his participation: "There are always those who will say 'There's a video designer, damn! This is going to be a very modern production. Couldn't we just let the music speak?'"[1] Far from a sign of insecurity, Braun's anticipation of resistance to video on the stage suggests familiarity with a long-standing hostility to a trend regarded by many critics as a creative fad. "Multimedia," wrote Lyn Gardner in *The Guardian* in 2006, "is a word I've come to dread in the theater. There was a period around five years ago when you could hardly step inside a theater to see a new play without encountering a bank of video monitors."[2] Diedrich Diederichsen recounts the similarly exasperated tone of a Berlin critic, who wrote already in December 2003 of her wish for the new year that the Berlin Volksbühne might resist using video projections just once.[3] Opera, meanwhile, has its own history of fascination with and resistance to stagings with video. The Toronto critic Peter Goddard wrote in 2008 of "opera's video projection fetish," quoting the director Astrid Janson on the "fashionable" use of "large projections, particularly in Wagner."[4] As part of the online publicity associated with its 2014 production of *Don Giovanni*, the Royal Opera House invited public debate via Twitter and web on the merits of what it called opera's "embrace" of video projection.[5] The reactions range from warm enthusiasm for what one commentator called "Opera 2.0," to qualified approval based on careful avoidance of overindulgence, to hostility that suggests opera's embrace of video projection is emphatically resisted by many in the audience.

Right or wrong, the skeptics are losing the battle: video's colonization of the stage (operatic and otherwise) continues apace, reinforced by technologies that streamline the production of video content and enhance the methods and appearance of projection.[6] This is not, however, to dismiss the video turn (if we can call it that) as a mere expediency underpinned by the availability of new methods and means. At their most compelling, these new practices suggest a recalibration not only of the materials but also of the terms of scenography. True, opera audiences will by now be wearily familiar with what sometimes feels like the inevitable video backdrop tracing some backstory or the projection that adorns a minimalist set, accompanying a scene of reverie with arty nature footage. But clichéd conventions suggest a wider poverty of imagination, pointing to a wider performative failure that does not necessarily hinge on video projection per se. Nor is it necessarily helpful to map these practices onto the kind of binary model proposed by Greg Giesekam, who distinguishes between, on the one hand, the critical and reflexive mobilizations of visual media associated with what he calls *intermedial* theater and, on the other, the mere embellishment and expansion of conventional mise-en-scène characteristic of multimedia applications of video on the stage.[7] Applied to opera's already-overdetermined media economy, these neat distinctions, as Tereza Havelková points out, have a way of blurring under scrutiny. To suggest that video projection merely supplements or extends opera's audiovisual or representational compact is to confer a certain coherence and stability on that compact—qualities that, as Havelková and others are at pains to point out, cannot be assumed.[8] Rather, video projection on stage can be understand to form another strand in opera's tangled weave, what David Levin describes as its "unruly surfeit of expressive means."[9]

Now to tangle the weave further. The three case studies that inform and underpin this chapter are televised or streamed remediations of opera-house stagings that themselves feature projected video. Each stage production references contemporary screen and video practices (social media, surveillance, computer desktops, dual screening) in ways that connect the stage reflexively to a wider audiovisual economy. The stage is at once a space occupied and shaped by screens—what Casetti calls a *screenscape*—and a representation of contemporary screen practices.[10] And all this is itself then telecast or streamed onto other video screens. This kind of reflexivity is not necessarily typical, as I observed above, but it offers a particularly vivid instance of an exchange operating more widely, even if less obviously. I want, that is, to interpret these case studies as acute iterations of issues that attend remediated opera more generally. If what we encounter here is a visual economy of staged opera, it is equally a *tele*visual economy, one shaped by the apparatus of multicamera production. This is true not only in the case of televised opera and its distribution on DVD but also in that of cinecasts and streams, which retain much, if not all, of this televisuality (the camerawork, the grammar of editing).

The relationship between staged opera and the televisual is no model partnership because it is typically no partnership at all. Owing to brief encounters (camera crews are typically guests on borrowed time) and a lopsided power dynamic (multicamera directors are strictly supplemental to the already-completed work of stage production), the video remediation of opera is rarely a collaboration, let alone a coherent project. I want to consider three of the issues that have haunted the relationship, and I present them as emblematic of the conflicted role multicamera production plays, at once respectful guest in the opera house and richly resourced apparatus with its own conventions and ambitions. I view these issues, in other words, as symptomatic not of creative cross-purposes (say, between stage director and multicamera director) but of juxtapositions of systems and means of showing, and of the contingencies of production that facilitate and limit what is possible.

The first might be called the *problem of duplication*: if video remediation is merely an encounter with an already-completed creative project, what we witness in the case studies featured in this chapter is video of video.[11] Do these video productions not flatten out the interaction of bodies and screen images on stage so that everything becomes an image? What does this encounter tell us about video remediation more widely, and is this merely an economy of loss or of reimagined theater? The second issue pivots on the collapse of theatrical distance: zoom lenses, the big guns in the multicamera arsenal, bring the stage and its occupants near—too near we are told repeatedly by critics. What are the implications of a video image that looks too closely at a video image, and how does this exposure expose the incompatibility between theatrical and televisual ways of seeing? Finally, by closing in on the stage, typically in combination with rapid cuts between perspectives, remediated opera leaves much outside the frame, something about which critics have complained endlessly. When video projections become, in effect, parallel scenes running behind, or on, or in front of the stage, what do the ever-active, ever-mobile cameras of the televisual apparatus capture, and what do they miss?

PARALLAX PERSPECTIVES

Arguably, no theater practitioner has done more to foreground the potential—and, many critics will counter, the limitations—of video on stage than Frank Castorf, whose long tenure as the artistic director of the Berlin Volksbühne is almost synonymous with the use of monitors and

28 | CHAPTER ONE

projections. For Marvin Carlson, the patterns of integration between stage and video evident in Castorf's productions raise the technological and aesthetic stakes by suggesting a whole new level of sophistication in the relationship between mediatized and nonmediatized images. Citing Thomas Oberender's distinction between *Einspielung* (the use of prerecorded video) and *Live-Produktion* (the live screening of video captured on camera in the theater), Carlson argues that the "hall of mirrors" effects of these emerging practices foreground new dimensions of critical spectatorship, ones that invite us to reexamine not only our engagement with video but also the very idea of "seeing" the actor or stage directly.[12]

Acutely aware of Castorf's practice and reputation, Bayreuth critics were unsurprised that his *Ring*, which weaves a loose narrative of rampant oil-based capitalism into a contemporary environment awash with consumerist paraphernalia, would assign video such a prominent role. Castorf duly obliged. All the hallmarks of his Volksbühne stagings are there: stages dominated by large edifices (what Birgit Wiens describes as "multilevel stage architectures")[13] stuffed with minute detail reminiscent of a film set, projection screens and monitors situated on the stage immediately above or integrated into the mise-en-scène, camera crews roaming the stage and peering intrusively at the actors, and action occasionally visible only via the live relay. If the foregrounding of the means of production broadly suggests a Brechtian politics of distantiation, Castorf has presented himself as a critic of what he regards as the Brechtian orthodoxies of theater in the German Democratic Republic (where he spent his early career). If there is a model for the video practices on Castorf's stage, it is, rather, the collage and montage techniques of Piscator's *Totaltheater*, even if, as Andreas Englhart notes, Castorf would cast doubt on the credibility of the *Überblick* (overview) that Piscator had associated with the presence of media on the stage.[14]

What is at stake, according to Castorf, is an engagement with realism summed up in the title of a collection of essays sponsored by the Volksbühne: *Einbruch der Realität*, meaning at once an invasion and a collapse of reality. Part of the invasion, as the video director and Castorf's longtime collaborator Jan Speckenbach puts it in his contribution to the collection, comes in the form of live video. If fixed cameras amount to a discreet apparatus of surveillance, the roving camera crews suggest an avowedly intrusive, voyeuristic tracking of subjects that draws on familiar media forms (reality TV, news gathering). But, Speckenbach adds, this entry of documentary reality in fact offers "citations of reality" only in ways that effectively defamiliarize both the language of television and that of theater. Edited in collage fashion, and displayed on screens positioned to juxtapose planes of stage and video presentation, the video feeds, according to Speckenbach, lose the "reality effect" associated with documentary television, while close-ups of actors and stage serve only to expose the materialities of makeup and paint in ways quite removed from the illusionist stage tradition that underpins theatrical realism.[15] And, as soon becomes clear, the refusal of unified perspective embodied in the incongruity of visual planes is matched by conflicting narratives: video and live action occasionally offer divergent accounts of the reality of what is happening on stage. Peter Boenisch likens the deployment of video on Castorf's stage to a "parallax" effect in which images appear to take on different forms depending on the perspective of the viewer. In its refusal to allow either stage or video alone to stand for reality, he argues, Castorf's practice offers a theatrical parallax, one that situates the spectator in a conflicted space between irreconcilable perspectives, between truths, between media.[16] Here, in other words, is another critical take on vision in the theater.

Layering this parallax theater onto the already-dense media economy of opera raises questions about saturation and perceptibility. Doing so in the cluttered territory of a Bayreuth *Ring* cycle—the most overdetermined work in the operatic repertoire at the most cultish of venues staged by a provocateur notoriously hostile to unified *Konzept* or even interpretation—was bound (and calculated) to generate controversy. The critics duly obliged. Amid the broader hue and cry about the *Stückezerstörer* (destroyer of pieces), critics singled out the problem of sensory overload.[17] "By directing the attention at stage and screen simultaneously," wrote Martin Kettle for *The Guardian*, "Castorf distracts from the music and words."[18] It was a view shared by many critics. Anthony Tommasini of the *New York Times* wrote that "the live videos, though involving, become very distracting,"[19] while the critic for *Der Standard* expressed annoyance that Castorf's "flood of images" made it "difficult to concentrate on listening."[20] The critic for *Spiegel Online* summarized the effect as "music and singing drowned in a flood of images,"[21] while Peter Hagmann of the *Neue Zürcher Zeitung* complained of *Das Rheingold* that "the screens add to the already complex network of levels in Wagner's music theater—one that particularly absorbs attention and makes listening difficult."[22] Some went further, alleging that the very essence of theater was under threat. In his review of *Götterdämmerung*, Hagmann went on to declare the deployment of video in the *Ring* depressing on several counts: close-ups of the singers reminded him of opera consumption in the movie theater and the roving cameras of the omnipresence of video in contemporary life, while glimpses backstage betrayed the essential secret of theater, "which knows a curtain behind which one should not be able to look."[23] Reflecting on his attendance at and reviews of performances of the Castorf *Ring* over several years, Mark Berry writes of the struggle, both at the time and even on mature recollection, to process such a saturated production: "Just how many narratives or standpoints on narratives could we see, let alone take in, simultaneously?"[24]

THE TELEVISUAL RECLAIMS ITS OWN (EPISODE 1)

What, then, to make of Castorf's practices when they are themselves remediated as video? Although cameras were occasionally invited into the Volksbühne during his tenure—his productions *Des Teufels General* (1997) and *Dämonen* (2001) were telecast—the televisual apparatus has historically played a more prominent role *on* the Castorf stage than in front of it. The Bayreuth Festival, on the other hand, echoed the wider enthusiasm in opera for live multicamera telecasts and recordings, and Castorf's *Ring* was a not unlikely vehicle for an encounter between onstage and offstage cameras. The production would have to wait, however, until the 2016 iteration of the cycle and a partnership between the festival and Sky Arts that would see the *Ring* screened on Sky's network of cable/satellite channels in Germany, Austria, Italy, the United Kingdom, and Ireland while the productions would remain available for streaming from its on-demand platforms.[25] That Castorf's *Ring* draws heavily on live projection of stage action might be read, at least retrospectively, as an anticipation of its own remediation. The visual grammar of much of the video footage displayed on stage resembles amateur reality videos characteristic of streaming platforms like YouTube, the very sites where pirated copies of the production have long been available. Meanwhile, the means of presentation on stage—deploying screens large and small, projectors, and monitors—foreshadows the range of devices and presentational media on which the production will be viewed. It is as if the Bayreuth audience had already been presented simultaneously with the two spectatorial registers that dominate opera today: in the opera house and in front of a screen.

But this impression of a collaborative encounter is nothing more than retrospection. Like almost all video productions of its kind, the telecast of the *Ring* was not a creative partnership but a supplement to a theatrical fait accompli. True, as Berry reminds us, changes were introduced each year the production was performed, in keeping with the festival's *Werkstatt* (workshop) principle of dramaturgy and performance.[26] But this was with a view to revisiting and revising the stage production. Questioned in an interview about the nature of her collaboration with Castorf, Myriam Hoyer tellingly refers only to her access to stage rehearsals for "improvements and inquiries," all with a view to "translating the intentions of the Bayreuth performance as precisely as possible into the audiovisual medium."[27] It is this institutionally and commercially prescribed role as external witness to an already-determined event—in this case, an event in its fourth year of presentation—that opens video productions of this kind to the charge that they merely copy or relay and in compromised form. And how deep is the compromise when a stage production featuring a combination of media forms is channeled into one medium, when refracted perspectives and juxtaposed planes are flattened into and as one screen? Is the reality effect of documentary television, the subversion of which is so pivotal to the Castorf project, not now reinstated on a metalevel when the stage production is enfolded by the documentary impulse of a multicamera production all too eager to present itself as truthful record of an event?

In fact, Hoyer's devotion to precision needs to be taken with a pinch of salt. The nine cameras at her disposal (all operated remotely) are mobilized to present angles, proximities, and planes worthy of the parallax effect Boenisch associates with Castorf's stage, or what Speckenbach calls its *gelebter Kubismus* (lived cubism).[28] Take the sequence of shots that follows the opening inward zoom in *Das Rheingold* onto the "Golden Motel" that is the permanent residence of the Rhine daughters. In the first minute from curtain up, the video production features nine cuts between shots from seven different cameras. Ranging from tightly framed upward-angled shots from the lip of the stage to stage-level mid-shots, the sequence can be understood as expository: it explores the minutely detailed, multi-layered set as a montage of contrasting images and perspectives. But such is the rate of cuts and the range of shots (later in the production vertical shots from cameras mounted above the stage will add yet more perspectives) that the telecast seems less to map or make coherent the collage of the stage than to revel in its details and overstuffed layers, fragmenting it, and reassembling it in sequences of contrasting perspectives and scales. It is a sign of things to come: throughout the telecast, bodies, edifices, and screens will be assembled in striking combinations both within the composition of individual shots and across the contrasting shots of the edit.

Contributing to the stage collage in *Das Rheingold* is one piece of apparatus that is out of place in the hyperrealistic environment of the Route 66 motel edifice that dominates the stage but thoroughly at home in a Castorf production: a giant video monitor perched above the motel, adjacent to its neon sign. What the monitor shows is an edited sequence of live footage of the characters coordinated and shot independently, as Hoyer explains, by Castorf's team.[29] That is, two multicamera productions are in play at the same time. Here, the reflected gaze I associated with the video remediation of the Bayreuth stage takes a more literal form when the telecast captures a parallel iteration of itself. And, if the two multicamera productions are independent, this does not preclude overlap in the form of shots of the onstage screens and direct feeds from Castorf's video production into the telecast production. The telecast, in a sense, claims video as its own.

The opening sequence of shots in *Das Rheingold* includes the first of these direct feeds. In fact, the last two of the seven shot types in the edited sequence are part of the stage production, here delivering reality-TV-style shots of the Rhine daughters. That the direct feeds from the cameras of the stage production are themselves edited sequences with their own cuts and shot rhythm only adds to the saturation, suggesting nested or competing layers of multicamera production. These direct feeds, featured throughout the *Ring* telecast, will play a prominent role in shaping its look and texture. Grainy, often unsteady, and monochrome, they draw attention to themselves and in turn to the high-definition color produced by the telecast cameras. Here, the telecast seems to take on board the duality implied in Speckenbach's reading of television's reality effect and apply it to its own terms of representation. By repeatedly interrupting the high-definition camerawork of professional multicamera production with raw, unvarnished footage of the performance suggestive of an encounter with reality, the telecast relativizes the documentary character of its default form, as though it were slickly produced fiction.

When the video produced by Castorf's team is remediated not by direct feed but by shots of the screens on stage, the adopted perspectives repeatedly juxtapose bodies, props, and architecture in ways that problematize the mapping and deciphering of the stage and complicate the act of witnessing by rendering it a form of frustrated voyeurism. In scene 4 of *Das Rheingold*, an encounter between Wotan and Erda is partially concealed in a motel room but made visible by a camera operator whose footage is relayed to other characters and to the Bayreuth audience via the large roof-mounted screen (fig. 1.1). In the telecast production, as Wotan and Erda kiss, a close-up of the motel room excludes the large screen (though it is seen in other shots), while the camera operator effectively blocks the shot (fig. 1.2). But the close-up makes visible another screen, the motel room's television, which carries the camera operator's footage. A screen virtually indecipherable for the Bayreuth audience now participates in the relay of images, negotiating private and public, visible and concealed, in ways more intimate than the large screen high above can. What Thomas Oberender calls Castorf's *drama of seeing* finds itself reconfigured by a parallel apparatus of vision, one that operates independently.[30] What the telecast audience witnesses, in short, is a video production of a video production of a stage production. If the telecast flattens the stage's juxtaposition

FIGURE 1.1. *Das Rheingold*, director, Frank Castorf, 2016 (original production, 2013). On-demand stream, Deutsche Grammophon Stage+, 2022.

FIGURE 1.2. *Das Rheingold*, director, Frank Castorf, 2016 (original production, 2013). On-demand stream, Deutsche Grammophon Stage+, 2022.

of live bodies and screens onto one screen, it invites the viewer to regard that screen as a composite of other screens and surfaces layered in ways that occasionally challenge the scopic organization of space familiar from multicamera production of opera. The telecast, that is, confronts in its own terms the problems—of narrative, of meaning making, of belief, of seeing—addressed by the stage production.

And there is more to say about the direct feeds. Formatted for display on screens with the almost square 4:3 aspect ratio, the video displayed on stage lends a retro effect to the mise-en-scène, but it needs to be adapted to the 16:9 wide-screen format of the telecast. The solution is to add mattes (bars) to the sides. The long-established convention for mismatched aspect ratios—for example, when wide-screen films were "letterboxed" for presentation on 4:3 television—is that these mattes are black, essentially rendering themselves invisible and directing attention to the image they frame. In the Hoyer video production, however, they are not black but blown-up, blurred versions of the actual footage (fig. 1.3). This technique of setting non-wide-screen footage against a wide-screen background composed of a digitally produced "Gaussian" blur of the same image is now widely used in television news and on social media to screen smartphone footage shot in vertical orientation. So widespread is its use, in

FIGURE 1.3. *Siegfried*, director, Frank Castorf, 2016 (original production, 2013). On-demand stream, Deutsche Grammophon Stage+, 2022.

fact, that it carries with it a certain trope or meme value as signifier of an on-the-scene capture of events—a striking occurrence, a confrontation, police brutality—not by professionals but by witnesses moved to record and disseminate. In the *Ring* telecast, its value as signifier—combined with the handheld, up close camerawork—is to foreground the sense of "eventness" and immediacy in the manner of reality TV or video posts on social media. Introduced only because of a gap between screen formats, the frame supplements the onstage video imagery in a way that draws attention to itself in televisual terms.

These frames, I want to suggest, are anything but peripheral. In *The Truth of Painting*, Derrida urges the reader to consider carefully the liminal function of the parergon (the frame) as transition between inside and outside of the painting as work.[31] The frame is a marker connected to and defining the boundaries of what lies inside, but it is equally an extension of the outside, defining by negation what the frame contains. This function as transition or supplement is itself framed when Derrida steps back to consider the frame's own identity as *separate* both from the painting and from the wall that surrounds it. The frame needs to be considered, that is, both as boundary and as something in itself, the liminal space no longer situated between inside and outside but between the very notions of connection and separation. To acknowledge the work of the frame, then, is to confront the role of the apparently peripheral in ways that have ramifications for what lies on either side of the frame; it is to nest apparently separate domains of thought and practice in a mise en abyme.[32] The relationship between video and matte in the Hoyer production invites just this kind of consideration: the blurred footage that forms the matte is based on the *periphery* of the source image, as though what we see are the edges of a complete image largely concealed by the superimposed source video. The effect is to imply a reversal of foreground and background, of original and copy, in which the unblurred video becomes a kind of matte placed over the (larger) blurred and now only partially visible video behind it. In this context, frames are anything but peripheral, and questions of priority and privilege—like the chronological priority of the stage production or the conceptual privileging of the stage as original event—are problematized.

THE TELEVISUAL RECLAIMS ITS OWN (EPISODE 2)

In its engagement with onstage video, the Hoyer production is not unique. Consider two opera telecasts aired within days of each other in July 2019. In the Kratzer/Braun *Tannhäuser* (2019) from Bayreuth, video projection expands the stage space with a mix of live and prerecorded footage. Dur-

FIGURE 1.4. *Tannhäuser*, director, Tobias Kratzer, 2019. Blu-ray Deutsche Grammophon 0735760, 2020.

ing the overture a filmed "backstory" is projected onto a large screen positioned in front of the stage. The screen returns in act 2, splitting the proscenium horizontally in two (see fig. 1.4). Projected on the screen is a range of live and prerecorded backstage footage reminiscent of the Castorf *Ring* but here directed to a metanarrative focused on the performance itself. Singers play versions of their backstage selves, their anxieties and interpersonal relationships projected above the stage in a way that combines opera with soap opera; characters intrude on the realities of the performance.[33] In the hands of the telecast director, Michael Beyer, this combination of stage and screen is intermittently shown in wide shot, but for most of the act it is interwoven as a series of monochrome cutaways from the (traditional) multicamera footage of the stage.

The result is that backstage footage is repeatedly presented *instead of* the stage rather than *with* it (as is the case for the audience in the Festspielhaus). As the performance unfolds, we witness a parallel drama backstage presented, like reality TV, by a mix of cameras both fixed and handheld. If, for the audience in the Festspielhaus, this parallel drama is spatially presented, in the video remediation it is temporally presented in the classic screen-media form of crosscutting. Beyer's production, in other words, takes the theatrical staging of a television genre (reality TV) and reverses the gesture, making the stage televisual, and returning reality TV to its native form. In so doing, it dares to take its eye intermittently off the stage, breaking from the traditional audience perspective, and allowing itself to be distracted by the view from backstage. A fixed camera positioned next to the stage manager's desk, for example, captures the stage from the wings (as well as the singers waiting to enter). As Elisabeth delivers the line "Der Sänger klugen Weisen lauscht ich sonst wohl gern und viel" (I used to listen with pleasure to the beguiling melodies of the singers), *we listen* to Lise Davidsen, only partially able to see her face, here obscured, thanks to the acute perspective, by Tannhäuser (Stephen Gould). Yet, in a clever rechanneling, a wide shot of the stage from the auditorium is partially visible within the shot (as is the conductor) via a monitor at the stage manager's desk (fig. 1.5).[34] The "direct" view of the stage is present in the shot but teasingly cropped and miniaturized; we monitor but only partially. The shot, that is, plays on the very possibility of seeing, at once framing and drawing attention to the act of framing. And, unlike the audience in the Festspielhaus, which can see this footage on the projection screen together with the stage, the viewer of the video production sees *only* this footage. Here, the spatial frame (the crop) is also a temporal frame (the crosscutting edit).

FIGURE 1.5. *Tannhäuser*, director, Tobias Kratzer, 2019. Blu-ray Deutsche Grammophon 0735760, 2020.

38 | CHAPTER ONE

THE TELEVISUAL RECLAIMS ITS OWN (EPISODE 3)

Only three weeks earlier, another production with a reflexive metanarrative had premiered at Aix-en-Provence. In his *Tosca*, coproduced with the Opéra de Lyon, the filmmaker Christophe Honoré takes the role of the eponymous diva as a cue to generate a mise en abyme of opera, here casting two Toscas: Catherine Malfitano as the mostly mute ghost of Toscas past and Angel Blue as her protégée. As in the Bayreuth productions, video is projected onto large screens, here mounted immediately behind the detailed contemporary interiors of Alban Ho Van's set design. Most of the footage displayed on the screens is relayed live from fixed cameras mounted on the sets and camera operators, who openly rove the stage, Castorf style, shooting close-ups in documentary fashion. (Part of the conceit of the production is that a rehearsal of *Tosca* is being filmed for a making-of documentary.) Telecast live in a production directed by Philippe Béziat, the video of the performance was later made available for on-demand streaming by the host, Radio France. In an approach quite distinct from those seen in the telecasts from Bayreuth, Béziat not only ignores but also studiously avoids shots of the projection screens that dominate the rear wall of the stage. This means avoiding key elements of the shot grammar so familiar from productions of this kind: no wide shots, no establishment or contextualization of the space as theater, no curtains parting to reveal the stage (though this is how the stage production opens).

Béziat's production, that is, seems to liberate itself from the outside broadcast mode of multicamera production so dedicated to mapping its environment and to the "authentic" representation of space. Instead, it relies on direct feeds of the footage from the fixed cameras and the onstage camera teams, interwoven with multicamera telecast footage consisting only of mid-shots and close-ups. In so doing, the production channels a different televisual grammar and aesthetic, one predicated on handheld cameras and close-ups. What comes across consistently is the claustrophobia and in-the-face immediacy of reality TV and video uploads. The effect is to suggest what almost never happens in the video remediation of stage opera: that cameras have been allowed to intervene on stage in a performance in front of a live audience. It is a glimpse, perhaps, of what might have been and what might be were video production less of an afterthought.

This mediality, however, is about more than claustrophobia. In an interview, Honoré expressed doubt about using video only as a "magnifying glass." The solution? To expand the video's terms of reference so that the projected images reach beyond what is happening on the stage or in the present moment. Supplementing the live relays are video clips from famous performances of *Tosca* as well as opera productions in which Malfitano has appeared, all grounded, Honoré tells us, in a desire to "converse with the past through archives."[35] This all comes to a head in the opera's signature aria "Vissi d'arte," accompanied in Honoré's production by mute excerpts ranging from productions produced for television (a 1976 Italian television film with Kabaivanska) to telecasts of the aria as an excerpt (Tebaldi on the *Bell Telephone Hour* in 1965).[36] The clips, unfolding on two screens behind Angel Blue as she sings, survey half a century of "Vissi d'arte" in performance, all framed by Callas in 1964 and Malfitano herself in 1992. If this "conversation" engages with a performance history—not least the diva cult associated with an opera about a diva—it is also an engagement with opera's media history, with the archive of *Tosca* on screen.

In Béziat's production, the sequence of excerpts is presented not via shots of the screens but as a montage linked with slow dissolves. It is a montage not just of singers or productions but of textures: monochrome/ color, film/video, blurred/sharp. Whatever these projections say about the diva, about performance tradition, about the melancholy of aging, they say much about the visual legacy of opera on screen. And, in Béziat's production, they say much about the relationship of performance with the archive. If on stage the clips form a "counterpoint" (to use Honoré's term) to Blue's performance, here they follow one another in full screen as a temporal montage. Each excerpt, each texture, not only displaces the other but also displaces Blue, who now becomes a live performer not simply overseen by her forebears but momentarily eclipsed by them. The archive here occupies the same place as the live performance; Blue's performance has itself been accessioned into the archive.

REALITY BITES

Just as instructive as these innovations and interventions, I want to suggest, are those features of the telecasts that seem to be the result not of a particular directorial strategy but of the consequences of live shooting and a limited opportunity for camera rehearsal. The production of *Tosca* made available for on-demand streaming was in fact a thoroughly revised version of the production telecast and streamed live. One of the pivotal aspects of the on-demand version—the direct feeds from the onstage cameras—is missing from the original telecast/live stream, which instead seems to operate as a completely independent production, relying exclusively on shots of the projector screens to access, by one remove, the video footage from Honoré's cameras. In some instances these shots are composed, as in the Hoyer *Ring*, to include a combination of stage, bodies, and projector screens, while, in other instances, tightly framed close-ups of the projection screens substitute for what will be direct feeds in the revised version.

Not only are these images, as copies of copies, much poorer in quality and resolution than the revised version (the glare of the screen has a blanching effect), but the absence of live feeds seems to generate a strategy that is the antithesis of the final version. For example, wide shots abound, and they serve a traditional establishing role, beginning with a classic shot of the curtains opening to reveal the stage. In the "Vissi d'arte" scene, the absence of direct feeds is even more keenly felt as a camera slowly pans between the two projector screens in a substitution for montage. True, the telecast/live stream version does include dissolves between these shots of the projector screens and close-ups of Angel Blue, but the impact of the revised version, with its thorough incorporation—its sense of ownership—of the archival footage, is here much diminished. Instead, the panning shots assume, like outside-broadcast productions, the role of mapping a space and documenting an event (see fig. 1.6, which juxtaposes the same moment as edited in both versions). It is an act of presencing devoted to being there.

Unlike Béziat, Hoyer incorporated direct feeds at the time of broadcast, but the *Ring* production appears not to have been revised from its live form, and the mammoth scale of the project shows in some rough edges. For example, the placement of cuts occasionally aligns in awkward ways with what happens on stage: a cut in the onstage video (itself a multi-camera production) will be separated by a split second from a cut in the telecast edit, creating a jarring double cut. Another mismatch occurs when a technical glitch on stage mars the closing moments of *Das Rheingold*. As the Rhine daughters lament the stolen gold and rain on Wotan's parade, prefilmed video footage shows them swimming underwater. The onstage screen, however, develops a fault: one of the video tiles that compose the composite image of the LCD screen begins to mismap, displaying imagery from another part of the image, as though a collage were being formed (note the tile superimposed on the body of the Rhine daughter in fig. 1.7). The effect might be taken as deliberate were it not for its inconsistency with anything the screen has displayed before. Tellingly, however, the telecast alternates shots of the screen with the direct video feed, which features no tiling or any disturbance of the image (fig. 1.8). On the one hand, the contrast opens a rift between stage and screen, accentuating the gap between evental failure in the auditorium and the intact image offered by the telecast's access to the video feed. On the other, the juxtaposition of flawed image and pristine image underlines the extent to which, like so

FIGURE 1.6. Catherine Malfitano and Maria Callas, "Vissi d'arte." *Tosca*, director, Christophe Honoré, 2019. (*Top*) Live stream, Arte Concert 2019. (*Bottom*) On-demand stream, Arte Concert 2019.

FIGURE 1.7. *Das Rheingold*, director, Frank Castorf, 2016 (original production, 2013). On-demand stream, Deutsche Grammophon Stage+, 2022.

FIGURE 1.8. *Das Rheingold*, director, Frank Castorf, 2016 (original production, 2013). On-demand stream, Deutsche Grammophon Stage+, 2022.

many television transmissions, the telecast is tethered to that eventness and shares the performative vulnerability of its presentation.[37]

The Hoyer *Ring* also reveals incompatibilities between conventions and systems of representation. In wide shots, the large LCD screen in *Das Rheingold* is vivid and legible but not always. The telecast features numerous close-ups of and slow zooms toward the onstage screen, and, here, the image quality transforms into something quite different. One effect of the close-up image is to render the screen's image as pixels, replicating the effect of looking too closely at a monitor. The composite effect of the pixels, so effective at a distance, is atomized into its components (fig. 1.9). When the telecast montage juxtaposes full-stage shots with close-ups, the effect is particularly pronounced: what is clear in one frame is obscured in the next. Worse, as a result of scanning conflicts between camera and screen, the close-ups render the video screen a noisy mess of waves and lines. This effect, known as *moiré*, is made worse by the motion of zooming, which generates a series of conflicting interference patterns (see figs. 1.10 and 1.11). In this oscillation between two perspectives on or renderings of the same image, the telecast again recalls the parallax view that Boenisch associates with Castorf's multiplanar stage. Drawing on Slavoj Žižek's quasi-Lacanian reading of the parallax, Boenisch characterizes Castorf's

FIGURE 1.9. Froh (Tansel Akzeybek). *Das Rheingold*, director, Frank Castorf, 2016 (original production, 2013). On-demand stream, Deutsche Grammophon Stage+, 2022.

FIGURE 1.10. *Das Rheingold*, director, Frank Castorf, 2016 (original production, 2013). On-demand stream, Deutsche Grammophon Stage+, 2022.

FIGURE 1.11. *Das Rheingold*, director, Frank Castorf, 2016 (original production, 2013). On-demand stream, Deutsche Grammophon Stage+, 2022.

practices as opening onto an encounter with the Real—that is, not reality but precisely that which resists incorporation into our experience of reality. The Real is not represented as such but emerges in the parallax space between incompatible perspectives. More specifically, the telecast presents the encounter with the Real as a problem of immediacy. If, like theater, desire depends on the maintenance of distance, *jouissance*, the excessive pleasure associated with the Real, is always "too close."[38] It is this collapse of distance that the telecast confronts when it closes in on video screens. Here, however, the parallax is not the outcome of a conscious creative strategy but an accidental encounter born of remediation and the conditions that attach to that remediation. More than manipulation generated by some individual artistic agency, this encounter suggests something that might emerge unbidden. Nor is this simply a matter of epistemology—of a difference of points of view. As Žižek argues, recognizing the dialectical character of the parallax raises the critical stakes. "Subject and object are inherently 'mediated,'" he observes, "so that an 'epistemological' shift in the subject's point of view always reflects an 'ontological' shift in the object."[39] In other words, the shift in perspective exposes something *in* the image, as though the remediation, far from linear, formed a circuit with the supposed original, inverting cause and effect, and rendering the image as what it always was. The tidy, meaningful representation we recognize from a distance turns out to be a chaotic mass of pixels.

Not that we need LCD screens to be confronted by the problem of proximity. One of the screens utilized in a number of recent opera productions is mounted not on or behind the stage but in front of it. In his productions of *Prince Igor* (2014) and *Tristan und Isolde* (2015), the director Dmitri Tcherniakov utilizes a stagewide scrim as a projection screen. Designed to allow light to pass through from behind (i.e., from the stage), the scrim reflects light cast onto it from the front, with the effect that it becomes a projection screen, one that partially obscures but blends with the image of the stage. Here, the dual identity of screen as both site for image and filter (screening out) is made manifest. The problem for video remediation is twofold. First, the giant images projected onto the scrim become mere shadows and abstract forms when viewed from any perspective other than a wide shot. Confronted by this problem, the telecast of *Tristan und Isolde* (video director, Andy Sommer) repeatedly cuts from mid-shots and close-ups to wide shots as soon as the projections appear. Awkward and jarring, the cuts seem forced and blindsided, like Hoyer's *Ring*, by the circumstances of production rather than following their conventional grammar, as though the video production were the titular pair interrupted in flagrante delicto by the arrival of King Mark and his cohort.

But there is a wider problem. Although the video projections are few and far between, Tcherniakov's production avoids the distraction of raising and lowering the scrim during acts and scenes. In *Tristan und Isolde*, this means that the scrim obscures and renders hazy the image of the stage for the duration of acts 1 and 2, all for video projections that last an accumulated five minutes. If this creates in the theater what one critic characterized as a "gauzy, filmic look," the impression on video is of poor definition reminiscent of an earlier generation of television telecasts and the VHS releases that accompanied them.[40] Although the Kratzer/Braun *Tannhäuser* makes more sparing use of a scrim, it too features scenes that compromise the video production. One particularly blurred shot in the live telecast was cleaned up for the DVD release (figs. 1.12 and 1.13). Just as problematic is the impact of shots that transform the gauzy effect into a grid-like overlay of the actual gauze of which the scrim is composed. Here, approaching too closely (if only optically) transforms the filtering effect of the scrim into something that resembles a surface texture, as though the screen were fashioned out of woven fabric (figs. 1.14 and 1.15 show the effect in *Tristan* and *Tannhäuser*, respectively).[41] Harnessed to a scopic grammar of closing in, of blowing up, the screen technology of the telecast inadvertently exposes the secret of other screens and the theater built around and through them.

FIGURE 1.12. Tannhäuser (Stephen Gould). *Tannhäuser*, director, Tobias Kratzer, 2019. Telecast 3Sat, July 27, 2019.

FIGURE 1.13. Tannhäuser (Stephen Gould). *Tannhäuser*, director, Tobias Kratzer, 2019. Blu-ray Deutsche Grammophon 0735760, 2020.

FIGURE 1.14. Isolde (Anja Kampe). *Tristan und Isolde*, director, Dmitri Tcherniakov, 2018. Live stream, Staatsoper Unter den Linden, March 18, 2020.

FIGURE 1.15. Tannhäuser (Stephen Gould) and the Young Shepherd (Katharina Konradi). *Tannhäuser*, director, Tobias Kratzer, 2019. Blu-ray Deutsche Grammophon 0735760, 2020.

HAUNTING SILHOUETTES

I have argued that the potential for these video productions to reimagine what they supposedly merely capture is undermined by the contingencies of production and the encounter of technologies and images. But they also find themselves in tension with deeply embedded conventions. Adventurous moments there may be, but they are situated within a very familiar context: a grammar of cuts between wide, mid-, and close-up shots that carefully establish and maintain spatial coherence and narrative continuity. Consider the establishing shots that introduce each "evening" of the tetralogy in Hoyer's *Ring*. As opening credits roll, a static wide shot from the rear of the auditorium captures the still-curtained stage and the seats filled with conversing spectators. In Bayreuth fashion, dimming house lights cue a hush (no applause for the concealed conductor) before the prelude begins. The camera slowly zooms in on the stage, gradually excluding the audience from the image frame as the characteristic "Wagner curtain" (the diagonal lift associated with Bayreuth) reveals a stage now surrounded by darkness.[42] Only then does the video production cut to other shots. With this establishing shot, the video production has reinforced and effectively reenacted the Bayreuth performance ritual as gradually directed focus on and revelation of the stage image.

And image it is, as Kreuzer points out. Emphasizing Wagner's conception of the stage as an animated image that generates the impression of depth through the "frontal plane" or screen defined by the proscenium, Kreuzer shows how the architectural design and features of the Festspielhaus—the narrowing columns on the side walls, a double proscenium frame, the placement and deployment of curtains—reinforce an impression of pictorial flatness that smooths out the stage's heterogeneity of materials, planes, and surfaces into an image.[43] Read with this Bayreuth effect in mind—or viewed through its frame—Castorf's multiplanar stage could be regarded as already flattened by the pictorial effect of the architecture and the theatrical apparatus that surround and frame the stage. Stage architectures they may be, but Aleksandar Denić's sets—already framed and pictorialized on the stage itself with cinematic lighting and ironic, arch-Wagnerian clouds of mist—are rendered imagistic by the meticulous framing of the Festspielhaus, as though the stage did not just house video screens but was itself a screen. In this context, the video production and its opening gambit of aligning image frame with proscenium frame seems less like an intervention or remediation than an encounter with its own reflection: video image meets stage image.

More explicit in its engagement with the proscenium is Beyer's *Tannhäuser* production. Here, the framing effect of the proscenium is reconstructed in the video production as a means of framing the image. As in the *Ring* telecast, Beyer must negotiate a variety of aspect ratios when the onstage video is relayed as a direct feed. Although the backstage feeds in act 2 are formatted in the 16:9 ratio native to television and require no formatting (the projection above the stage crops this image to fit what is effectively a "Cinerama" aspect ratio of 8:3), the prerecorded films displayed variously in front of and above the stage require adaptation. In act 2, a cutaway sequence depicting fictional action outside the auditorium requires black letterbox mattes to accommodate its 24:10 "ultrawide" format in a televisual presentation. But, like the introductory backstory screened during the overture, this film is also presented in places as a full-screen image, taking its aspect ratio from the almost square dimensions of the Bayreuth proscenium. The telecast image requires mattes not at top and bottom but, as in the Hoyer *Ring*, at the sides. Unlike the Gaussian mattes of the Hoyer production, however, these are black, matching the letterbox mattes of the wide-screen footage.

Yet there is something different here. On each side of the image near the top is a curve or bulge in the black matte (fig. 1.16). Not quite symmetrical, the curves intrude oddly on the otherwise clean lines of the frame. The clue as to their source is provided in the opening seconds of the telecast when, in a full-stage shot, the curtain is lifted in signature Bayreuth fashion (the Wagner curtain again) to reveal the film that opens the production. The screen, however, is not visible in its entirety. Situated immediately behind the dual proscenium arches, it is slightly cropped by the decorative moldings that kink the side and the top of each arch (for the view of the stage in the Hoyer production, see fig. 1.17). Although the video is clearly a direct feed in the telecast and not camera footage of the projection screen (a dissolve transitions from one to the other), the effect of the moldings is retained as stylized curves in the matte, as though they were present in silhouette. It is a gesture that draws on the long-standing visual trope I touched on in the book's introduction: a stage silhouette frames an image, packaging it as spectacle. It simulates what is essentially a theatrical impediment, and it conceals the traces of its televisual intervention (the direct feed) to suggest that it is in fact merely filming a screen. As an immediacy effect, it is overdetermined. Not quite symmetrical, the curves on either side seem to suggest a slight skew in perspective from the auditorium, as though they were the product of a literal tracing of the outlines of the obstruction as seen from a specific point in

FIGURE 1.16. *Tannhäuser*, director, Tobias Kratzer, 2019. Blu-ray Deutsche Grammophon 0735760, 2020.

FIGURE 1.17. *Die Walküre*, director, Frank Castorf, 2016 (original production, 2013). On-demand stream, Deutsche Grammophon Stage+, 2022.

the auditorium. A gesture so site specific as to be almost fetishistic in its attachment to Bayreuth, it resonates with the self-reflexive concept of the stage production. By replicating the view of the stage right down to a slight skew, tracing it and modeling it as a matte, the frame suggests something more in Bayreuth than Bayreuth itself. And the there in question is also a then. When the curves break up the otherwise clean lines of the frame, something of the decorative nineteenth century disturbs and haunts the symmetrical minimalism of contemporary screen media.

VERSIONS OF REALITY

Even the apparently most unconventional gestures of these telecast productions—the intrusions of reality in the form of interpolated live monochrome footage—are at the same time presented precisely as citations, neatly packaged as the characterful, manufactured other of the telecast. This compartmentalization is emphasized when, in proper televisual fashion, the telecasts favor temporal over spatial montage. While the Kratzer production owes its impact to the simultaneous presentation of two screens (one for projection, the other a stage), the telecast only very occasionally offers a wide shot of the two together. When it does, the video screen comes across as underilluminated and at times barely decipherable in comparison with the brightly lit stage (this is a technical problem evident in telecasts and streams of other productions featuring projections). More typical is the alternation of multicamera coverage of the stage with direct feeds of the monochrome footage. But even these interpolations constitute only a fraction of the overall edit. It is the stage that dominates the telecast, leaving the direct feeds in the much diminished role of occasional cutaways. There is, in a sense, a form of containment or marginalization at work in this rebalancing of simultaneities into an uneven temporal montage dominated by one aspect of the staging.

I argued for the subversive potential of substituting spatial with temporal montage when it marginalizes the stage. But, when the Hoyer *Ring* compartmentalizes the collage of Castorf's stage into a sequential video edit, it could equally be read as domesticating the challenge of spatial montage so remarked on in commentary on the stage production. Now the collage is parsed and atomized into a series of fragments focused on this or that segment of the stage. Take scene 3 of *Das Rheingold*, when Loge and Wotan manipulate Alberich into donning the magical Tarnhelm to assume forms. In Castorf's staging, Alberich's transformations—first into a serpent, then a toad—are captured in monochrome by a prominently visible onstage, dolly-mounted camera to which the Nibelung plays like a media-obsessed reality-TV star. In a cheesy video sleight of hand, the supposed live feed of Alberich at the door of his trailer dissolves into a still of the same scene minus Alberich. The effect? Alberich vanishes. Crucially, however, this video is displayed on the giant onstage screen *simultaneously* with the live action of Alberich merely retreating into his trailer (not vanishing). It is one of the many juxtapositions of mediatized and live action in this production, juxtapositions that call into question the reliability of representation by combining two versions of the same reality.[44]

The telecast, however, carries only one of these versions of reality: via a direct feed, we see the mediatized sleight of hand as Alberich disappears. Despite the copious use of cameras, angles, and cuts before and after this scene, the telecast production shows us nothing of the stage and its duality when Alberich disappears. Instead, we witness only a magical transformation. For all the telecast's devotion to capturing the multiplicity of Castorf's stage, a pivotal moment that poses a critical question about representation is flattened into a singularity. True, framing both live action and screen in a single shot may have posed technical challenges (a wide shot of the large stage would surely have rendered both Alberichs rather small), yet there is something about the single feed that is telling here, as though the lure of this moment of enchantment and the need to capture it up close trumped Hoyer's stated goal of honoring the intentions of the production.

Even the revised version of Béziat's *Tosca* cannot quite hold back the weight of tradition. As I explained earlier, the production dispenses with wide shots that would reveal the projection screens on stage and instead focuses on a more claustrophobic view based on a combination of Honoré's roving camera teams and close-ups from Béziat's own cameras. Yet, strangely, after consistently—one might say insistently—shunning the wide shot throughout act 1, suddenly, as the concluding Te Deum reaches its climax, the production cuts to a full-stage shot, revealing, for the first time, the projection screen with its live relayed image. "Where has this been?" the video spectator might ask. "What have we missed?" The same is true of act 2, which again avoids revealing the screen until the end of "Vissi d'arte," when the represented space is suddenly transformed by the revelation of two screens that, we now realize, *were there all along.*

What to make, retrospectively, of all those archival images that dissolved, dreamlike, into one another, displacing and giving way repeatedly to images of the two Toscas on stage? Now it seems as though they hovered on screens behind those singers, not supplanting but shadowing them. On the one hand, the phantasmagoria of the on-screen dissolves is dispelled with the revelation of the all-too-real apparatus of the projection screens. On the other, the ghostly doubling of the onstage performers by images of their predecessors (something unseen by the video spectator until now) is itself doubled by the realization of what has been left out of the frame. This seemingly random mismatch between theater and multi-camera production, like the reduction of Alberich's vanishing in the Hoyer production, leaves the frustrating impression of having missed out on something. Worse, it can frustrate interpretation and legibility. Comparing the live stream and the theatrical experience of a production featuring a split between stage and projection screen, Joshua Barone notes that the camera's reluctance to show stage and screen together makes for a "confusing resolution that is easily legible in the house."[45]

MISSING OUT

Writing on Castorf's theater, Boenisch observes that being deprived of the full picture is no accident or failure: "Far from preventing us from seeing the real thing, this missing out *is it*."[46] It would be tempting to read these video productions as iterations of a similar critical impulse. I fear, however, that this would a generous interpretation. Do they not register, rather, an encounter between two mismatched systems or modes of (re)presentation, one predicated on planned failure, the other on the relentless pursuit of capture? Recall Davis's claim that in multicamera production "the best technique highlights that which is important, eliminates that which is unimportant, and obliterates itself by its own perfection."[47] This statement of principle is testament to the desire of multicamera production to don the Tarnhelm and render itself invisible. Here, the vanishing mediator is rooted in a notion of selectivity or filtering that grants the shot choice an air of inevitably: because a certain happening calls for the camera's gaze, and because this is apparently the only natural focus, the work of the directorial hand is concealed, the edit naturalized. If there remains a sense of missing something, this is no critical twist but an indication that the goal of self-obliteration has not been met.

Still, reading these productions as awkward encounters between a critical, radical theater and the conventional, congealed practices of multicamera production risks overlooking some nuances. On the one hand, claims made on behalf of parallax perspectives need to be carefully weighed up. In her analysis of intermedial opera productions, Havelková wonders whether the capacity of a multiplicity of perspectives to question homogenizing or totalizing views of the world also risks generating a perspective cloaked by that very multiplicity, as though, liberated from any one perspective, the everything and the in-between offered their own immediacy with the thing represented.[48] Like the oscillations theorized by Bolter and Grusin, hypermediacy here pivots to immediacy in ways that risk undermining the supposedly critical stance this theater adopts. When the apparatus of multicamera production assumes its own perspectiveless perspective, it perhaps merely responds to something it recognizes on stages like the ones considered here.

On the other hand, the question of what counts as conventional or uncritical is relative. In the cautious tradition of remediated opera, even incorporating video textures and colors other than default transmission standards or deploying camera techniques other than professional best practice comes across as adventurous. Over a decade ago, I wrote of the impact of slow-motion and night-vision-style footage in a 2005 telecast (also released on DVD) of a stage production of *Tristan und Isolde*. The video still stands out because so many of the conventions have remained intact.[49] In this context, the three video productions considered in this chapter join select company. Admittedly, my words damn with faint praise.

I identify something innovative and challenging only because, as I see it, the bar is set so low. My abiding sense of remediated opera—and this will be a recurring theme of this book—is of opportunities missed, of turns not taken. Perhaps this is all inevitable: even to ponder what is missed is to rage against the machine. How could the institutionalized partnership between large opera houses and long-established forms of audiovisual production—between one set of vested interests and another—ever hope, one might ask, to produce something innovative? Not to mention the business logic of a model that seeks to monetize a marketable event. That even the modest sense of adventure evident in these examples seems carefully licensed by the event they purport to serve is a sobering reminder of the commercial and institutional parameters at play here. In chapter 2, I turn to other productions to tease out these questions further, revisiting the sources of my critical frustration while remaining alert to gestures that might challenge the operatic-televisual compact as I have presented it.

CHAPTER TWO

Split Loyalties

In the book's introduction, I cited Stanley Cavell's observations on television's handling of staged opera. These observations are part of a wider consideration of multicamera production. If the basis for the shooting of an event—a game show, a sitcom, live sports, a performance—is simultaneous coverage from multiple cameras positioned to provide a range of perspectives, what the viewer at home sees, Cavell points out, is an edited selection of those perspectives presented as a sequence of single images to a "sole receiver." Although it might be impractical, "in principle," he adds, "we could all watch a replica of the bank of monitors the producer sees."[1] That is, we too could become editors of sorts, positioned to select from several options presented simultaneously. For Cavell this hypothetical apparatus serves an argument about the material distinctions between television and film. Pragmatics may require transmission of the images "one at a time," he goes on to argue, but this should not obscure the pivotal role of simultaneity in television. Whereas the edited succession of images in film is determined by meaning, cuts between perspectives in television are dictated by the opportunity to cover an event. It is the event that determines the form, Cavell concludes, and the result is that meaningful succession is displaced by what amounts to a "switch of attention from one monitor to another monitor," as though the director were a security guard seated before an array of closed-circuit video screens and waiting for something to happen.[2] In this chapter, I want to take Cavell's characterization of television as a provocation to probe the pragmatics and poetics of the multicamera production of videos of staged opera. In keeping with my claim that a reflexive encounter represents a particularly rich site for investigation, I will focus on video productions of two recent stage productions, both directed by Katie Mitchell, that themselves foreground some of the questions raised by Cavell: of simultaneous but separate feeds, of monitoring, of surveillance (not only visual, but also sonic).

First, a historical caveat. Published in 1982, Cavell's essay reflects practices, conventions, and technologies arguably much developed in the meantime. The traces of these developments of and within the televisual apparatus are visible—and audible—in many of the video productions I consider in this book, including the ones that will feature in this chapter. Image resolution, screen size, audio quality—these characteristics have changed substantially since 1982, and camera and audio recording techniques have arguably shifted with them. I am unconvinced, for example, by Brian Large's suggestion that the grammar of video productions of staged opera has changed little since the era of black-and-white images and mono sound.[3] But this does not mean that there is not continuity. Large's argument, presented in response to a question about the impact of cinecasts on his practice, amounts to resistance to assumptions that smack of technological determinism: yes, the technology has changed; no, my creative principles have not. The argument does also highlight something of the durability, even rigidity, of some of the conventions and grammatical norms that attend these productions and multicamera production more generally.

Take the windowed and split-screen effects much facilitated by digital production beginning in the 1990s and made familiar in television by twenty-four-hour news channels. Could this configuration of the screen, which amounts to a composite of several screens, not be read as a realization of Cavell's replica of the director's bank of monitors? Once hopelessly miniaturized, these split effects surely become more legible with the scale of screen now available, making redundant the need for a bank of monitors in the home. Yet, although this fragmentation of the screen, emblematic of what Bolter and Grusin call *hypermediacy*, has become a standard feature of television genres such as news and live sports, it has only occasionally registered in television dramas, sitcoms, talk shows, or what Cavell calls *cultural coverage* (concerts, ballet, opera).[4] Here, the single frame holds fast, and exceptions (e.g., in title sequences) serve only to prove the rule. The technology is available; missing is the desire. Video productions of staged opera, like those of theater and ballet, have only fitfully adopted these configurations of the video screen, even as splits, frames, and windows have increasingly featured on the stages they shoot and record. This chapter is about the implications of this disparity.

DISTRACTING STAGE

If any term could be said to function as a recurring motif in reviews of Katie Mitchell's production of *Written on Skin* (Aix-en-Provence, 2012), it is *distraction.*[5] The problem, it seems, lay in the need for the audience to split its attention between the primary action (associated with the singers delivering the opera's vocal parts at any given time) and parallel, silent action taking place in adjacent but narratively noncontiguous spaces. Sounding not unlike the overwhelmed survivors of Castorf's *Ring*, critics repeatedly write of their frustration at having to attend to two or more scenes at the same time. No screens here, as in Castorf, at least not in the literal sense. What Mitchell and Vicki Mortimer present, rather, is a segmented stage divided by screenlike rectangular frames, each encompassing an interior space. Based loosely on the life of the troubadour Guillem de Cabestaing, Martin Crimp's libretto fragments the action into two temporal layers linked by the fictional compilation of parchment folios: contemporary "angels" oversee and intervene in the medieval narrative of a love triangle between a landowner ("the Protector"), his wife, Agnès ("the Woman"), and "the Boy," commissioned to create an illuminated manuscript celebrating the Protector's wealth. And it is this temporal split that underpins Mitchell's staging and Mortimer's design. Whereas Tom Rogers's design for a production of *Written on Skin* at Opera Philadelphia (director, William Kerley, 2018) takes the imagery of the illuminated manuscript as the basis for scenic form (decorative flats, vividly colored props), Mortimer's design takes its cue from a more recent aesthetic. A two-story grid of compartments is juxtaposed with a hypernaturalistic, minutely detailed conservation laboratory (white coats, fluorescent light, industrial shelving) with an earthy, "medieval" domestic interior, the latter's historical constructedness foregrounded by the prominent modern-industrial struts that support the ceiling, as though it were a restoration projection.[6]

With this striking stage architecture, the palimpsestic premise of Martin Crimp's text (the restoration and reenactment of a past concealed in layers) takes the form of a forensic investigation in which Crimp's angels become lab technicians, their interventions with narrative complicit in the violence of the events set in motion by that narrative. Critical to the production's play on temporalities is the simultaneity of the contemporary and historical layers: action in the past is always accompanied and framed by an industrial-scientific present populated by conservators who not only monitor events but also intervene. In transitions between scenes (signaled by cool-white, high-contrast lighting cues and triggered by the flick of a wall switch in the lab), the angels/lab technicians dress and position the medieval protagonists of the narrative, functioning like metatheatrical backstage personnel who coax the protagonists into (re)playing their roles. Consigned once more to a framing role when the scenes begin, they move in varying rates of slow motion, visualizing in gesture a juxtaposition not just of historical moments but of rates of time. This is not only, in other words, a real-time montage of remote spaces but also a layering of remote times and temporalities in keeping with the opera's metanarrative. As the gesture of closing the cover of the illuminated manuscript signals the close of the work, the motion of the actors is frozen altogether.

For the critic Andrew Clements, it was all too much, too "distracting" from "a work that seems perfectly self-contained dramatically anyway," and Clements goes on to claim that it is George Benjamin's score, otherworldly yet impassioned, that properly propelled the performance, not Mitchell's "directorial glosses."[7] Sounding remarkably like the critics Manuel Braun anticipated when interviewed about *Tannhäuser*, Clements summons the tried-and-tested canard, "Couldn't we just let the music speak?" The problem is in part one of genre and expectation. Writing on the theatrical avant-garde—or what he terms *postdramatic* theater—Lehmann stresses the role of the simultaneity of separate zones or layers of signification as a means of making explicit the illusory nature of the quest for organic wholeness. Unable to reconcile the demand for attention at once to the particular and to the totality, the frustrated spectator is confronted with the "fragmentary character of perception."[8] Lehmann's mobilization of this *programmed* frustration as a defining characteristic within his sweeping taxonomy of contemporary theater could itself be accused of an illusory wholeness. Mitchell's theater, for example, sits comfortably with Lehmann's emphasis on the pivotal role of simultaneity, but, with a manifest commitment to Stanislavskian textual analysis and the critical potential of naturalism, it makes an odd bedfellow with the postdramatic and the narrative of radical, postrealist theater that attends the concept.[9]

Still, in the institutional context of opera—even when the opera is new and even when grid stagings like this have become increasingly common in opera—the kind of critical resistance that met Mitchell's production of *Written on Skin* has an air of inevitability.[10] Like the critics who had complained about the multiplicity of narratives in *After Dido* (2009)—Tim Ashley declared that Mitchell's production of the Purcell opera "adds confusion to a work that for many is a model of narrative clarity"—and the critics who would later complain about the distracting effect of the divided stage in Mitchell's *Lucia di Lammermoor* (Royal Opera House, 2016), Clements here speaks to a frustration centered on what Lehmann might term a thoroughly *dramatic* conception of how opera should be staged.[11]

There is a parallel here, I want to suggest, with commercial videos of staged opera. They too sit awkwardly with the question of genre and medium, and they too provoke complaints about distraction and fragmentation, typically focused on an authenticity paradigm in which close-ups or frequent cuts distort the stage production they should be merely relaying or capturing.[12] In a case of purported mission creep, that is, video directors stand accused of taking it on themselves to add layers of interpretation when they should be minimizing their intervention or fragmenting spectatorship when they should be honoring the stage production *as theater* by, in effect, documenting the event and simulating attendance.[13] I will return to this question of and desire for virtual presence in chapter 4. For now I want to ask how this anxiety about intervention might be complicated by a stage production that already seems to anticipate its own remediation on screen.

LIVE CINEMA

High-contrast lighting, spatiotemporal dislocations, slow motion, freeze-frame, detailed—one might say, forensic—naturalism: all are suggestive of a theater that aspires to the condition of cinema, a theater whose fourth wall is already a screen.[14] Mitchell/Mortimer's mise-en-scène is a *mise-en-écran*, its compartments a set of richly detailed film or television sets ready-made for the magnifying gaze of the zoom lens. The stage, in short, resembles a studio awaiting the camera crew. This dual character of stage and studio is made explicit and literal in one strand of Mitchell's work: in productions such as *The Waves* (2006) and . . . *some trace of her* (2008), camera operators, like those in Castorf's *Ring* and Honoré's *Tosca*, roam the stage, feeding live images to a large projection screen situated immediately above the set. But, whereas the combination of live action and projection in the theater of Castorf and Honoré can be understood as a means of presenting and complicating the live stage, Mitchell incorporates the cameras and projections into a screen-media production process. In what she dubs *live cinema*, the theater audience witnesses the shooting, editing, and screening of a digital film in the real time of a theater performance. *Live cinema* is also the term used by the Royal Opera House to market what is a quite different encounter between theater and cinema (its cinecast series), but both applications capture the same paradoxical quality of a cinema produced and experienced as live performance. They also share a rhetorical elision. Just as the live transmission of opera to cinemas writes out the televisual basis of its production in the name of a more prestigious and marketable encounter (something to which I will return later in the book), so Mitchell's live cinema, with its simultaneously active cameras and live-edited video, glosses over its debt to the televisual.

Written on Skin features no onstage camera crews or projections; it would seem to form no part of Mitchell's live cinema project. Yet the production's camera-ready quality complicates any clear demarcation. Its defining visual characteristic—the grid of compartments—can be usefully compared to something that critics have observed in live cinema productions. Reflecting on the combination of live action and projection in *The Waves*, Paul Taylor characterized the production as one that "bangs its brow against the limitations of the theater of permanent long-shot."[15] Dividing the stage into separate spaces may not generate the close-ups that cameras and projections make possible, but it does break up that singular, permanent quality that Taylor invokes, fragmenting the stage image into multiple imaginary spaces viewed from multiple imaginary perspectives. Mitchell foregrounded just such a link when she characterized the divided stage of *Lucia di Lammermoor* (again designed by Mortimer) as a "split screen."[16]

But this anticipation of the cameras was not entirely in vain, and the screen has not always been imaginary. In two early performances, *Written on Skin* did play host to multicamera production, not, as in live cinema, incorporated into the production, but as dissemination *of* the production: first at Aix-en-Provence in 2012 in a live telecast on the Franco-German arts channel Arte (director, Corentin Leconte), then at the Royal Opera House in 2013 (director, Margaret Williams). In a kind of corollary to live cinema, though the Williams production was shot live, it was clearly edited in postproduction, telecast on a delayed basis by the BBC, and released on DVD on the Opus Arte label—in other words, the televisual in its recorded, not live, form. Delayed broadcast of material edited in postproduction is not uncommon in performing arts programming on television, and of course postproduction is essential for titles released on DVD. As we have seen, too, live streams can be edited to produce archival versions. The extent of the editorial intervention varies, although video productions shot in the opera house typically retain an as-live quality. In the DVD production, for example, the performance is presented *as* a performance, framed by standard audiovisual codes: the orchestra tuning up, shots of the conductor (in this case, the composer) entering the pit to applause, curtain calls at the conclusion.

CINEMASCOPE OPERA

Less typical is another form of frame: not the temporal bookends of the performance but the aspect ratio of the video. As flagged in the marketing copy on the cover of the DVD, *Written on Skin* is presented in Cinemascope format (1:2.35). Developed to accommodate this and similar wide-screen formats on the less elongated 16:9 format of wide-screen television and

FIGURE 2.1. *Written on Skin*, director, Katie Mitchell, Royal Opera House, 2013. Blu-ray Opus Arte, OABD7136D, 2013.

DVD, black bars are added to the top and the bottom of the image. It is one of the most familiar codes for remediated cinema. But what is it doing here on an opera DVD, a media form that has almost invariably adopted the 16:9 format since wide-screen television established itself in the early postmillennial period? The answer would appear to lie on the stage. Mortimer's stacked compartments form a grid that is rectangular in shape, but not just any rectangle. The proportion of its height to its width is almost exactly 1:2.35.[17] In other words, the Cinemascope format allows the video production to match the format of the mise-en-scène: the grid occupies almost the full width of the image, while its top and bottom are tightly framed by black bars (see fig. 2.1).

Compare the live telecast from Aix-en-Provence, which adopts the standard wide-screen format. Here, accommodating the full width of the grid means including areas above and below it. Above the stage we witness the glow of the in-house surtitles; below the stage are the heads of the musicians in the back row of the orchestra pit (fig. 2.2). Here is the evental real so neatly framed out on DVD. Having introduced the production with an invitation to virtual presence in the opera house, the latter now covers over the traces of that presence with black bars, invoking an immediacy that is at once the antithesis and the epitome of virtual attendance: the epitome in that it extends the focusing function of the darkened audi-

FIGURE 2.2. *Written on Skin*, director, Katie Mitchell, Festival d'Aix-en-Provence, 2012. Live stream, Medici.tv, July 14, 2012.

torium (its channeling of attention and shrouding of distraction) to the absolute opaque of black bars, the antithesis in that it extracts the stage from its performative context, rendering it a film with operatic soundtrack. And what this alignment of stage image with video image seems to license is something else unusual in video productions of this kind: a directorial willingness to dwell on this wide shot, to linger with it, to return to it often. It is, in this sense, the fulfillment of the fantasy underlying the persistent call for videos to feature only a static shot of the complete stage: the fantasy, that is, that the immobilized body of the theatrical spectator would find a proxy in the immobilized single camera. It equally addresses the accompanying complaint that video directors force the viewer to miss out on something. In a stage production in which that something is happening—as parallel action in separate compartments—*all the time*, the wide shot becomes a form of assurance. You are not, to use Boenisch's phrase, "missing out," or, given the fragmentation of perception already at work in the theater, you are not missing out on missing out. As far as possible from the televisual simultaneities Cavell associated with his imaginary bank of monitors in the home, this static wide shot nevertheless channels simultaneity by pointedly bearing witness to it in the stage architecture. To put it another way, the video production here registers frenetic fragmentation of perspective with a shot type characterized by its patience and wholeness.

Except, of course, that the *multi-* in *multicamera production* has only so much tolerance for the singular and static. Or, to put it more precisely, the *edit* will resist only so long the impetus of conventions, of a grammar, predicated on the temporal sequencing of its multiple perspectives and realized in the form of crosscutting between camera feeds. Take scene 8, the pivotal confrontation between the Protector and Agnès. Repulsed by Agnès's intimate approaches, the Protector dismisses her as a child and attempts to force her to say so. In the angry confrontation that follows, Agnès reveals her infidelity with the Boy: "Ask him who I am!" In the Mitchell staging, this primary action, located in the medieval interior on the lower level of the grid, is accompanied by scenes in three other compartments: two played out in slow motion in the contemporary conservation labs stage right and the third on the upper level, a medieval exterior with window through which the Boy appears to eavesdrop on and visibly react to the exchange below.

The means by which the two video productions configure this multiplicity is telling. In what is by this point a familiar pattern in each video production, the scene transitions are associated with wide shots, with the effect that the approximately eight-minute scene is bookended by a kind of establishing or master shot. In the Arte telecast, this is all we will see of the complete stage. The shot mix in the scene consists almost entirely of mid-shots and close-ups of the encounter between Agnès and the Protector. Only one shot departs from this focus: a single cutaway to the Boy in mid-shot, followed by a slow tilt downward to the scene below. Compare this to the DVD production, which features no fewer than four separate cutaways to the Boy, ranging from mid-shots to close-ups. One reading of the prominence of this cutaway shot would be to suggest that multicamera production here simply incorporates—one might even say, domesticates—the spatial montage of Mitchell's stage into familiar cinematic/televisual territory. Given that the scene from which it cuts away (the principal encounter) features a familiar grammar of close-ups and mid-shots, and given that throughout the rhythm of the cut seems seismographically linked, as it so often is, to affect and gesture, the response might be to consider this cutaway as assimilated into a quite conventional context. The spatiotemporal implications of the grid—that the Boy is at once contiguous with and separate from the space occupied by Agnès and the Protector—seem lost, that is, in a classic reaction shot. Where now is the tension of witnessing separate spaces simultaneously if this is merely the classic cutaway of televisual drama, perhaps the kind of eavesdropping so familiar from soap opera?

We might complicate this reading by observing that the capacity of the

FIGURE 2.3. Angel 1/the Boy (Bejun Mehta). *Written on Skin*, director, Katie Mitchell, Royal Opera House, 2013. Blu-ray Opus Arte, OABD7136D, 2013.

camera to scale the image in effect extends the range of juxtapositions of perspective, of sights and sites: one close-up of the Boy reveals his anguished face (which is turned away from the audience) reflected in the window at which he stands (fig. 2.3). Like the closed-circuit-style images from the fixed cameras mounted within the set (another feature of the video production), these close-ups offer perspectives unavailable to the theater audience or at least difficult to discern. In the context of a production that combines spaces and bodies imagined to be separate, the video production presents to its viewer other proximities of bodies or fragments of bodies, other configurations of space that supplement and extend the juxtapositions on stage. The impression is of ownership, of adaptation rather than remediation.

PART AND WHOLE

But there is something else here. I mentioned that in this scene the Arte telecast offers no glimpse of the full stage between the bookend shots. This is not the case in the DVD production, which interpolates an additional three wide shots of the full stage into the edit. Consistent with its emphasis on this shot type throughout, the DVD production in this scene insists on foregrounding the full stage. Where the Arte telecast briefly maps the stage space by scanning it with a tilt from the upper level to the lower, the DVD contextualizes and situates its fragments in a different way: by cutting back and forth between part and whole. The close-ups and rapid cuts, the DVD edit repeatedly reminds us, map to *this whole* (the full stage). It is a gesture consistent with the *documentary* impulse of live multicamera production—consistent, that is, with its hesitancy to challenge spatial coherence. At the same time, the repeated interpolation of this shot type into an already-generous and restless mix has the effect of expanding the range of perspectives and of further accelerating the cut rate: more shots, more cuts, more fragmentation.[18] And all this to present a wide shot that is itself a scene of fragmented space (the grid stage). So the very shot type that might offer to map the stage space, to make spatial sense of it, is itself an image of divided space, while the insistence on returning to this shot type within the edit further agitates and fragments the temporal montage in ways that foreground the medial intervention of the video production and draw attention to its mediality.

If this were not enough, consider that the cutaway to the Boy presents a scene of listening: he stands by an open window not to look through it but to eavesdrop on the inhabitants of the house. His own silence is of course textually mandated—in the libretto and the score he is absent from this scene—but justified in Mitchell's visual metanarrative of observation and monitoring as one of the angels/conservators who set the narrative in motion. Angel 1 here takes up his part in the narrative as the Boy and listens as he becomes the subject of a heated exchange. It is one manifestation of a complex *staging* of sound—imaginary and actual—in Mitchell's production. Imaginary: it is not the capacity to speak but to hear that is privileged, to hear voices from elsewhere, to be able to hear the orchestra as sonic trace of a metanarrative (something the angels seem able to do). Actual: while the lower layer plays host to noisy voices, the upper remains silent throughout, its compartments mute. Yet, if only some compartments produce sound, all resonate with it, vocal and orchestral; they are all bound together by music. That is, the division of the visual field into separate spaces is not matched by a fragmented sonic stage. Shaped in performance by a literary/musical text unconcerned with this compartmentalization, *Written on Skin* sounds as and within a single space, like a sonic equivalent of the permanent long shot. Remediated within a video production, however, this single space of sonic production—the space of the opera house—fragments and divides across a different kind of stage.

68 | CHAPTER TWO

SOUNDSTAGE

Recorded sound has long been likened to a theatrical stage. Théberge et al. note the role of the théâtrophone, Clément Ader's 1881 telephone-based experiment in transmission of sound from the stage, in establishing a stage imaginary for recorded sound in scientific and journalistic discourse.[19] Reinforced in recent decades by some of the key literature in the field, the heuristic of sound recording as stage has thoroughly embedded itself in the language of audio production and reception, both in the industry and in consumer-oriented commentary. It is above all the term *soundstage*, defined in William Moylan's much-reissued textbook and manual *The Art of Recording* (1992) as the "perceived performance environment," that has crystallized the association and gained discursive traction.[20]

For Théberge et al., the value of the term *soundstage* and of the broader conception of audio recording as a form of staging lies not in its mobilization of a model of fidelity—understanding recorded music as a good or bad copy of an original sonic event—but in its potential to problematize this model by taking its bearings from a *structural* likeness: the resemblance between the artifice of recorded sound and the artifice of the stage. Thus imagined, the space of the audio recording becomes, as Théberge et al. put it, "a technical representation of that which was already a representation."[21] My own motivation for thinking through recorded sound in these terms is different. I want to consider not how the stage as metaphor might enrich our understanding of recorded sound but how the soundstage of audio recording might map indexically back onto the stage space it purports to model.

Like virtually all video productions of opera, sound in *Written on Skin* was recorded using a multitrack technique that mixes sources recorded at discrete (and discreet) locations throughout the opera house. As Haigh et al. explain, microphone choice and placement at the Royal Opera House are modeled on studio techniques initially developed by the producer John Culshaw for the celebrated Decca stereo studio recordings of opera in the 1950s and refined in the following decades until the studio recording of opera became financially unviable toward the end of the century. So, for example, an array of microphones consisting of stereo pairs is positioned at intervals across the lip of the stage. The effect is to divide the stage into zones of pickup reminiscent, as Haigh et al. point out, of the grid marked on the recording stage that was a feature of Decca recordings. Just as singers in those recordings would be positioned on the grid to achieve spatial effects in the recording, so the (unmarked) grid defined by microphone location offers to place voices—what Haigh et al. repeatedly refer to as the *imaging* of voices—on a sonically rendered stage when the multiple tracks (each mapped to specific microphones) are laterally assembled (panned) within a stereo or surround-sound mix.[22] The video production of *Written on Skin*, then, is doubly defined by grids. Mortimer's vertically stacked architectural grid (so prominently featured in the wide shots of the video edit) complements an imaginary, horizontally conceived sonic grid defined by microphone placement. Both can be understood as combining remote spaces but to different ends. Where the architectural grid divides actually adjacent spaces on stage to generate the impression of a simultaneity of remote points of view, multitracking mixes actually remote sonic spaces to generate the impression of a single and coherent point of audition.

Much emphasized in the account of the production goals outlined by Haigh et al., the question of a coherent sonic space is defined in terms consistent with the broader discourse associated with the soundstage. So, for example, the focus on precise imaging of voices (including lateral movement across the stage) tallies with Moylan's taxonomy of image types—fixed points, "spread," and moving images—within the soundstage.[23] And when Haigh et al. consider the wider sonic environment of the opera house—the radio microphones worn by singers to capture vocal detail, the microphones installed in the rigging above the stage for voices (including chorus) positioned further upstage, the large array of microphones positioned within the orchestra pit, and microphones positioned in the auditorium to record ambient sound—they do so in ways consistent with Moylan's characterization of the soundstage as a space that potentially contains and combines subspaces placed side by side or overlapped or at varying perceived degrees of distance. Admittedly, Moylan is primarily concerned with studio recording: he refers repeatedly to the "illusion of live performance."[24] Focused, by contrast, on recording in an actual space of live performance, Haigh et al. confront not only the logistic challenges associated with on-site recording but also the assumed burden of *re*-creating an original. Yet the dynamics of illusion—of a manufactured real—remain the same. "The result," Haigh et al. observe in prefatory remarks on their "philosophy" as recording engineers, "must be believable even if it contains a great deal of artifice."[25]

MIXING FOR PICTURE

Haigh et al. also confront another problem: how to record and mix sound for screen media. Here, a number of competing interests come to the fore. What to do, for example, about what they call *perspective realism*, the practice of manipulating the audio mix so that the sound is perceived to match the perspective adopted by the image at any given time. True, they point out, a wide shot might be accompanied by a greater focus on ambient sound sources, and close-ups invite a prominent role in the mix for the singers' radio microphones as a means of focusing sonic image during close-ups. But any fader manipulations, they stress, should be "very slight" and "subtle," drawing attention to themselves only in very obvious moments, such as a singer exiting while singing.[26]

In *Written on Skin*, perspective audio is barely discernible in the stereo or the surround-sound mix. To my ears, wide shots of the stage architecture offer no more ambient sound than closer-range shots of the various compartments, and the busy cut rate that alternates between silent and noisy compartments and between close-ups and mid-shots within those compartments is not tracked by the audio mix. Haigh et al. offer two justifications for this kind of restraint. The first is based on genre: not the conventions of recorded opera or music but those of television dramas and soap opera, which, as they point out, have historically avoided any mimetic mapping of dialogue audio onto shot type. The second is based on the classic logic of fidelity to music in performance: shifting sonic perspective in the middle of a musical phrase, they argue, would draw attention away from the music and toward the mediation, pulling the "viewer/listener out of that moment." Since this is an undesirable effect—and the underlying assumption is that it is—the emphasis is on continuity: "Consistency of sound is prioritized over perspective realism."[27] The audio mix, that is, owes its allegiance to music, not to the screen.

At the same time, Haigh et al. acknowledge that "mixing for picture" calls for special considerations. So, for example, while advising against what they describe as "large fader moves" to boost the singers' radio microphones during close-ups, they highlight the need for the mix to offer greater vocal detail than it might were there no picture. Implied visual perspective or proximity, it seems, demands a corresponding gesture from sound. The solution? A compromise in the overall static balance: "To cater for close-up images without sudden audio perspective changes, the recorded sound for picture might need to be slightly more detailed." Another potential problem is particularly associated with surround sound (a mix featured not only in the DVD release but also in the Royal Opera House's cinecast series). Panning the stage microphone sources across the mix (whether stereo or the front channels in a surround-sound mix) generates an "appropriate width," Haigh et al. explain, to the soundstage—appropriate because it maps the soundstage onto opera-house dimensions. That is, the sonic scale of the presentation of opera—and specifically here the Royal

Opera House—demands width in the soundstage if it is to offer what they describe as a "believable sense of perspective."[28]

But there is a constraint. A lateral spread in the vocal images, Haigh et al. warn, must be carefully managed to avoid any conflict with the spectator's orientation toward the screen. Too much width in the soundstage, and sound begins to compete with the forward-facing orientation demanded by the screened stage. If a sound-only recording might aim for the impression of a wide, enveloping mix, the priority when "mixing for picture" is a soundstage that "keeps the stage action contained in front of the listener."[29] What emerges here is an operatic equivalent of the anxiety associated with the "exit door effect" in cinema, when surround-sound effects are perceived to draw the audio viewer's attention away from the screen and toward perceived sources in the auditorium.[30] Opera on video, in other words, calls for a certain sonic deference, not necessarily to any image per se, but to the place and orientation of the screen in the act of viewing.

What we encounter visually in the video production of *Written on Skin* is the simultaneous presentation of stage spaces imagined to be remote (whether presented as a wide shot or across the temporal montage of the video edit); what we encounter sonically is an audio mix drawn from an accumulation and blending of multiple separate sonic perspectives. Understood in *audiovisual* terms, the production presents these simultaneities simultaneously, as a dance of deference and independence: image composition and edit are attributed to the rhythms of musical text and its sonic realization but equally to the visual and spatial configurations on stage; sound is mixed to reinforce the perspective generated by image but preserves its own coherence.

THEY ARE WATCHING YOU

In Emma Dillon's reading of *Written on Skin*, the dual temporality of the parchment, at once object of conservation and catalyst in an unfolding narrative, foregrounds the work of philological inquiry and its attendant apparatus.[31] Also at work in Mitchell's staging, I want to suggest, is the apparatus of scientific observation of live subjects. What the angels/conservators set in motion becomes an unfolding experiment, a set of behaviors that they document and monitor: they watch, they listen. The compartmentalized staging is decisive here because it consistently makes visible both experiment and scientific inquiry, subjects and observers. And recall how the Boy takes up a position from which he can overhear the Protector and Agnès: he plays the double role of scientific monitor (he remains on the upper level, the level of observation and listening) and participant-observer (one who dons the costume of his subjects and plays a part *within* the experiment).

Williams's video production takes a cue from this apparatus of observation/monitoring and gives it specific form. Dispersed throughout the production are shots fed by cameras mounted strategically within the set. Static, wide angled, and monochrome, these images carry the unmistakable imprint of closed-circuit television (CCTV). More than presenting just another camera angle, this footage draws attention to itself; it monitors not just a scene but the monitoring of a scene. It raises the questions, Who is monitoring? and, To what end? In short, it pushes observation and monitoring in the direction of discipline, control, and security, invoking the shadow of surveillance by mobilizing its apparatus. In this, the Williams production is not unique: as though belatedly taking a cue from the surveillant imaginary long mobilized in the camerawork of cinema and of television drama, video productions of opera have occasionally incorporated feeds reminiscent of CCTV (we have seen, e.g., how monochrome shots fed from mounted cameras figure prominently in the video productions of the Castorf *Ring* and the Kratzer *Tannhäuser*). What is rare about the Williams production is the independence of these shots from the stage production. In the Bayreuth productions, the footage is already projected on the stage; by contrast, the CCTV footage in *Written on Skin* (fig. 2.4) is new to the video production and forms no part of the mise-en-scène in the theater.

By harnessing the visual rhetoric of CCTV surveillance, the Williams production signals that it knows something about the narrative that the stage production cannot or will not acknowledge: it knows that surveillance is in operation, and it mobilizes, while at the same time exposing, the surveillant gaze. But does this self-awareness extend to the metagaze of multicamera production? Is there a recognition, in other words, of the surveillant character of its real-time monitoring of an unfolding event? By folding the *explicitly* surveillant imagery into a montage that otherwise features a familiar range of multicamera shot types, the production might be understood to generate a certain equivalence, as though affirming the televisual capacity—proclivity, even—to monitor/observe events in real time. It is all surveillance, the production seems to suggest. Yet this video production is a recording and an elaborately postproduced one at that. This is no monitoring in real time because that real time has already taken place. This is no raw relay but a carefully assembled, professionally produced edit.

Thomas Y. Levin addresses this issue when he considers the cinematic

Split Loyalties | 73

FIGURE 2.4. The Protector (Christopher Purves) and Angel 1/the Boy (Bejun Mehta). *Written on Skin*, director, Katie Mitchell, Royal Opera House, 2013. Blu-ray Opus Arte OABD7136D, 2013.

engagement with surveillance. What concerns Levin is not merely how surveillance is represented but how, in a more fundamental reorientation beginning in the 1970s, cinema structurally incorporated real-time monitoring as modeled first by live multicamera television and CCTV and later by webcams. The effect was to foreground a "temporal indexicality" rather than the spatial indexicality that had been guaranteed by cinema's photochemical means of production.[32] But, Levin adds, if television is at home with surveillant observation, it too confronts a challenge in the form of what he calls the *anxiety of postproduction*, which presents the possibility of distortion of an otherwise authentic real-time capture. The *post-* syncopates the temporal indexicality that is supposed to be the televisual guarantee of observational truth and replaces it with that which has already happened; substituting real-time observation, recording undermines the claim to truthful record. Precisely the postproduced, recorded polish of the *Written on Skin* DVD—its cinematic aspect ratio, its elaborate and flawless montage, its rich range of shot types (including the surveillant imagery)—can be read as challenging its surveillant character by implying that, far from monitoring passively, the production intervenes and manipulates. From this perspective, the live telecast from Aix-en-Provence, in which multicamera production assumes its characteristic role as inconspicuous observer tracking an event in real time, more authentically channels the surveillant quality of multicamera production, despite the absence of explicit surveillance-style footage. To tease out this question of multicamera production as surveillant further, I turn to a Mitchell staging that weaves surveillance explicitly into the mise-en-scène. How, I want to ask, does this theme of surveillance register in a more reflexive encounter—when, in other words, surveillance on stage is itself subject to surveillance?

PEEP-BOX OPERA

In *Judith* (2020, Bayerische Staatsoper), a staging of *Bluebeard's Castle* follows a forty-minute silent film prologue (director, Grant Gee) accompanied by a live performance of Bartók's *Concerto for Orchestra*. As in Kratzer's production of *Tannhäuser*, the film presents a backstory, in this case a detective narrative in the mold of television crime thrillers. Judith, the film reveals, is not the overinquisitive feminine ingenue of Balázs's libretto but an undercover detective investigating the disappearance of three escorts (the three wives of the libretto). Posing as an escort, she lures Bluebeard into hiring her and enters his "castle," here a penthouse apartment. *Judith* is, as Mitchell puts it, a feminist "overwriting," one that takes into account a history of feminist readings of the *Bluebeard* fable but that also rejects "traditional images" and gives the "female figure more room to maneuver."[33] In narrative terms, this maneuvering room takes the form of an inversion in which Judith becomes the agent of a sting operation and Bluebeard its target. The imagery, however, might be more conventional than Mitchell allows: several critics bemoaned the familiar televisual imagery in Gee's film, likened by one to a "middling Netflix thriller."[34]

More convincing, critics argued, was a hypernaturalistic theatrical mise-en-scène that meticulously—forensically—matched the props, sets, and lighting of the staging to the film.[35] The overt apparatus of Mitchell's live cinema technique is absent here, but its visual language is very much in evidence, as though the production represented a diachronic, reversed unfolding of the typically synchronic presentation of live cinema: not simultaneous shooting, editing, and projecting the work of live actors but a film that *retrospectively* comes to be seen as though it were the product of a live staging.[36] In the set design by Alex Eales, the seven rooms of the opera are configured as a linear sequence of compartments that scroll slowly across the stage, two visible at any given time, as though the grid in *Written on Skin* had been placed on a conveyor belt. The rooms enter from one wing and disappear into the other as Judith penetrates deeper into Bluebeard's claustrophobic domain (see fig. 2.5).[37] The effect, wrote the critic for *Bachtrack*,

FIGURE 2.5. *Judith*, director, Katie Mitchell, Bayerische Staatsoper, 2020.

is of a "sophisticated peep box [*Guckkasten*]," a comparison elaborated on by the critic for *Die Tagespost*, who observed that, "like a film, the peep-box images [*Guckkasten-Bildern*] move from right to left past the viewer."[38]

That *Judith* is saturated with representations of looking is perhaps unsurprising given its narrative theme of criminal investigation. The detective (Judith) scrutinizes visual evidence of crime: photographic records left behind by the missing women, images on social media, case files presented on computer screens. And repeatedly it is not just the imagery itself that is represented but the act of looking at the images: the detective's eyes are seen in reflection or superimposed in a dissolve, and the most recent victim is portrayed as a keen amateur photographer, her own gaze repeatedly foregrounded together with her photographs. Although Bluebeard's face is never seen in the film, his presence is repeatedly invoked in the form of silhouettes and reflections, his gaze in the form of extreme close-ups of his eyes. One of these close-ups captures the object of his gaze: the monitors of a CCTV security system (fig. 2.6). The monitors themselves feature repeatedly in the film, as do the mounted cameras that feed them images. In the *Bluebeard* staging, the CCTV system returns in the form of a bank of seven monitors, each connected to a fixed camera in one of the rooms Judith will visit. Beneath them is a composite monitor that allows the individual camera feeds to be combined and tiled (fig. 2.7).

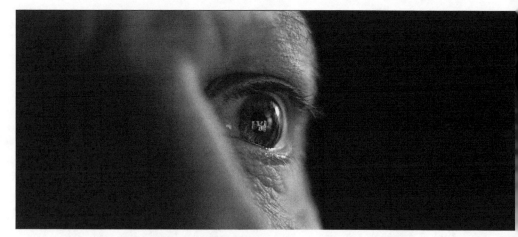

FIGURE 2.6. *Judith*, director, Katie Mitchell, Bayerische Staatsoper, 2020. Live stream, Staatsoper.tv, 2020.

FIGURE 2.7. Bluebeard (John Lundgren) and Judith (Nina Stemme). *Judith*, director, Katie Mitchell, Bayerische Staatsoper, 2020. Live stream, Staatsoper.tv, 2020.

SWITCH OF ATTENTION

The monitors foreshadow the configuration of the set itself in their very arrangement: horizontally arrayed, they anticipate, in narrative order, the scrolling peep boxes as Bluebeard and Judith penetrate ever deeper into the bunker. They also mirror another CCTV system: that of the multiple cameras linked to a bank of monitors in the media production suite of the Staatsoper. The monitoring, that is, does not end on stage. *Judith* was streamed live and available on demand for one month as part of the company's Staatsoper.tv platform and on BR-Klassik. The streamed video (director, Christoph Engel) begins with a direct feed of Grant Gee's film and follows that with a conventional live multicamera presentation of the *Bluebeard's Castle* staging. The stream, that is, channels its own likeness. In the film, the camera dwells on the bank of monitors and their panning, tilting images, which occasionally cut to other feeds from an array of CCTV cameras. When the monitors return on stage, the Staatsoper cameras introduce them by panning across the array, mimicking the very motion the monitors feature while adding one other effect not demonstrated by Bluebeard's cameras: zoom. Armed with the PTZ (pan-tilt-zoom) motion widely associated with surveillance, the Staatsoper cameras close on their subject to offer details of the content of each screen surely out of reach of the naked eye in the auditorium. An alternative might have been to adopt the CCTV feeds directly to create the kinds of effects we saw in chapter 1. Instead, like so much video production of staged opera, the stream limits itself to observing from the auditorium: panning, tilting, zooming. It is a shooting technique that will feature throughout the video production. Perhaps because the naturalistic detail and precise *Personenregie* (direction of the actor) on stage invite close-ups, the cameras tightly frame the protagonists and must then pan and tilt to track them as they traverse the conveyor belt of peep boxes.

The stream imitates Bluebeard's monitors in another way too. Just as the images on some of the monitors cycle across the array of feeds one by one, so the edited stream cycles through feeds from the several cameras set up in the Staatsoper auditorium. Both depend on a configuration in which cameras link individually to a wall of monitors while also feeding into a sequenced combination. Likening multicamera production to CCTV surveillance calls for some qualification. Certainly, televised/streamed coverage of this kind does not amount to surveillance understood as an instrument of control or discipline in the manner Foucault associates with the "panopticon," Jeremy Bentham's concept for a system of prison surveillance. At the same time, the panoptic impulse—the desire to "see everything constantly," as Foucault puts it—finds form in the multicamera array and wall of monitors, an apparatus devoted to *coverage* of the stage enabled by diverse, simultaneous angles and ranges.[39] Not that the viewer is to see everything; rather, it is the director who sees all and selects on that basis.

This raises the question of agency. Surveying the monitor-like quality of our contemporary screenscape, Casetti reminds us that closed-circuit surveillance systems are often automated and recorded—that there may be no one watching until "after something has happened."[40] Bluebeard may or may not be watching his monitors at any given time, but the feeds continue to cycle automatically, and the system is presumably armed with recording capability and motion-detection algorithms. No such automation drives live multicamera production, which places the director in the position of selecting images from the multitude available. Someone is watching. Cavell is reminded of a security guard "glancing" at a "bank of monitors," the selection process, as we have seen, a "switch of attention from one monitor to another monitor." It is an image of passivity at one with Cavell's broader account of television as a medium in which image selection is driven not, as in cinema, by meaning but by the opportunity to direct attention. It is, he concludes, "as if the meaning is dictated by the event itself."[41]

Video direction can be compared to surveillance, then, because both imply a ceding of agency and intervention in the face of what is being captured. Cavell's argument is borne out at certain points in the live stream. When the direct feed of Gee's film is interrupted seven times for wide shots of the conductor and/or orchestra, it is as though the live stream had to remind the viewer repeatedly that this is taking place in the opera house—that this is a live screening, not just another soundtrack. Yet these cutaways come at a cost: the viewer misses moments in the film. One film scene involves a close-up of car lights, creating a blinding sheet of white light textured with flares. The live stream, however, cuts to a wide shot of the orchestra pit and the front rows of the auditorium, the blinding white light evident only thanks to the reflected light that suddenly bathes the orchestra and audience. When the live stream cuts clumsily back to the film, the viewer sees the white screen for half a second before the film cuts to the next scene. It all seems haphazard as a sequence and driven by a desire for multiplicity of perspective and blanket coverage.

Conversely, arguing that this kind of practice in television recalls the security guard's switch of attention between monitors, as though this were a lower order of observation, may do a disservice to surveillance in both these settings. We can glean a quite different attitude to the work of monitoring and security from social scientists engaged with questions of human-technology interactions in working environments. Writing on the

Split Loyalties | 79

surveillance operation rooms in train stations, Marcus Sanchez Svensson et al. are keen to challenge what they regard as problematic assumptions in scholarship, not least about the passive quality of the work undertaken by operators in surveillance environments: "Station supervisors and other control room personnel . . . do not passively monitor the displays waiting for 'something to happen' or just glance at the screens to gain a general awareness of the activities occurring within the station. They actively discriminate scenes and have resources that enable them to notice . . . what needs to be noticed."[42] In this reading, the work of surveillance is driven by a capacity to interpret and anticipate, not merely by passive observation. Just as the surveillance operation room maps the space of the station and makes visible the events unfolding within those spaces, so the bank of monitors in the production control room sees and maps the stage. Granted, there is a distinction to be made between shooting a rehearsed event and the unrehearsed nature of public surveillance. But Svensson et al. emphasize the skill associated with active discrimination—that is, with the ability to isolate what seems worthy of attention. And this is a performative skill arguably as relevant to public surveillance as it is to the scripted but pressured environment of live multicamera production (which is typically afforded little rehearsal time anyway).

WEARING A WIRE

There is another form of surveillance featured in Mitchell's production. As Judith pleads for him to open the last door, Bluebeard, his suspicions aroused, reaches into her dress to find a microphone and a transmitter: Judith is wearing a wire. In uncovering her secret, Bluebeard has also touched on an operatic secret or at least a practice that some institutions and practitioners seem reluctant to discuss. As Haigh et al. observe of recording practices at the Royal Opera House, the array of fixed microphones is typically supplemented by small omnidirectional radio microphones (also known as body or lavalier microphones) to offer "detail and image stability" to individual voices within the mix.[43] But this is all carefully managed to keep the intervention concealed because the microphones must not interfere with the illusion of theater. Like agents wiring up an informant, a team of specialist radio microphone operators works closely with the singer. As Haigh et al. explain: "Fitting radio microphones to performers so that they are hidden in clothing and wigs is a specialist job that requires excellent interpersonal skills." But there is a double motivation at work here for concealment. Theatrical illusion is complemented in opera by an investment in the authenticity of vocal production. Amplification of voices in live performance is one of opera's unmentionables, but even the recording of voices for broadcast and streaming generates suspicion and anxiety that clandestine assistance is at work.

It is an issue taken up, half in jest, by the *New York Times* music critic Anthony Tommasini in an article tellingly entitled "Wearing a Wire at the Opera, Secretly, of Course." Having confronted the Met general manager, Peter Gelb, with questions about radio microphones in *Met: Live in HD* productions, Tommasini is not reassured to learn, first, that it does occasionally happen and, second, that it is concealed: "I get nervous hearing Mr. Gelb talk of camouflaging wires on singer's bodies. And the Met has certainly kept this practice secret."[44] Part of the anxiety associated with radio microphones among purists, it seems, is that, in an economy of performance reputed increasingly to privilege mediated over live sound, audio engineering artificially compensates for smaller voices. Wearing a wire at the opera may not serve a sting operation, but it does participate in a clandestine audio practice replete with conspiracy theories, insider knowledge, and even the familiar surveillance narrative, played out in *Judith*, of the wired operative whose secret is known. As the bass-baritone Eric Owens quipped: "You want to be heard? Go and sing in so-and-so's wig!"[45]

But there is more to this than visual concealment. The vocal detail made possible by radio microphones, Haigh et al. explain, will add an important dimension to the sound, but that dimension must be deployed "*without ever allowing the presence of the radio microphones to become discernible.*"[46] In his article, Tommasini interviews the Met audio producer Jay David Saks, who declares absolute confidence that the use of radio microphones could never be detected by the listener. This story, he tells Tommasini, "started from something someone saw, not from something someone heard."[47] Maintaining that inaudibility, the audio producer Jonathan Allen observes, means confronting two challenges. One is a question of timing. The vocal sound recorded via the radio microphones will precede the sound captured by the main array of voice microphones installed at the lip of stage and needs to be delayed to synchronize with the rest of the mix. As the singer moves away from the float microphones, Allen explains, the delay increases. The response in live transmissions is to "chase" the delays manually. The second challenge concerns the proximity of the radio microphones to the voice. With detail, Allen points out, comes the potential for an artificially dry and "boxed" sound that fails to register the full "body" and "color" associated with a form of vocal production predicated on projection at distance.[48] As Haigh et al. add, the sound must not privilege the close-miked voice, as in pop and musical theater, but should be subtly and flexibly integrated into a mix that is focused on a wider acoustic ambience.[49]

BUGGING THE ROOM

Writing on *Invisible Cities*, a 2013 site-specific production by the Los Angeles opera company The Industry, Megan Steigerwald Ille observes a logic of mutual determination in which a specific listening experience—the work is conceived for an audience equipped with wireless headphones—is shaped by but also determines compositional practice and vocal production. The network of listening and hearing—or "aurality"—at work in *Invisible Cities* is characterized, Steigerwald Ille argues, by an intimacy of vocal production designed for headphones and modeled in part on pop aesthetics and practices.[50] What Allen and Haigh et al. articulate, by contrast, is the conventional aurality from which *Invisible Cities* departs. They too recognize a sonic model, but here it is shaped by the acoustics of the opera house, by listening to voices on a large stage. To (re)construct this projected sound in recording requires, paradoxically, an intimate engagement with those voices. The role of the audio engineer, then, is shaped by a logic of adaptation and concealment in which sound technology must conform to and reproduce the effect of existing practice; it must intervene artificially while remaining undetected.[51]

The image of concealed audio engineers remotely monitoring and adjusting levels to refine and chase the vocal sound recalls the cinematic representation of audio surveillance, classically illustrated in *The Conversation* (director, Francis Ford Coppola, 1974) when the audio engineer Harry Caul tweaks and filters a bugged conversation to clarify voices against background noise.[52] Do audio engineers not effectively bug the opera house when they plant concealed microphones throughout, then monitor and manipulate the feeds and levels, either in real time (as in the *Judith* live stream) or in postproduction (as in the *Written on Skin* DVD)? Yet, whereas Harry Caul will begin to register doubts about the apparatus as some objective trace of sonic reality, audio engineers like Saks and Allen display an unshakable faith in their capacity to mobilize technology to craft, undetected, a convincing sonic fiction. "I would bet everything I own," Saks told Tomassini, "that from listening to the broadcasts you could not tell which singers and which productions used body microphones."[53]

SPLIT-SCREEN OPERA

One of the screen configurations widely in use in CCTV systems features prominently in both the film and the stage segments of *Judith*. If a bank of monitors offers one way to display closed-circuit feeds simultaneously, another technological solution is the split screen. Bluebeard watches screens with individual feeds, but he also watches a screen divided into four tiles, each carrying a separate feed. It is this composite screen that is reflected artfully in Gee's film in an extreme close-up of Bluebeard's eyes, and it the same screen that takes pride of place in the mise-en-scène of Bluebeard's monitoring room, where it sits on a desk beneath the bank of seven monitors with their individual feeds. An interface between the separate feeds, this screen also occupies an interstitial location between media technologies. It is at once a television monitor within a closed-circuit loop and a computer monitor that displays a configuration generated by surveillance software.

As television, it recalls the split-screen form cultivated in particular by multicamera genres like live sports and twenty-four-hour news channels; as computer screen, it recalls the windowed arrangement of applications, images, and feeds on desktop monitors, laptops, and mobile screens. And this double allegiance is itself doubled when the stage production is remediated as a live stream. The production process is that of multicamera television (itself reliant on computer technology), while distribution relies on web-based streaming technologies to link servers, hubs, and networks to web browsers on computer screens and phones (with the possibility of playback via a television screen). Sitting at the very heart of these interfaces is another split screen: in the production room among the bank of monitors carrying individual camera feeds is a composite image that combines and labels all the camera feeds on one screen. Like a map of the process, this television/computer monitor watches over everything, in effect presenting a miniaturized model of the bank of monitors around it.

For Cavell it was economic constraints alone that prevented the viewer at home from viewing the bank of monitors. No such limitation applies to this digitally produced composite. Indeed, nothing technical prevents a composite image of this kind or any subset of it from being selected as the image for transmission or streaming. Here, in other words, is one possible realization of Cavell's imaginary bank of monitors in the home: in place of the temporal montage of multicamera editing a spatial montage that displays multiple perspectives simultaneously. Yet at no point in *Judith* does the screen split to offer multiple perspectives simultaneously—this despite the potential to render in screen-media form the split stage (peep boxes) of Mitchell's production and/or the multiple CCTV feeds that capture and are displayed within those compartmentalized spaces. For the live stream it is a case of business as usual. In its camerawork, the *Judith* live stream follows the conventions adopted by the Staatsoper live streams more generally, but these conventions are in turn consistent with decades of multicamera production of opera, with thousands of telecasts and streams. Split screens rarely figure in that history. In this, the video production of staged opera takes its cue not from live sports but from recorded multicamera genres such as sitcoms or talk shows.

There are exceptions, of course, but they tend to be productions with a conceptual hook that motivates a particular treatment. So, for example, Philippe Béziat's video production of *La pietra del paragone* (2008) takes the novel intermedial staging by Giorgio Barberio Corsetti and the video artist Pierrick Sorin (it featured live video remediation, including blue-screen effects) as a cue for multiple split-screen effects. It is a staging that, as Senici puts it, "opens up unusual technical and aesthetic possibilities to video recording," but these, he stresses, are only ever possibilities.[54] Opera North's semistaged *Ring* cycle (2016) was effectively staged on video thanks to a production telecast in part on the BBC and subsequently made available in complete form as an on-demand stream.[55] Directed by Peter Mumford, the video featured copious use of split-screen presentation, including fixed-camera shots of the conductor and the orchestra. Perhaps the project that most closely resembles the composite monitor of the multicamera production is the Royal Opera House's "Opera Machine," a web interface that presented viewers with a "camera grid" of seventeen perspectives from which they could choose individual feeds (in combination with three audio feeds) to curate their own video production of act 3 of *Die Walküre* (stage director, Keith Warner; "machine" director, Jonathan Haswell, 2014). The "Opera Machine," then, even incorporated the interactive quality of the composite monitor (the viewer in effect becomes a director who chooses from the available feeds), but in this it bears little resemblance to standard practice in multicamera video production, which of course offers the viewer no input on camera selection.

One notorious case illustrates what happens when video productions mobilize split-screen effects without what critics regard as a compelling conceptual or visual cue from the stage production. As I have discussed elsewhere, critics were incensed when Barbara Willis Sweete introduced split-screen effects in *The Met: Live in HD Tristan und Isolde* (2007). The director herself is quoted as likening the response, presumably tongue planted firmly in cheek, to a "fatwa." Although the production features sustained passages with standard edits based on cuts between full-screen images, it repeatedly breaks the full screen into tiles so that cuts give way to a simultaneous presentation of multiple camera perspectives. Confronted with the opera's expansive phrasing and long stretches of "inner" action (all presented in a sparse staging directed by Dieter Dorn and designed by Jürgen Rose), "what," Kay Armatage asks sympathetically "is the director of an HD transmission to do?"[56] Anything but this, came the response from critics, who perceived the split screen as a violation of the illusion of theatrical presence and an unwelcome reminder of the mediation at play—in short, the production had strayed from the path of transparency. Though she would direct dozens more productions in the series, the director retreated to the relative safety of conventional practice with its temporal montage of full-screen images.

Why the furious rejection? And why so little counterresistance from practitioners? Writing at the turn of millennium, Lev Manovich predicted that an exponential growth in image resolution in digital cinema would license a reemergence of forms of spatial montage suppressed since cinema's early history in favor of sequential editing devoted to narrowly temporal conceptions of narrativity. If the technology of video and film had emerged in forms predicated on the delivery of single images in sequence, he added, all this was about to change.[57] But, though the resolutions have grown (both in cinema and especially in the home via streaming technology), the revolution has not materialized. That accounts of split-screen presentation still dwell on the innovations of *Timecode* (Mike Figgis, 2000) and the series *24* (Surnow and Cochran, 2001–10) says much about the still-limited reach of the split screen in cinema and narrative televisual genres.[58] Elsewhere, Casetti observes, split and multiple screens proliferate: in the arrangement of our computer and mobile screens, in the videos (including music videos) that proliferate online, on the facades of our urban-consumer palaces, in the surveillant image. These configurations exemplify what Casetti terms *display*, understood as a form of presentation and engagement unbound by the presumption of attentiveness. "The display shows," he writes, "but only in the sense that it places at our disposition or makes accessible. It exhibits, but does not uncover; it offers, but does not commit."[59]

Yet Casetti recognizes a certain cinematic resistance embodied in a mode of presentation still loyal to apparently untimely notions of attention, of narrativity, even of truth and the realism of the image. Do we not still gather, he asks, in darkened theaters and even equip our domestic spaces to emulate these spaces of attentive viewing?[60] We might say the same of narrative television genres: if the so-called prestige or quality television featured on streaming and premium cable services increasingly competes with cinema as a vehicle for visual innovation, it does so (at least visually) in cinematic terms. Like cinema, television of this kind still seems to demand an attentive eye, and its screen remains whole, never subject to splitting. It is from these prerecorded television genres and their associated modes of spectatorship, not the arguably more comparable live production of sports and news programing, that the remediation of staged opera seems to take its bearings, even as these opera videos find themselves increasingly disseminated as streams and downloads to be viewed as one window among many on a computer desktop or on one of several screens within reach of the viewer's gaze.

TEMPORAL MONTAGE

This investment in narrative in the form of what Manovich calls *temporal montage* informs the conventions and grammar of these productions. Explaining their role, multicamera directors in opera repeatedly identify storytelling as a priority. "The first principle is narrative," Haswell explains. "I have to communicate the story of the show."[61] Large characterizes the video director as a storyteller who adapts via moving image.[62] And Halvorson likens his work in opera to his experience with sitcom scripts: "You start with the story and you work your compositions and your shot movement and everything else to tell that story the best way you can, pictorially."[63] Consistently, it seems, the best way to tell a story within the apparatus of multicamera production is to arrange shots sequentially, even, as we have seen, when the stage production in question configures its narrative in explicitly spatial terms. This sequential presentation amounts to a mapping of the space, an unfolding devoted to the formation of spatial coherence via the comprehensible (because conventional) ordering of shots: wide shots to establish spatial context, mid-shots to mediate with close-ups, and so on.

Written on Skin deviates from this pattern in its insistence on the wide shot, but more telling is something in the DVD that does not feature in the video of the performance itself. Among the paratextual features of the DVD is an animated interactive menu comprising a wide shot of the stage grid (in the cinematic aspect ratio of the video) and some discreet clickable navigation cues. Or, rather, it comprises a montage of separate images of each compartment in the grid separated by thick black frames. Silent, the menu is initially still before coming to life as each compartment in turn is animated by short sequences of video drawn from the production. As each sequence ends, it dissolves back to the still photograph from which it emerged, just as the next compartment comes to life. What we see here resembles the paratextual materials and techniques identified by Carlo Cenciarelli in opera DVDs. Drawing on Manovich, Cenciarelli considers the allusions to computers, video games, and narrative cinema in the looped presentation, interactive screen, carefully designed picture frames, and cinematic codes (including the conventions associated with feature films on DVD) that package and frame the video feature within the DVD. The value of attending to these paratexts, he argues, lies precisely in the way they conflict with the main feature, gesturing toward possibilities excluded by the "conceptual strictures of the televisual."[64]

In the case of the Williams video, the grip of these strictures, as we have seen, is partially loosened, and the features of the DVD menu can be read as anticipating and resonating with qualities in the main feature, not least its cinematic aspect ratio. What really distinguishes the menu, however, is precisely what is absent from the video production: a split screen. The menu animation realizes the possibility that the video overlooks, rend(er)ing the stage production into the very split-screen form the grid emulates.[65] One of the animated sequences even features the slow-motion movement adopted by the stage production, itself modeled on screen media. The menu sows doubt about the source of the slow motion. Is it performed that way, or is it a video effect? Summoned here is less the cinematic than video art, with its history of manipulated playback speeds. Meanwhile, the looped and multiscreen presentation recalls the temporalities and narrative forms of video installation and in ways that seem more in keeping with the palimpsestic layers and juxtapositions of the text and of Mitchell's production than do the storytelling sequences of the video production proper. Like a corrective to the cinematic rhetoric so pervasive in the discourse around Mitchell's work, the menu gestures toward another screen-media lineage. In this sense, it interacts with—reveals something about—qualities in the stage production that the subsequent video production will be content merely to capture.

CONCLUSION

I have been arguing that the encounter between multicamera production and the divided stage represents a missed opportunity—that televisual convention allows video production to let itself be seen and heard only fitfully, only in fragments and in the margins. Let me conclude, however, with two observations that at least reframe, if not quite dispel, my critical frustration and disappointment that more is not ventured or risked in these video productions. One comes courtesy of Mitchell, who has this to say about split stages in opera: "If I just hold to one setting and one situation, I'll be really struggling to fill it with drama, because the music goes so slowly and there are all these long gaps. Having simultaneous action and environment makes it easier for me to fill the music."[66] Theater, in this view, abhors a vacuum, and opera, encumbered by so much music, risks precisely that. Far from the fidelity to music that Senici identifies as the dominant paradigm in the rhetoric of opera directors (and in the discourse of operatic staging more widely), what Mitchell outlines here is a poetics of plugging gaps.[67] And, just as the split stage affords Mitchell access to modes of action and configurations of space with the potential to fill a void, so multicamera directors can draw on the bank of monitors to banish the possibility of a black screen. Take, for example, the closing seconds of *Judith*, when the stage goes dark but the music continues in the form of Bartók's hushed closing pulses in low strings and timpani. It is a mere few seconds of darkness, but Engel's video production does what these productions habitually do when confronted by the possibility of a black screen: it cuts to the conductor, someone unseen for the entire staged portion of *Judith*, as she beats those pulses.

Like Senici's stage directors, multicamera directors are discursively beholden to the notion of fidelity—to music but also to the stage production and to the event (recall Brian Large's insistence that the video director should above all demonstrate respect for the work and the performance being shot and recorded). In moments like these, however, when they fill gaps with images available only to the cameras, these directors come closer at once to the panoptic visuality of television and to the fear of blank spaces articulated by Mitchell. True, the performance of music is here foregrounded but only thanks to its *visualization*. As Armatage writes of Willis Sweete, "What is the director to do?" It is a reminder to be conscious both of the independent mediality of the video production and of the values it may share with the stage production, values not necessarily predicated on *Werktreue* (fidelity to the work) or on the veneration of music but on the fear of voids and the need to sustain a sense of event.

A second observation comes from something Cavell had to say about opera on television, and it concerns the question of independence from what is being filmed. I cited a phrase from this passage in the introduction, but it is worth quoting in full:

> I would like to have useful words in which to consider why the opera and the ballet I have seen on television in recent years have seemed to me so good, whereas films I recall of opera and of ballet have seemed to me boring. Is it that television can respect the theatricality or the foreign conventionality of those media without trying, as film greedily would, to reinterpret them? And is this well thought of as television's ability to respect the independence of the theatrical event?[68]

We return once again to that respect that Large considers so important. But Cavell perhaps hints at something more here: that the independence the televisual affords is a form of generosity predicated not simply on self-abnegation but on a resistance to the greedy notion of absorption or adaptation that underpins cinema. And could this be understood as a form of simultaneity in its own way? While film seeks to fold opera into singular terms—its own—the televisual allows for parallel modalities. While cinema swallows in a way reminiscent of the totality and organic wholeness Lehmann associates with conventional theater, the televisual allows theater to coexist with it—to coexist precariously and fitfully, perhaps, but to coexist nevertheless. The televisual, that is, stages two spaces at the same time.

Part 2

CHAPTER THREE

What Time Is It in New York?

In *Echographies of Television*, Derrida and Stiegler direct a critical gaze toward the medium regarded as the dominant form of mass communication in the second half of the twentieth century. It is television, the book argues, that bore witness to the momentous as it unfolded, that relayed the specific time and place of a sports event to a global stadium, that expanded the immediate audience for a music performance (say, three tenors in concert) to a mediated audience in the millions. But, Derrida and Stiegler caution, this very grip on the flow of information and the monetized dissemination of content—on our very conception of time and event—demands scrutiny. What does it mean for television to insist on the "now" and the "once"? They are not alone here: one of the recurring themes of television studies is a suspicion about its claims to liveness. Is televisual liveness—what Mary Ann Doane calls its *insistent presentness*[1]—a matter not of ontology or even of epistemology but of corporate strategy, even ideology?[2] According to this critique, television has constructed itself as the medium of instantly communicated knowledge and experience, but this should be regarded as marketing, framing, packaging, not some vast actuality of networked immediacy.

Television, the critics warn, does more than register or communicate the a priori singularity of the event; rather, by mapping the act of witnessing onto the very idea of singularity, it insistently and persuasively constructs the evental terms it purports merely to relay. Its impression of the singularity of the event, happening once and unfolding in real time, is always shadowed, Derrida observes, by the knowledge that it is mediated by "the most sophisticated repetition machines."[3] Equally, television's purportedly instantaneous dissemination of information, packaged as a simultaneous sharing of the act of witnessing on a global scale, is actually an engineered conceit, what Stiegler calls a *synchronization machine*. Singularity and simultaneity: these are the terms, the characteristics, the qualities at stake in televisual liveness. But they are contested terms: singularity is shadowed by repetition, simultaneity by the suspicion of empty homogenization.

I want in this chapter to unpack these twin concepts as they relate to remediated opera and one form of remediation in particular. The transmission of live and as-live opera to cinemas preserves much of the vocabulary of telecasts. More than that, these cinecasts are underpinned by the technology of television: what audiences see and hear in their local cinema is based on the same kinds of satellite signals beamed by television broadcasters to dishes mounted on domestic dwellings. True, the image is projected onto a screen of cinematic dimensions, while the speaker array dwarfs anything available in the home. But the video signal is the resolution of HD telecasts (1080i or 720p), the multichannel audio the same 5.1 configuration that home audio systems and soundbars can process. Content providers like *The Met: Live in HD* market their product as an encounter between opera and cinema, and with respect to venue it is. But the medium is televisual: that the cinecasts are effectively television writ large gets no mention.

What does get mentioned, repeatedly, is the kind of rhetoric of liveness cultivated by television. These cinecasts are presented as events shared globally; they instantaneously capture a distant and unrepeatable happening and permit simultaneous engagement across a network of cinema audiences. The Metropolitan Opera wastes no opportunity to trumpet the number of cinemas receiving the transmission worldwide, while the marketing slogan featured in one of the trailers emphasizes the momentous nature of the performances in a way that draws together the two implications of the term, at once fleeting and important: "At any moment a *great moment*."[4] It is one of the Met's cinecasts that will be the focus of my inquiry, but I want to situate it as one of several moments in recent history, each with its own claim to the momentary and to the momentous. I want to ask, that is, what constitutes the live in the Met cinecast as simultaneity across space (its nowness) and unrepeatable event (its onceness).

JUNE 15, 1920: A SONG TO THE WORLD

The claim that something happening elsewhere is happening *now* is so commonplace in the era of digital networking and transmission that it takes on a deceptive banality. Yet, as Peter Galison shows, the impetus to pose the question, "What time is it now somewhere else?" and to propose answers arises from a confluence and interaction of technologies, materials, and ideas associated with modernity—not least the economic and scientific modernity of fin de siècle empire.[5] This is not, Galison stresses, to imply the invention of coordinated clocks in the late nineteenth century (this had happened already in the early decades of the century). What the period witnessed, rather, was the emergence of models of scientific inquiry, economic progress, and social cohesion that lent particular urgency to this question and offered fertile ground for the contested pursuit of answers. The late nineteenth century, Galison concludes, *produced* simultaneity, understood in terms that ranged from philosophical models of intuition (Henri Bergson) to the rational-scientific framework of theories of relativity (Albert Einstein).[6]

One of the key conventions underpinning and in turn reinforced by the imaginary of simultaneity is the coordinated spatial division of the globe into zones of simultaneity, a project initiated by railroads and telegraph networks dependent on synchronized schedules. Synchronized clocks coordinated networks of transportation, facilitated exploration and the exploitation of resources, and established order and uniformity across nations and colonial territories. Key to this synchronization was the network of communication established first by the telegraph and later by telephone and radio. Seemingly instant communication over long distances created the impression of immediate contact and facilitated the synchronized regulation of spatially remote locations.[7] Mobilized to transmit messages and relay positions and bearings, these networks could also generate communities bound by shared information and knowledge, even while spatially separated. And what began as point-to-point communication became broadcast communication when, after the Great War, radio (and, for longer distances, combinations of radio relays and telephone wires) transmitted programmed content over vast distances.[8] Now news, political speeches, and coverage of state events and ceremonies could be relayed instantly to dispersed audiences, while arts and entertainment programming could assemble a listenership into remote but simultaneous audiences.

The imperial dimension of all this was on display when the *Daily Mail* sponsored a broadcast of excerpts sung by Dame Nellie Melba from the Marconi wireless factory in England on June 15, 1920. Just as it had done with the technologies of the phonograph and the telephone, opera would serve as a high-profile vehicle for experimentation with the radio broadcast. Hailing the success of the transmission, the *Mail* concluded: "Art and Science joined hands, and the world 'listening-in' must have counted every minute of it precious."[9] Unlike a prewar experimental transmission from the Metropolitan Opera (a signal picked up only by local receiving stations) or a 1919 opera broadcast from Chicago that, according to *Radio*

Amateur News, had reached "over one hundred miles," the Marconi experiment would transmit Melba's voice on an international scale.[10] The titles of the *Mail* articles say it all: "Melba's Song to the World" (June 14), "Melba's 1,000-Miles Song" (June 15), "Melba at 1,033 Miles" (June 21). The *Mail* even published a list, supplied by Marconi, of ships equipped with wireless receivers and likely within range: "Megantic (Liverpool for Canada), Caronia (Liverpool for New York), Mandala (Gibraltar for London), Walmer Castle (Cape for Southampton). . . ." Mr. P. S. Smith, on board the SS *Baltic* bound for New York, claimed the greatest distance when he confirmed that, with nothing more than an amateur crystal wireless set, he had received the signal at a distance of 1,506 miles. Hardly the global span claimed by the *Mail*, but with an artist from one of the dominions and a recital that ended with Melba singing "God Save the King," a coup for the empire nonetheless.

But empire is trade, its global coordination a means of organizing the flow of capital, of fashioning its territories as markets. Although radio in Britain would soon come under the public-service remit of the BBC, this early experiment was a commercial partnership between two companies, one eager to showcase its potential, the other eager to sell newspapers.[11] Boasting that it had secured the services of the "queen of song," the newspaper claimed that the event heralded a new era for a technology hitherto confined largely to an informational and navigational role. What entertainment radio had hitherto featured was strictly amateur fare offered by Marconi employees and the hobbyist operators who formed the bulk of the wireless community. Now a professional artist had inaugurated another path, and the *Daily Mail*, with a week's worth of publicity articles, lost no opportunity to hype this celebrity event as the beginning not just of a new era of entertainment but of a new notion of audience. Assembled by a signal, this network of listeners would attend from their own space but at a unified time.[12]

When the Met launched its cinecast series in 2006, it did not need to carve audiences or behaviors entirely out of nothing. National live broadcasting of the Met's Saturday matinees had by then been a feature of US radio programming for seventy-five years, international broadcasting for only slightly less. Just as the radio broadcasts had arisen out of a Depression-era financial crisis (the recently founded NBC network paid $150,000 for the broadcast rights), so *The Met: Live in HD* owed its origins to Peter Gelb's search for a solution to declining audiences and revenue.[13] Here, Gelb would rely on the Met's cultural capital, on the assumption that experiencing an event at the Metropolitan Opera in the same moment as the New York "master audience" is worth the inconvenience. As an enterprise, the *Met: Live in HD* phenomenon depends, that is, on the hegemonic position of the Met as a powerhouse among producers of opera.

But the cinecasts make no assumptions about the Met's cultural status or the appeal of the new format. Tirelessly, relentlessly, the series promotes itself, reminding its patrons of its value and, like the *Daily Mail*, its reach. With impressive paratextual evangelism, the cinecasts' introductory titles boast that each performance reaches an audience of 350,000 in 150 countries, while hosts backstage lavish praise on the endeavor and its source, the "corporate headquarters of the initiative," as James Steichen puts it.[14] The cinecasts repeatedly remind us that this global networking of cinemas, this multiplicity of audiences, is new and extraordinary, even after a decade and a half. In the process of delivering the cinecast, that is, the Met promotes both the cinecast itself (an audience of 350,000 cannot be wrong, can it?) and, in a reflexive turn that Steichen labels *institutional dramaturgy*, the product's producer.[15]

The jury has been out for a very long time on the question of whether the initiative has done anything to enhance attendance at the Met or to diversify audiences (the suspicion is that the answer is no and no), but *The Met: Live in HD* now enhances the company's otherwise shaky financial picture, contributing 8–10 percent of revenue.[16] Having remade its matinee broadcasts in cinematic form, the Met now dominates the format, at least among opera producers (other opera companies with similar offerings have nothing like its reach), and the figures reflect that success. Perhaps, too, the cinecasts enhance the Met's institutional hegemony understood as cultural capital: what share of *that* revenue does it contribute? But above all the cinecasts invest in themselves—invest, that is, in the very notion that they assemble a global audience and in novel form. *The Met: Live in HD* refashions the technological means of the Marconi broadcast, but it sustains its imaginary. Just as Melba's "song to the world" had paired technology and promotional rhetoric to confront the limitations of simultaneity, so the cinecasts invest rhetorically in the magic of the connected cinema and in sustaining that magic even as the commodity ages and risks becoming familiar. Not for the Met the humdrum of established broadcasting norms and certainly not of television. Rather, a reenchantment of opera and cinema and a reinvestment in the wonder of the global moment.

JANUARY 21, 1927, CHICAGO: COLD DINNERS

When in 1927 the Chicago Grand Opera Company became the first US company to broadcast nationally, the *New York Times* marveled at the implications of its simultaneous reception across the country: "Radio grand opera, broadcast from the stage of its actual performance for a generation long since grown callous to these miracles of modern life, was heard by more millions in American homes last night than ever before listened to opera at one time."[17] Seven years after the Marconi experiment, the anonymous correspondent sets the event against the backdrop of a blasé familiarity with technological wonders, implying that this national broadcast of the "Garden Scene" from Gounod's *Faust* ought surely to amaze. But the article goes on to speculate on one of the odd effects of the broadcast. Contrasting the local times of reception across the time zones, it concludes that listeners "further out on the Pacific Coast must perforce have let their dinners grow cold until the first 'national opera' experiment was over."[18] This conflict between local and nationally coordinated time is an issue that will arise repeatedly in press accounts of live opera broadcasts, amplified further when relays of whole operas become a feature of broadcast schedules.

Returning to the problem in a 1931 article, the same newspaper allowed that individual arias and excerpts suited radio well—"there has been no objection of late on that score"—but concluded that the medium "could never do full justice to the complete opera."[19] Reviewing a broadcast of act 2 of *Wozzeck* from the Philadelphia Metropolitan Opera in March 1931, Orrin E. Dunlap Jr. quoted its conductor, Leopold Stokowski: "We are broadcasting only the second act of this opera, because we felt that the whole opera would be too long to broadcast and to listen to if one could not at the same time see what is happening on the stage."[20] An anonymous article in the 1932 *B.B.C. Year-Book* concurred. These complete operas had a problem, it pointed out, and it was a "problem of time." Was it not asking too much of listeners, the author asked, to expect them to listen to an entire opera broadcast? "Everything heard by wireless seems to last longer than when heard directly, and a whole evening of opera through the loud-speaker would bore many of those listeners who would enjoy an equal time spent in the opera house."[21] Writing in 1934, the composer and radio producer Ernst Schoen explained the reluctance of radio producers in Germany to embrace the broadcast of complete operas: "They wondered if, at best, the radio listener of a stage opera performance was not in the position of the opera visitor who is late and, as a punishment, is condemned to press his ear on the wall and to listen to all the complicated sounds of this performance without making out their real scenic meaning."[22] In a sense, then, there is a double time-zone issue at play. Not only might listeners at home occupy a different time zone geographically, but, outside the opera house and deprived of the sight of the stage, they found themselves resituated phenomenologically, facing a problem of duration, of endurance.

One of the oddest aspect of the cinecast experience is the intermissions. Typically about forty minutes in length, they are determined not by local needs or conventions. Rather, the intermission complies with opera-house convention, itself based on a combination of practical needs (rest for artists, scene changes) and the ever-present social and commercial dimension of foyer mingling and refreshment. Recognizing the less than appealing prospect of being cut adrift for forty minutes to try to duplicate these conventions in a cinema lobby, the cinecast intermissions feature backstage interviews and other features. These, however, typically end about halfway through the intermission, and it is then that a countdown clock appears, superimposed on live static-camera footage of backstage preparations. It is at this point that cinecast audiences are left to their own devices: they can stay in place and watch static-camera feeds of set changes in preparation for the next act, or they can relive the practice of cinema intermissions, a staple of the double feature common in screenings until the 1960s and retained as breaks in long films into the 1970s. Should they choose to leave the auditorium, audiences can head for the popcorn stand or take a comfort break, albeit guided by an on-screen digital countdown that was never a feature of cinema screenings, whether during intermissions or before a screening.[23] Watching the clock tick down, the audience will never be more aware of the strange empty time they now occupy: not so much an audience for an opera but an audience for another audience, waiting, as observers, for the observed to assemble.

Part of what seems to be invoked here is the widespread use in screen media of countdowns as marketing and promotional tools, even if, as Peter Kirwan points out, cinecast audiences have already bought their ticket and need no further inducement.[24] It may also invoke the screen clocks once a familiar feature of sign-on, continuity, and sign-off segments, particularly among European and Asian broadcasters. In this context, the timer (which also features before the performance begins) might be understood as one of the self-promotional paratexts I discussed above, but above all it serves as a guarantee of eventness. Overdetermined in a cinematic context, this timekeeping repurposes the movie theater as a networked space; it insists that the movie theater is synchronized with other, similar spaces and with the master venue, even if oceans and time zones separate them.

That cinecast audiences on the US West Coast are prepared to adapt to the experience of what one blogger described as a "morning at the opera" in one sense merely revisits the delayed meal imagined in the *New York*

Times.[25] Distant devotees of the Met, first on radio, then in the movie theater, have long straddled the same imaginary of distance and synchronization that prompted Susan's question to her husband in *Citizen Kane*: "What time is it in New York?" On Saturdays, opera time is New York time. Still, a morning by the radio is not a morning at the movie theater. To expect that potential audiences would be willing to take the term *matinee* literally and attend a performance in the morning rather than the afternoon was to chart new territory and new time. It was a call for audiences to invest *their* time in new ways but also to pay for the privilege. But it is this *public* dimension of the cinecast that recasts it. The claim in the press materials released by Fathom Events (the Met's US distributor) that the series is "transmitted live from the stage of the Met into movie theaters worldwide" overlooks the dissonances between local and global time that make simultaneity an impractical proposition in much of the world.[26] For example, audiences in Tokyo (where live screenings would begin at 2:00 a.m.) are accustomed to attending Met cinecasts scheduled as minifestivals (or what opera companies would recognize as *stagione* seasons) comprising multiple screenings of several productions weeks and even months after the live transmission. Cochrane and Bonner even report "wry laughter" from Australian audiences viewing the much delayed live cinecasts from the Royal Opera House.[27] If, as Ellis argues, "television made the act of witness into an intimate and domestic act," cinecasts have offered a public alternative.[28] By returning a visit to the opera to the public sphere, the cinecasts undermine the compact of global simultaneity formed in the last century on the basis of private consumption. By making the audience assemble, they recalibrate the simultaneous; they revive the live as local.

DECEMBER 11, 1952: HOPE FOR THE FUTURE

Already in the 1930s, television was being proposed as one solution to the problem of opera on radio. Having, as we have seen, explained the rationale for offering only a portion of *Wozzeck* in the 1931 broadcast, Stokowski adds: "But we all look forward with great eagerness to, we hope, the near future when, by television, we can send out to you or anyone who wishes to listen the impressions of the eye and the impressions of the ear synchronized of *Wozzeck* and any other of the great operatic works." Earlier that year, the *New York Times* had published a feature section entitled "Television Seen as New Hope for Radio Opera." In it, the correspondent had identified a sense of anticipation that opera's radio problem was about to be solved: "Now . . . the devotees of opera and its singers are looking ahead to the day when opera can be sent through space on radio's wings because television will add sight to the sound waves. It can be seen through interviews with operatic stars that eventually they expect that opera will be one of radio's greatest performances, but not until television emerges from the experimental stage and enters the home."[29] This last caveat proved prophetic. Set back by global depression, then war, the development of a television industry to rival that of radio had to wait until the 1950s. Until then, television sets remained much too expensive for the average household, and the meager broadcast offerings hardly justified the investment. As for the transmission of opera, some of the doubts raised by Orrin Dunlap in a 1937 *New York Times* article echo the doubts expressed about radio: "A sixty-minute television opera in the home may prove to be long enough, at least until large screens and distinct pictures are available. By that time, television, because of time limitations and commercial commitments, may find it impossible to devote from two to four hours to opera."[30]

The large screens Dunlap imagines did materialize but not in the home. One of a series of experiments and pilots with closed-circuit transmission to movie theaters, Theater Network Television (TNT) launched in 1951 primarily as a means of transmitting live sports to US movie theaters via coaxial cable. In a tentative partnership with the Met, TNT distributed two productions to its network. *Boxoffice* magazine reported that TNT's transmission of *Carmen* in December 1952 was "something less than a box-office sensation" but concluded that, despite mixed reactions in the press to the quality of sound and image and concerns that the 5:30 p.m. start time on the West Coast was problematic, it represented a publicity coup for theater operators seeking "novelties to bring in new patrons and bring back old ones."[31] *Variety* reported much improvement in sound and image and better box receipts for the transmission of the Met opening-night gala in November 1954, although it too noted that the start time (in this case, 4:45 p.m.) "was an awkward hour for the Coast" and judged the initiative a "stunt by the Met for cash and publicity purposes."[32] Although the Met and TNT had announced a three-year partnership earlier that year, no further transmissions were presented, and TNT itself soon went into decline, hobbled by the impracticality and expense of installing and maintaining special projectors in its cinemas.

Given that a half century would pass before the Met returned to the movie theater, it may be a stretch to imagine this short-lived endeavor as some kind of precursor or nascent gesture on the path to *The Met: Live in HD*. But, if TNT and other competing closed-circuit initiatives faded from public consciousness, remembered only in media histories, the circumstances that propelled the project were not single historical iterations. The articles in *Boxoffice* and *Variety* identify industries and institutions in search of new answers: the Met sought solutions for its shrinking audience and its financial difficulties, while movie theaters looked on anxiously as television took up residence in the living room. With the digitization of cinemas around the turn of the millennium came the opportunity for exhibitors to find alternative content to supplement flagging box office, while the Met was in search of a solution for its shrinking audience and its ongoing financial difficulties.[33]

Until then, it would be broadcasts on the small screen—in the Met's case beginning tentatively in 1940 and becoming a regular feature in the 1950s—that embodied the promise of addressing radio's lack. And it was television that would cultivate a visual grammar for remediated opera, all while honoring the eventual quality of operatic performance by mobilizing its signature capacity for distant simultaneity. With this historical divergence in mind, can we not regard the return of the televisual image to the movie theater in the form of *The Met: Live in HD* as an (re)encounter of competing and long-estranged media forms, one granting the gift of simultaneity to the other? "[Television] was unlike cinema," Ellis argues, "because performers and viewers were held in the communion of a single moment, rather than being separated by time."[34] Yet this distinction arguably calls for a more nuanced reading. Critical of what he regards as the presentist view of media history underwriting this perspective, William Urricchio challenges the association of film exclusively with storage while overlooking a discourse around cinema's future that had long imagined the possibilities of synchronized transmission—what he calls a horizon of *televisual expectation*.[35] Besides, as Michael Cowan observes, cinema had been instrumental in cultivating what he describes as "media fantasies" of "global simultaneity." He cites, for example, the cinema's interwar fascination with representations of the emerging technologies of instantaneous communication (radio, telephone) and its cultivation of montage techniques as a cinematic registration of simultaneous action across space.[36] Cinema, in other words, may not historically have relied on or developed instantaneous transmission outside experiments like TNT, but it had invested in and enriched the imaginary of simultaneity, and the genealogy of moving pictures includes the possibility—or hope—that, like television, cinema would communicate in an instant.

JUNE 25, 1967: OUR WORLD

Adopted and further enabled by the global networking of media technology, the convention of simultaneity became, as Kevin Birth puts it, a foundational illusion in "modern cultural models of time." Birth cites the example of a 1979 examination for entry into the French police force. In the French territory of Martinique, in the Caribbean, the examination was held at 3:00 a.m. to synchronize with the examination happening simultaneously, at 8:00 a.m., in France. According to the model of unified global time, this is the same moment, yet, as Birth points out, 3:00 a.m. is *not the same time* as 8:00 a.m.[37] An abstract concept of now, established in imperial modernity and maintained in the name of postcolonial unity, has been prioritized over the bodily, cognitive, and cultural experience of time. This postcolonial exercise of power finds an analogue in what Arjun Appadurai calls the *global now* of modernity, understood as the West's attempt to assert control not only over the flow of commerce and information but also over the very terms and measures by which that flow is measured and regulated.

Media technology, Appadurai argues, has been critical to the globalist impulse of modernity and its project of flattening out and assimilating the temporal multiplicities of the local.[38] Yet Appurdai's global now takes no account of the role played by communication satellites in the formation of this imaginary of simultaneity. He is far from alone, as Lisa Parks is at pains to demonstrate. So striking is the dearth of scholarly engagement with the impact of satellite technology, Parks argues, that it takes on the role of a "structuring absence" in cultural theory, at once instrumental in the flows and measures that define the "global imaginary" yet hidden in the periphery of critical visibility.[39] Without the network of geostationary satellites first established in the 1960s, the global, live reach of video transmission is unthinkable, yet even the field of television studies has, in large measure, overlooked their role. Parks shows, for example, how the early mobilization of satellite feeds in television established patterns of rhetoric and presentational syntax that have persisted in live programming, not only in television, but also in forms of web-based communication that continue to draw on televisual norms. One event in particular illustrates a combination of characteristics—a foregrounding of the program's liveness, a self-conscious and self-advertising global reach—familiar from television news, sports, and live arts programming and now evident in event cinema forms like the Met cinecasts.

Our World, a two-hour live, global telecast to an estimated fifty million viewers on June 25, 1967, was the first television program to avail itself of the recently established network of communications satellites. Conceived by the BBC producer Aubrey Singer, and hosted by the European Broadcasting Union, the program was touted in a press release as a triumphant demonstration of the communication in the space age: "'Our World' . . . will utilize the magic of space-age electronics to flash sound and visual images across lands, seas, and time zones, fusing 'yesterday,' 'today,' and 'tomorrow' into a globe-encircling 'now.'"[40]

As Parks notes, the program, divided into forty-two short features from fourteen countries, highlights global inequality but seems fixated on the threat of global overpopulation and perpetuates a binary narrative of the West's progress and achievement in elevating itself above the problem of basic need and survival. One strand in that achievement—and the focus of several segments of the telecast—is the arts, or, as the narrator puts it, the "restless striving to stretch mind and spirit." While the British would steal the show with footage of the Beatles in a recording session for "All You Need Is Love," *Der Spiegel* reported that the broadcaster ARD had originally proposed a feature on the Harmonica Orchestra Championships in Karlsruhe as Germany's contribution to this segment. Singer, however, rejected this as not "typically German," and instead live coverage of a rehearsal at the Bayreuth Festival was chosen.[41] The segment begins with an exterior, nighttime shot of the Festspielhaus, zooming into the festival flag flying above it. "It is twenty minutes past nine," the German host announces, "and here they're rehearsing *Lohengrin* with an enormous orchestra: ninety-two musicians." Panning shots from within the orchestra pit and the auditorium establish the space, before the director, Wolfgang Wagner, with impeccable timing, jumps to his feet at the rehearsal desk and heads for the stage. What follows is the most staged of stage rehearsals, ending with Wagner's proclamation, "We've got exactly what we wanted!" and his call for a ten-minute break, just in time for the telecast to bid farewell from Bayreuth.

The impression in *Our World* is of having gained access to a privileged space and of having glimpsed something unpredictable in the act of unfolding: Wagner's dynamic directorial performance, framed by the host's observation that things may get "stormy," lends the telecast an eventual quality. Stay tuned, the telecast says, because anything could happen. At the same time—and this too has been a feature of televisual liveness— the very act of monitoring the world suggests something of the routine of other lives at this moment: a day in the life of the planet. For all its focus on events, live television can convey the now as ordinary: even newscasts combine coverage of events with a monitoring of the state of play locally, nationally, and internationally. As the host in Bayreuth observes at the end of the segment: "The storm that has been promised hasn't happened yet, and so we bid hail and farewell from Bayreuth." Wagner has been the professional, and the rehearsal has unfolded in a collegial, even routine manner.

It is this tension between television's construction of liveness as an event unfolding in the unpredictable now and the routine, everyday quality of what typically unfolds that interests me. It is a tension evident in the presentation of opera on television and inherited by the Met cinecasts. Although the cinecasts only occasionally feature rehearsal footage, the backstage interviews and behind-the-scenes intermission footage echo the sense of privileged access that *Our World* had channeled and commodified. Supposedly revealing and immediate, the interviews, like the host segments, are actually carefully choreographed yet often come across as awkward or just plain tedious. And we might detect the same tension with respect to the performance itself. For all its evental potential, the weight of routine drags on the machine that is opera: at any moment, another moment.

JUNE 3, 2000: *TRAVIATA* IN PARIS

In an essay included in the DVD release of his *La traviata in Paris* (2000), Andrea Andermann, the producer, singles out the opera's "timeless contemporaneity."[42] Like his earlier *Tosca: In the Settings and at the Times of Tosca* (1992), *La traviata in Paris* uses live, on-location television transmission to transform real locations into operatic stages. In the absence of the kind of specific locales identified in the libretto of *Tosca*, however, *La traviata in Paris* turns to generically striking historical interiors, such as the Hôtel de Boisgelin, formerly the site of the Italian embassy. Fin de siècle props, costumes, and hairstyles seem to contradict Andermann's insistence on the opera's contemporaneity, but there is a twist, as he explains: "Utilizing the intrinsic nature, the raison d'être of television, this *Traviata* comes to you live, in the regular daily language of television—the news—when the anchorperson, amongst the other stories of June 3rd, 2000, tells us of an event that is taking place to which we are immediately transported. And there we are in the festive Paris of June 3rd, 1900, right in the middle of the Exposition Universelle."[43] What Andermann imagines, then, is the superimposition of moments in time (2000, the now of the production, and 1900, the setting for the mise-en-scène) as reports in a live television news broadcast, each a story summoned by a news anchor and presented instantly before our eyes. But where television news purports to join spatially distant events at the same time, Andermann imagines different times coexisting in the same location: Paris. Television here becomes the vehicle for the temporal corollary of distant simultaneity, a concept that, as Max Jammer points out, has been little theorized and lacks even an agreed-on term (Jammer offers *local recurrence*).[44]

If only *La traviata in Paris* were quite as intriguing in practice as Andermann's conceptual framework. Alas, the combination of roving television news cameras, historical costume, and singer close-ups resembles something more like period soap opera than the radical encounter of television and opera that Andermann imagines.[45] What does give the production an innovative edge is that this televisual present is at once conceptual and actual: the opera is divided into four "episodes" (three acts, including two scenes in act 2), each performed, shot, and telecast live at the time of day represented in the action: Saturday, June 3, at 8:30 p.m., and Sunday, June 4, at 12:50 p.m., 8:30 p.m., and 11:30 p.m.[46] These staggered telecasts not only map the performance to the stage time but synchronize both times with a kind of real-time spectatorship. In effect, everything is folded into the present, including a represented past, which becomes a segment in a television newscast; it is a story climaxing with a late evening Sunday bulletin about a tragic death.

Early observers of television spectatorship were struck by the medium's capacity to generate and capitalize on an impression of simultaneity. "In live programs," wrote Richard Hubbell in 1950, "there is that sense of immediacy, of actuality. One knows that what he is seeing and hearing is actually taking place at that moment."[47] For Rudy Bretz, the question of the here and now, taken for granted by the copresent audiences of theater, becomes in television something to be reinforced: "An audience before a television screen . . . is fascinated by the actual and the real. The more they can be kept conscious of the fact that the show they are watching is going on at that very moment in a very real place, the better they like it."[48] This "keeping conscious" is a task assumed by the practices of the industry, from marketing and programming to the grammar of broadcasting. Reflecting on the success of this project, not least its effectiveness in securing the participation of the viewer, Ellis traces the persistence of a "rhetoric of liveness" even when much television programming content is recorded.[49]

MARCH 15, 2017: ENCORE!

At a *Met: Live in HD* presentation of *La traviata* in 2017, around the movie-theater audience the murmur of another audience can be heard: it is the sound, distributed by walls of speakers, of the assembling Met patrons. The picture fades in on mezzo-soprano Isabel Leonard. In a "walk and talk" between the music stands of the backstage banda, she welcomes the remote viewers and informs them that she is "so excited to be [their] host today." Leonard's in-the-moment enthusiasm, presented, it has to be said, with some considerable confidence and polish, summons the familiar televisual trope of the live piece to camera, while her reference to audiences "like you" in cinemas around the world summons for imagination the simultaneity of the network of which they are a part.

It is precisely this first-person, present-tense address to camera, Mimi White argues, that has been instrumental in constructing, via news telecasts, the very notion of televisual liveness. And, she adds, this form of address has been strongly associated with an "insistence on a privileged spatial and temporal proximity" to the events relayed.[50] Leonard is conspicuously located in the thick of the action, passing backstage chorus members poised by stage entrances and huddled instrumentalists performing, with mixed success, the studied nonchalance of bystanders who know they are on camera. As she introduces the principal cast and conductor, we hear a temporal marker of operatic liveness: the sound of the audience applauding the entrance of the conductor to the pit. These six seconds of applause and the silence that ensues at once frame Leonard's presentation (we know that only so much time will now elapse until the beginning of the performance) and generate a kind of intermedial polyphony that sets the unfolding of a televisual set piece against the temporality of operatic ritual. The movie-theater audience is invited to become, like the viewer of live television, a witness to events *as they unfold*.

There is a problem, however. This is not the live Saturday transmission but its encore presentation offered the following Wednesday. It is a recording, a replay of something once live yet presented a though it were still live. Other providers of opera and other forms of cinecast have similar practices. A report commissioned for *NT Live*, the cinecast series from the National Theatre, stresses the need "to preserve a sense of event" in repeat presentations.[51] For Nicholas Hytner, formerly the director of the National Theatre, something about delayed simultaneity "seems to work," even if success is possible only when the audience "performs the mental trick" of belief and investment.[52] If Hytner is right—that some kind of performance is required of the audience—then the televisual apparatus is critical to the facilitation of the performance. In this context, the in-the-moment hosting, the countdown clocks, and the (no longer strictly necessary) intermissions seem less like empty replicas than performative gestures capable of reanimating a lost live. Critical here is the *as* in *as live*: the cinecast frames the theatrical performance *as though* it were happening now; the audience reciprocates with the *as though* of Hytner's "mental trick." At the end of the encore presentation, when applause from New York is channeled through the surround speakers, it is supplemented with local applause—hesitant, admittedly, but enough to compete with the array of speakers. The audience seems to be joining, via a recording once presented as live, an audience once live in the theater. This ensemble, this apparatus that hovers between past and present, is the cinecast's repetition machine.

Other cinecast series, such as the Royal Opera House's *Live Cinema Season*, offer proof of this now in the form of social media. Tweets from the audience (though only the positive ones) are displayed on screen during the intermission, generating a form of interactivity that reinforces the sense of a happening in the moment. Not that any of these practices represent a guarantee of liveness. The marketing language claims the event is happening simultaneously, the countdown clock suggests a link to something about to happen, and the social media interaction implies live feedback. But, as Margaret Jane Kidnie points out, nothing in the screening can be taken as hard proof that the performance is happening now; only a knowledge of external "points of reference" (e.g., awareness of the Met's schedule) can confirm the actuality of the event.[53] Or not. The encore cinecast of *La traviata* coincided with a performance of Gounod's *Roméo et Juliette* at the Met. Even interactivity via social media requires that only the screening be networked now, not the performance that it purports to relay. What this compact of liveness relies on, it seems, is a combination of trust that institutions like the Met are doing what they claim to be doing and a collective investment in or desire for the idea of simultaneity. This is the cinecast's synchronization machine.

Is the encore presentation not a classic illustration of the capacity of media technology to duplicate and a demonstration of its inability to do anything *but* duplicate? Aware though she is of the tolerance for delayed liveness, Kidnie registers her own disappointment with a cinema presentation of a recorded performance she had previously attended in the theater. Gone was the frisson generated by the uncertainty of live performance, replaced by the dull predictability of archived content: "Nothing could go wrong with that performance precisely because it was not live."[54] Part of what Kidnie registers as disappointing is the machinic perfection of repetition: the cinematic presentation is unengaging because we know that everything will be all right on the night. But this is not always the case. True, some of the technical difficulties that can affect the live Met cinecasts (the infamous stage machine that dominates the Robert Lepage *Ring* delayed a cinecast for forty-five minutes in 2011)[55] can be edited out in the encore presentation. Yet, as the Met's FAQs acknowledge, transmission problems are possible too. Among the questions is one on "technical challenges" with a response that reads like an attempt to deflect blame: "Even though all live programs are subject to technical issues, the problems often rest with the individual movie theaters."[56] Encore presentations are not insulated from these issues. They too rely on a chain of transmission subject to technical glitches in the local cinema (file playback, projectors, satellite receiver). There is, in other words, a fragility in the dissemination, both original and encore, that is performative.

Conversely, the production featured in this cinecast is a repetition machine in its own right. Directed by Willy Decker, it became something of a franchise after its initial Salzburg Festival (telecast and released on DVD). It was then seen on loan in Amsterdam and Valencia, had already been presented twice at the Met (including a 2012 cinecast) before this 2017 iteration, and has generated a formidable archive. Viewing that archive reveals a striking degree of conformity between the iterations, despite there being almost no duplication of casting across the performances. The lack of variation in musical execution, for example, may be symptomatic of a trend toward standardization of interpretation of core repertoire much remarked on by critics (something for which recording technology may itself be partly responsible), but it is striking nonetheless.

What emerges as well is the conformity in *Personenregie*. Clearly, each Violetta brings to the role a gestural vocabulary and bodily comportment of her own, yet the grip and resilience of *Regie* is starkly on display in the tightly choreographed sequences of gestures that return in each performance. Perhaps the combination in opera of auteur director and the choreographing impact of music is bound to produce a certain standardization. That is, if productions are to become franchises not only of sets and props but of directorial signature reinforced in revival either by the auteur or by his/her proxy, then the giddy creativity so treasured by performance studies—the agency of the actor, the improvisatory freedom of rehearsal—proves fragile. Combine this with the rhythmic imposition of a seventy-piece band and the standardized tempi imposed by the international conducting fraternity, and the conformity is stifling. "Performance," writes Schneider, "becomes itself through messy and eruptive reappearance. It challenges . . . any neat antinomy between appearance and disappearance, or presence and absence through the basic repetitions that mark performance as simultaneously indiscreet, non-original, relentlessly citational, and *remaining*."[57] Performance, that is, revisits and reenacts memory not as something linear but as *retroaction*, not as an unfolding of a present that immediately fades and is no more but as a repeated recovery that takes place in and through time lags.[58] The encore cinecast replays a performance that was itself already a form of encore. If the cinecast sustains the illusion of a now-lost singularity, it punctures that simultaneity with the repeats and returns not just of a video recording but of performance itself.

As for synchronization, we might say that media technologies have

108 | CHAPTER THREE

produced the modern imaginary—or, as physicists put it, convention—of simultaneity. But this should not be taken to imply that the televisual is ontologically rooted in liveness, somehow hardwired for simultaneity. As Auslander, Feuer, and others have argued, the associations between media technologies and liveness are constructed via practice, not derived from the essence of the medium. Equally, the imaginary of simultaneity does not depend on media technology. Consider this: the first Met cinecast of the Decker *Traviata* began at 1:00 p.m. EDT on Saturday, April 14, 2012. At that very time, as the performance was beginning in New York, two performances of *La traviata* began in Europe, one at 7:00 p.m. CEST in Prague, another at 7:30 p.m. CEST in Lübeck (a third would begin at 9:00 p.m. CEST in Salerno). That day, several performances of *La traviata* overlapped; two, in New York and Prague, unfolded more or less simultaneously. The discursive silence on this kind of synchronization is no aberration: in opera's repetition machine, the likelihood of simultaneous performance of a canonic work somewhere in the world is high, yet *this* form of simultaneity, unproductive in the commodification or fetishization of liveness, is not one rehearsed in the marketing and promotional rhetoric of the opera industry or cultivated among opera's devotees in blogs and social media.[59] As though demonstrating the role of discourse in shaping the investment of the imagination in a global now, this simultaneity does not register: it does not exist.

CHAPTER FOUR

You Are Here

Mounted on the wall at the Lakeside Terrace entrance to London's Barbican Centre is a map of the local area. The map includes a grid and numbered references to key venues in the Barbican, but its most eye-catching feature, in bold lettering immediately above the map, is a phrase familiar to tourists and visitors to public amenities: "You are here." The phrase is duplicated in tiny form next to a marker placed at a point on the map corresponding to the map's location. It is a conceit but a familiar one. I am of course not literally there at the physical point indicated on a wall; nor is the map's bold lettering intended to remind me, redundantly, that I am present in the place where I stand. Rather, in a learned act of conceptual "mapping," I associate my physical environment with a two-dimensional representation of its layout. By aligning that representation both with my current location and with my intended destination, I can decide which direction to take.[1] In this case, my destination is through the adjacent doors to the Barbican Cinema, one of many London venues to screen the *Met: Live in HD* cinecasts. The cinecast begins, and with it comes another conceit: the host welcomes me to the Metropolitan Opera in New York. Again, I know, because I have learned, that such greetings are not to be taken literally.

Live and even recorded broadcast media have for decades invited their listeners and viewers to an "electronic elsewhere" in ways that encourage them to overlook the distance involved in the traversal.[2] My body is not in New York, and the words of welcome are not naively imagined to reconfigure space. Yet the imaginary in this invitation is a powerful one: I am invited to suspend disbelief and invest in the here of this elsewhere, just as illusionist theater (including opera) had long played on the pleasurable and productive tension between, on the one hand, knowing distance and theatricality and, on the other, investment and belief in the imagined worlds it presents and *makes present*. As in the theater, sitting in front of a cinema screen and being welcomed to New York gestures to a negotiated space between belief and knowledge, presence and absence. In this gesture, the cinecast also recalls the map on the wall outside. True, the cinecast implies the imagined collapse of great physical distance, yet the conceptual transfer—between a represented here and my physical location—is not dissimilar: both cinecast and map invoke a split but colocated self when they propose that "you are here."

In the three chapters that follow, I unpack the concepts of presence invoked in opera cinecasts, asking what they assume, negotiate, and reconfigure when they purport to overwrite distance with immediacy. Promoted on the premise that they can extend or offer communion with a master presence in the opera house, the cinecasts are judged according to conventions and attitudes not unlike those associated with the electronic transmission of live organized events: just as sports telecasts mobilize techniques and devices in the name of vicarious attendance at an event, so the cinecasts immerse remote audiences in the eventness of a performance at the Met. If the ubiquity of sports telecasts has normalized mediated sports spectatorship to the point at which stadium-based events need to incorporate screen media into the on-site experience, the grammar of the telecasts nevertheless suggests an economy of compensation: how to respond to the absence of physical copresence. The cinecasts not only retain this logic but, according to the rhetoric associated with their promotion and reception, also seem to amplify it. What they also share with sports broadcasting is the impression of overdetermination (overcompensation?), seeking to offer, via camera perspectives and privileged forms of access, a kind of superpresence unavailable to the audience on site. In this sense, the proposition of *The Met: Live in HD* is that "you are more than here." But, just as maps can confuse and theater alienate, so these presencing effects and gestures can underwhelm or even backfire, reminding cinema audiences that they are in fact distributed across a network of elsewhere. Besides, *here*—which is to say, a movie theater—can always assert its own presence in ways that do not necessarily contribute to and may even compete with the impression of liveness and immediacy that underwrites the cinecast project. In this way, the cinecast is always locally contingent, vulnerable—in its own way, performative. You, as it turns out, are not here.

THE NEXT BEST THING

When the Metropolitan Opera issued a press release in 2006 to announce the as-yet-unbranded series of transmissions of its matinees to cinemas, it included quotes from representatives of some of the key partners, including the distributors and the unions. One was from Ellis Jacob, the president and CEO of Cineplex Entertainment, the distributor that would exhibit the cinecasts in Canada. "The combination of the Met's superb musical productions and our giant screens and Dolby Digital Surround Sound," read the quote, "will make these events the next best thing to actually being there."[3] As promotional copy, Jacob's phrase strikes an ambivalent tone. Understood as simulacrum, the cinecast is state of the art: it mobilizes technology and resources to channel the impact of live performance in new and marvelous ways. Yet it will never quite compete with the original, which it can only mimic. It is a double characterization that anticipates the promotional rhetoric the Met would adopt for the cinecasts. Peter Gelb, for example, would later frame the impact of the cinecasts in similar terms: "Although nothing is comparable to being at the Met for a live performance, these larger-than-life big-screen transmissions provide an alternative experience for our national and international constituency." This rhetoric of "almost but not quite" is only one manifestation of a logic of absence and compensation that had long accompanied the electronic transmission of opera. True, early experiments in trans- and intercontinental radio transmission of opera prompted statements of astonishment in the press at the perception that geographic distance had been overcome. When, in 1924, opera excerpts were transmitted via shortwave from the recently established BBC to a North American listenership largely composed of amateur wireless operators, the *New York Times* reacted enthusiastically: "The clearness with which the sextet from *Lucia* crossed the sea from 5NO, Newcastle, on Tuesday night made many listeners feel that the distance between America and England had been greatly reduced. It hardly seemed that 3000 miles of sea intervened between the piano in Aberdeen and the headsets in the United States."[4] A decade later, a period in which commercial radio broadcast established itself and live relay from opera houses established itself in radio programming, this same sense of wonder was still being harnessed in marketing language.[5] Announcing sponsorship of the Metropolitan Opera national broadcasts in 1936, David Sarnoff, the president of RCA, is quoted in the *New York Times* as saying: "Through the magic of radio a front row seat in the most famous opera house in America will be made available to every music lover in the land."[6] Here is the promise of radio.

Yet this glowing assessment of the potential of opera on radio was accompanied by more critical perspectives. We saw in chapter 3 that enthusiasm for the way opera was remediated by new technologies quickly ran into disappointment when idea met actuality. Radio generated concerns about its perceived medial deficit: it was incomplete without image because opera was incomplete without image. This, as we saw, was one of the themes of the 1931 *New York Times* feature on television and opera. One of the artists quoted there, the soprano Rosa Ponselle, alighted on just this problem: "One must see and hear the opera to get the fullest appreciation, but I believe we are rapidly approaching the day when radio and the opera will be entirely reconciled by the addition of television to sound programs."[7] This hope for an imminent televisual future had already been articulated in Germany in 1929 by Frank Warschauer:

> Consider that tomorrow opera in its entirety will be delivered to residential dwellings like gas and water. Far removed from all cheap triumphs, what glorious progress we have made; far removed from an infantile *a tout prix* optimism in regard to technology, it must nevertheless be said that with the realization of television, already at the point of technical utilization, a startling novelty in the history of culture will make its appearance: opera as an everyday event in one's own home. This is contrary to the whole idea of festival performances: opera with beer and house slippers.[8]

What Warschauer summons is the corollary of being there: presence as transporting from there to here, the same virtual opera in the living room with which I opened the book. But this promise would itself fade under scrutiny—or, rather, shrink under scrutiny because the size of the television screen and its poor resolution proved so unsuitable.

This is not what Harry Stephen Keeler had predicted when his mystery novel *The Box from Japan* (1931), set ten years in the future, imagined a remote live screening in New York of a theatrical production from London. Mounted not in a small device in a living room but on a large wall in an exhibition hall, the screen is of cinematic proportions, its impact amplified by 3D glasses and complemented by equally impressive sound:

> So real was the illusion to him that he was simply seated in the front row of a big empty theater, Halsey continued to stare upward without word—like a man who dares not speak lest he interrupt a carefully acted-out performance of some sort. The myriad small sounds carried by the fine sound-reproducing apparatus, itself not anywhere in view, however, were so convincing in themselves, let alone in conjunction with the extremely real figures less than fifteen feet from him, apparently, that he reached down with a thumb and forefinger and pinched himself that he was not merely dreaming a dream that he was a specta-

You Are Here | 113

tor of such a super-perfect fantasmagoria as was this, much less that he was not in London itself.[9]

Actors appear as though in the room, sound is rendered with detail and fidelity, and distances seem to collapse. It is an imaginary fulfilment of the promise of transmitted sound and image, a vision of the future (or future vision) that combines television and cinema.

BEST SEAT IN THE HOUSE

If Keeler's "super-perfect fantasmagoria" would remain in the realm of science fiction, isolated experiments in transmission of signals to movie theaters began at least to demonstrate the possibility of television on the big screen. It was, however, the interest demonstrated by the Hollywood studios and cinema exhibitors in the immediate postwar period that offered to make this combination a practical and commercial reality. Movie theaters would need to be equipped with specialized projectors and linked with appropriate forms of transmission, but this was an investment deemed necessary and timely by an industry anxious to respond to the threat of television in the home by offering a competing form of presentation.[10] I want to revisit one manifestation of this investment to consider it from a different perspective. As we saw in chapter 3, TNT partnered with the Met to transmit its 1952 production of *Carmen*. Part of what was deemed novel about the initiative was its introduction of the live quality of television into the movie theater. But I want to explore the entirely untelevisual but utterly operatic scale of image and sound and the public, theatrical space of encounter—to explore, that is, the question of presence.

Utilizing three static cameras, *Carmen* was, as we have seen, transmitted in whole, according to the trade weekly *Boxoffice*, to 67,000 spectators in thirty-one cinemas across twenty-seven cities in the United States.[11] Summarizing the press reaction, *Boxoffice* noted that observations ranged from expressions of astonishment at the technology, to complaints about indecipherable images and poor sound, to concerns about attendance figures falling short of expectation. It concluded, however, that lack of planning had compromised the event and that the extent of the coverage in itself confirmed the value of the experiment as a means of raising the profile of theater television and its potential content: "Chief interest in the experiment from the exhibitors' point of view rested on the drawing strength of opera as a possible use for TV installations."[12] The next event to put this hypothesis to the test was the Met's opening-night gala, part of an announced three-year contract, and screened, reportedly, with considerably more preparation, on November 8, 1954.[13] Although the issue of disappointing attendance figures resurfaced in some reports, critics also compared the quality of sound and image favorably to the *Carmen* transmission, and press coverage was extensive once again. *Variety* reported that the event received front-page newspaper coverage in fourteen cities and grossed an estimated $180,000.[14] With a contract in place, the future looked bright; perhaps, *Billboard* noted, the future would be in color.[15]

Observations on the telecasts by Nathan L. Halpern, the president of TNT, summarized in what amounts to a promotional article in *Opera News*, are worth quoting at length:

> In a recent interview Mr. Halpern expressed his belief that Theater Network Television has brought members of the audience closer to the opera house than they could possibly come sitting beside their home TV sets. The theatrical atmosphere is indispensable to grand opera, he believes, while the reaction of a theatre audience contributes much to the individual's enjoyment. The largest available screens are essential to the reproduction of a stage like that of the Metropolitan. It is true, Mr. Halpern admits, that the eye of the television audience is not free to focus at will on any part of the stage. The eye has become a camera, which is directed by an engineer, not by the viewer. But although TNT is no substitute for attendance at an actual performance, Mr. Halpern believes that it has some advantages, such as improved visibility, by which the entire public occupies, as it were, the best seat in the house and can move toward the focal point of the stage action as it unfolds.[16]

Evident here are some of the themes that run through much of the press coverage of the TNT telecasts: the advantage of the large screen, the proxy audience experience represented by the movie theater, the offer of the ideal seat, the capacity to reproduce the stage spectacle. These are perspectives that will resurface half a century later in association with the new cinecasts. Halpern also anticipates two caveats that will accompany *The Met: Live in HD*. One, the claim that nothing beats being at the Met, will be key to the promotional intent of the cinecasts; the other, perhaps the major thread in critical reaction to the cinecasts and to telecasts of opera stagings more widely, is the persistent complaint that the spectator's eye is commandeered by a video director. I will return to these perceived limitations, but I want to focus for now on the rhetorical themes of proximity and reproduction.

In a front-page review of the 1954 gala telecast, the *New York Times* offered a glowing assessment: "From all over the country there were reports of good sound and improved visual projection. For most of the viewers in theaters other than the Metropolitan, the action on the stage was brought up close. It was as though each spectator had a front-row seat. There was the intimacy that one gets with television in the home and the size and clarity that one gets in the films."[17] In this best-of-all-worlds reading, the transmission mobilizes the signature attributes of both television and cinema to offer what is imagined as the most desirable experience in opera: front row in the opera house. It is a perspective echoed repeatedly in press reactions to the transmission and one that will have sat well with Halpern. Assessing the telecast in *Étude* magazine, Rose Heylbut cites Halpern, whose ambition for the transmissions, she writes, "is to enable people to feel that they are actually present at the event." Heylbut goes on to note that four cameras were positioned in the auditorium and a further four in the lobbies and in Sherry's Lounge to capture the gala as a social event. The result, she concludes, in an appraisal very much in tune with the marketing language associated with the TNT telecasts, is a palpable sense of the "buzz" and "excitement" and "the illusion of really being there."[18]

HD: AT A THEATER NEAR YOU

Step forward to the reincarnation of the TNT telecasts in *The Met: Live in HD*, and the language is all but identical. "Superb camera work and image mixing," wrote one appreciative Facebook contributor after the transmission of *Nabucco* (2017). "Thank you so much, you make me feel I was there (though I am some 3000 miles away)."[19] If, as we have seen, Gelb and Jacob carefully enclosed the Met itself as a privileged space, the language of access and proximity is nevertheless striking. Repeatedly, the marketing and promotional material generated by the Met and by distributors and exhibitors emphasizes the directness of the transmission, discursively streamlining mediation as a form of *im*mediacy: "The operas will be presented live in HD, via satellite, from the Met Opera's stage directly to the screen at . . ."[20] The acronym *HD*, foregrounded of course in the branding, is often expanded in marketing copy to *high definition*, as in the launch press release of 2006, which uses the term no fewer than seven times.[21] In either form, the term was at the forefront of the marketing and branding of broadcasting and consumer electronics in the immediate postmillennial period. This was the period in which broadcasters and manufacturers were gradually adopting a new standard (HDTV) for image resolution and frame size, made possible in part by the development of digital compression standards for signal transmission and file storage.

This new standard would affect devices (televisions with new screen sizes and resolutions, new disc formats and disc players), television broadcasting resolutions, and, ultimately, video streaming. In short, HD was everywhere, and the branding of the Met's new series fully capitalized on the market moment. In fact, in the absence of an agreed-on term for this new form of transmission and dissemination—variously referred to as *broadcasts, telecasts, livecasts, simulcasts, event cinema,* and, my own preference, *cinecasts*—commentators filled the gap by referring to it with the shorthand *HD,* as in "the HD season"[22] or "the HD schedule"[23] or even simply "the HDs."[24] In a form of semiotic distillation, the series is not only shot and projected in HD; it *is* HD, as though image resolution were its very essence. That the acronym *HD* is hived off *HDTV*—as proposed in the late 1990s by the "Grand Alliance" consortium of manufacturers, broadcasters and researchers—is not something apparent in any of the promotional literature for *The Met: Live in HD.* Nor do we ever learn that the signals transmitted by the Met's broadcast partner Fathom are the same high-definition television signals available to home viewers via satellite. The signals are not even encrypted and can be intercepted by determined viewers equipped with motorized satellite dishes and armed with the correct transmission information, as shared by a dedicated online community.

The Met's *Live in HD* FAQ acknowledges that what is screened is video, not film: "The HD broadcasts are shot in high-quality video for a live performance. Video looks different from film on any size screen."[25] But there is no reference to television, which seems to be the hardest word for the Met to say, as it is for all promoters of live content in cinemas. These transmissions, we are told, are an encounter between an event (opera, ballet, theater) and cinema; the only acknowledgment of the role of television broadcast technology is reference to the use of satellite transmission, which here becomes, as we have seen, a cipher for immediacy and simultaneity. It is as though invoking television lowers the commodity value of event cinema and needs to be written out in the name of a more exclusive and direct encounter.

Is this simply one strand in the wider process of convergence we are told is now the fate of media such as television and cinema? Does the exchange of aesthetics between media (the rapid cinematic montage in television, the televisual editing in cinema), not to mention the convergence of screen sizes, not suggest that the era of medium specificity is on the wane? Reflecting on these questions, Marcia Citron argues that, in parallel with the decline of television as a medium, recent scholarship on opera on screen has understandably directed its focus away from its medial impact. Citron means to imply not that television and cinema have somehow blended in an "amorphous" way but merely that their "theorized characteristics" should not be overemphasized.[26] My focus here on cinecasts in part affirms this view—Citron is right, I think, to view *television* in historical terms—but I am not so convinced that moving on from a consideration of the *televisual* serves us well. Precisely because it is no longer confined to television, the televisual, I suggest, demands the attention of opera studies.

This is, in my reading, not a question merely of theorized properties but one of shared practices, conventions, personnel, technologies, and materials—in short, the televisual apparatus. The rhetorical erasure of television in the promotion of *The Met: Live in HD* stands in contrast to what I want to suggest is its profound debt to the presentational and production techniques of live television genres. Granted, as I argued in chapter 2, the split-screen effects so characteristic of news and sports programming are nowhere to be seen. But in other ways and above all in the presentational packaging that frames the actual operatic performance—the intro and credit sequences, the walk-and-talk host, the live interviews and backstage access in the style of television news gathering—the model is the televisual live. As though compensating for what is still the novel—and, if commentators are to be believed, odd—experience of attending a live event in the movie theater, *The Met: Live in HD* offers something familiar and decipherable. Whether referencing the tradition of live telecasts from opera houses and concert halls (and many among the cinecast audiences, often already operaphiles, will have acquaintance with this history) or the wider televisual practices of live multicamera broadcasting (marketing research shows that cinecast audiences tend to be an older demographic representing the era of television's dominance), this is, if not television, a remediation vividly modeled on the televisual. More specifically, it is the televisual as witness to events, medium of the immediate, conjurer of the impression of being there.

THANK YOU FOR JOINING ME

Although the scripts vary, the language of the *Met: Live in HD* hosts often begins with a greeting that implies direct contact: "Thank you for joining me" (Susan Graham, *Tristan und Isolde*, March 22, 2008); "Thank you for joining me for this new production" (Renée Fleming, *Carmen*, January 16, 2010); "Hello, and welcome to the Metropolitan Opera live in HD" (Natalie Dessay, *Peter Grimes*, March 15, 2008); "Welcome to today's performance" (Eric Owens, *Wozzeck*, January 11, 2020). This is language with a pedigree in the Met's live radio broadcasts, introduced, for example, by the host,

Peter Allen, with the words: "Welcome to the Metropolitan Opera House in New York City."[27] But it is familiar, too, from televisual presentation, both live and recorded. Thanked for joining the host, or welcomed to the location they occupy, we are greeted in terms that are at once immediate and intimate. These are addresses pitched not to an audience en masse but to an imagined individual, the personal dynamic generated in part by the direct address to the camera and the close-up framing of the image, often preceded by the slow approach of the camera to its subject, as though I, the viewer, were walking toward the host.[28] Nor is this debt to the televisual isolated to the Met cinecasts. As Janet Wardle notes of the *NT Live* cinecasts, impressions of intimacy and immediacy, from the host's address to camera to the tone of "chatty bonhomie," directly recall the presentational style of television genres such as breakfast shows and live sports broadcasts.

TELLING TWO STORIES

But what of the presentation of the opera proper? What happens when the house lights go down? One of the recurring themes of televisual discourse—scholarship, critical commentary, observations by practitioners—is an emphasis on the service of televisual grammar to the construction of a coherent narrative. This is true not only in the case of explicitly narrative genres such as television drama but also in that of live, multicamera coverage. There is no compulsion, Jeremy Butler observes, for nonnarrative television genres to "tell a story," yet visual storytelling habitually underlines the shot grammar, the articulation of space.[29] As Paddy Scannell puts it, live television news coverage defines itself according to the "work of finding the story," of articulating the "meaning and significance of the 'event-as-story.'"[30] Recall the observations by Haswell, Large, and Halvorson on the importance of storytelling in their work as multicamera directors. Halvorson, for example, likened *The Met: Live in HD* to his work on sitcoms: both, he argued, were forms of visual storytelling. But there is at work in the remediation of opera a kind of narrative doubling. While multicamera direction is the native domain of the sitcom—the performance is *for* the cameras—staged opera is an event already complete in itself. Video remediation, that is, tells two stories: one about the event (a live performance), the other an adaptation of a dramatic narrative delivered on the stage. The event-as-story is evident in the paratexts of the presentation: the assembling audience, the buzz in the auditorium, the host sequences, the intermission features, the closing applause—all carefully sequenced and made spatially coherent. Framed within these paratexts is the explicit, already-formed narrative of the plot, and this story is adapted—in a sense, retold—in the conventions of multicamera direction. In a sense, the video remediation replicates the tension already embedded in the theater between foregrounding, on the one hand, the evental quality of the performance (its execution and realization) and, on the other, the fictional spaces/worlds represented on stage. But, like much video remediation of opera, *The Met: Live in HD* works hard to shape this tension by privileging the illusionist investment in the world of the stage. Once the lights go down, the cameras devote themselves to immersion in and adaptation of *that* story, omitting anything—a glance at the auditorium or backstage, the face of a spectator—that might redirect attention explicitly to the event. The cameras model our gaze as ideal, undistracted spectators of illusionist opera. Event will always manifest itself—close-ups of singers, for example, can reveal the labor of performance—but the investment, as the directors affirm, is in narrative immersion.

But why the emphasis on story as opposed, say, to the sensory impact of the images and their mobilization into forms of montage, or the potential to transform and reimagine the mise-en-scène, or even, heaven forbid, the potential to challenge aspects of the production? No doubt, as Frances Babbage argues, privileging story in theater is a "popularizing" gesture, one with the potential to renew the appeal of theater to traditional audiences and invite new ones.[31] The Met gestures precisely in this direction when, in its *Live in HD* FAQs, it responds to the question, "Is this program just for opera fans?" by affirming that all the productions "feature great storytelling."[32] But Babbage wonders, too, whether story in theater is what seems most "shareable" for the purposes of adaptation, in the sense that it precedes the codes and conventions of particular theatrical forms and means. Story, that is, suggests the archetypical and universal; here the director responds not necessarily to verse forms, cavatinas, and visual cues on stage but to arcs and denouements. Discursively, citing story becomes a means of licensing shot types. Asked to explain how he chooses a shot, Large singles out the close-up as "incredibly important for storytelling."[33] From this perspective, the recourse to storytelling carves out for the video director a meaningfully creative role within a narrow space framed by a commercial mandate as spin-off and a genre identity as derivative. More than relay or reproduction, the directors imply, the video production finds its own means of telling a story but without overstepping the mark or undermining what Large characterizes as the need for "respect."

This respect manifests itself as well in adherence to the ebb and flow dictated by the score. The shooting script for the productions is guided by the score. Layered with Post-it notes and instructions, it becomes a detailed cue sheet, a multicamera equivalent to the heavily annotated scores that guide stage direction. Camerawork can also respond in a more directly mimetic way to the music. Large speaks of the possibility that a close-up might be "dictated . . . by a specific change in the composition, whether it be dynamic, whether it be orchestra, or whether it simply be part of the construction of the score itself. . . . It's a musical feeling."[34] Cuts and shot choices can map to the beats, accents, and phrasing of the music. For example, in slow and lyrical passages, cuts are often limited to phrase endings, while forceful musical statements trigger synchronized cuts with a similar rhetorical charge. Fast tempi and forceful dynamics seem to license rapid cutting rates, lyrical introspection a lingering shot. Camera movement, too, often seems to react to musical intensity, dynamics, and rhythmic impetus, as though propelled by its energy. Commenting on Willis Sweete's use of the jib-mounted cameras, Armatage observes that "soaring or swooping" movements seem to construct a "visual architecture" in response to the swells and climaxes of the musical line.[35]

It would be misleading, however, to suggest that the editing seismographically tracked the gestures of the score. Rather, directors typically balance this kind of alignment with a more contrapuntal relationship that forgoes direct correspondence. The convention, that is, involves a mixture of audiovisual alignments: this is what we as spectators have come to expect. Were a director relentlessly to map the rhythm of the edit to the music, it would, by breaking with the conventions of mainstream audiovisual production, draw attention to itself and undermine the compact of presence at work in the cinecasts. At the close of the "Marche hongroise" in part 1 of *La damnation de Faust*, a five-bar cadential flourish is dramatically prepared by a pregnant set of three emphatic downbeats, each followed by a cymbal crash. In Willis Sweete's cinecast production of 2008, each cymbal crash is synchronized with a cut progressing from mid-shots to a culminating wide shot of the stage, as though reinforcing the gestural rhetoric and framing function of the music. But, in the five bars that follow (including the final cadence), the full stage shot is held unchanged: suddenly the video edit is unmoved by the music's rhetoric and steps back. This is only one illustration of countless instances in the cinecasts and in remediated opera more generally in which editing and movement seem to resist the mimetic or kinetic impulse, as though aware of the obviousness of mapping themselves naively to musical gesture.

THE SOUND OF SURROUND

Marketing the Met's cinecasts, distributors and venues typically twin the term *HD* with the sonic equivalent of sensory plenitude. Tom Galley, the chief operations and technology officer of National CineMedia, one of the distributors of the Met cinecasts, suggests as much in the launch press release: "The High-Definition quality, big screen and cinema surround sound in our theaters allows patrons to really become immersed in the experience."[36] The term *surround sound* will hardly confound cinema audiences, which have encountered it in promotion and marketing materials since the rollout of digital surround-sound technologies from the early 1990s.[37] Nor will the characterization of the experience as *immersive* seem odd, reflective as it is of a broader market-driven focus in film production and exhibition on the potential and attraction of immersive effects, whether the impact of projected images on visual perception or the capacity of sound to envelope the audience.

In a gesture of venue mimesis, the movie theater attempts to reconstruct with speakers and screen the audiovisual configuration of the Met auditorium: delivered by speakers behind the screen, the left, center, and right channels carry the sound recorded, as the Met media engineer Mark Schubin explains, by almost twenty microphones positioned across the lip of the stage and in the orchestra pit; the surround speakers, situated on the walls of the movie theater, offer a blend of these vocal/orchestral feeds with ambient sound recorded by three microphones situated farther back in the auditorium.[38] In this way, the speakers behind the screen colocate the vocal and orchestral soundstage (as audio engineers and audiophiles call it) with the image of the stage projected on the screen while the surround speakers carry the recorded reverberation of that sound, generating virtual ambience in a space typically constructed to suppress reverberation.[39] As the *Met: Live in HD* audio producer Jay David Saks put it, the goal is to simulate the sound from a "really good seat."[40] And the cinecast invites attention to ambience even before the music begins: the soundscape enveloping the movie theater as audiences arrive is a surround-sound feed of the noise of the assembling audience at the Met. The movie-theater patrons do not so much *join* the Met audience as find themselves sonically enveloped by it. Situated within or, better, contained by, the ambience of the master venue, the spectator/auditor takes up a place in a Met 2.0 (or 5.1), a here sonically rendered as though there.

In its next-best-thing reluctance to reveal or foreground its mediating role, the mimetic sonic space of the cinecast embodies the same ideals of transparency as are evident in the language and practices of multicamera direction. This is no accident: the televisual notion of transparent immediacy and presence rests on more than cameras or vision. Theorists of television have noted that the medium's roots in the electromagnetic technology and live presentation of radio is reflected in its privileging of sound—privileging, at least, in comparison to classical cinema.[41] Rick Altman has observed, for instance, that television as a medium is bound up with the historical apparatus of its delivery, the television set, which is often heard in the home without necessarily being seen.[42] And, when Chion characterizes television as a form of radio illustrated by images, he defines it in its classic mode of live relay, precisely the mode at work in the cinecasts and something they share with their genealogical forebears in the Met matinee radio broadcasts.[43]

More recent scholarship has sought to account for the development of increasingly sophisticated modes of sound production and delivery in television, but it has done so by borrowing from theories of film sound, stressing the alignment of these new practices, including multichannel sound, with cinema.[44] It is an association that mirrors a wider understanding of cinema as the native soil of surround sound. Despite the increasing availability, from the early years of the twenty-first century, of multichannel audio options for select programming (notably drama series), surround sound finds its home, at least in the public imagination, in cinema; to the extent that the term *surround sound* invokes the televisual, it is in the form of home cinema, not broadcasting. Both as practice and as promotional label, then, surround sound has the effect of foregrounding the cinematic in the cinecasts while obscuring televisual precedents that lack the cinema's cultural capital.

A similarly hidden precedent can be found in multichannel audio recordings of classical music for home consumption. When high-resolution audio on disc became commercially available on the Super Audio CD (SACD) in 1999, the format provided for a multichannel option marketed as "SACD Surround." While rock, pop, and jazz releases often featured discrete audio channels, recordings of classical instrumental music typically captured or simulated the acoustic environment of concert and recital halls, with the bulk of the sound distributed across front channels and surround channels reserved for subtle (for many reviewers, much too subtle) ambience.[45] Perhaps because it required investment in dedicated equipment, the format was a commercial failure and is now offered almost exclusively by niche labels: a technical precedent for the surround-sound offering of the cinecasts, then, but hardly a familiar one.

More directly relevant to the cinecasts are the 5.1 Dolby and DTS surround tracks available on DVD releases of opera. Like their SACD counterparts, these mixes restrict the surround channels to ambience, while the front, center, and left speakers share the burden of carrying the directly recorded sound from stage and pit. Owners of these DVDs will have encountered the multichannel option not only on the disc cover and in the accompanying booklet but also in on-screen menus for setup. Whether they will have been in a position to select the option is another matter. As I argued in chapter 2, surround sound is the hidden format of remediated opera. Included as an alternative to stereo on most opera titles released on DVD from around 2000 on, and a standard addition by middecade, multichannel audio calls for a home-theater system with suitable receiver and speaker array.[46] Although the film distribution and consumer electronics industries began promoting and facilitating a cinematic experience in the home via DVD from the 1990s, the market for multichannel audio in opera occupies a doubly niched place in the catalog: within the already-specialized market for opera on DVD, the option to access the multichannel mix seems, at least according to online forums for audiophiles and home-theater owners, to have been little explored. It is a layer of sound widely available but seldom heard, a trace of labor largely unrecognized, and a commodity unconsumed. Into that void, the Met and its distributors project some alluring language. In the absence of any widely shared reference point for the multichannel recording of opera, the term *5.1 surround sound* promises an experience largely unknown: sonic immersion in a distant opera house.

FOLLOW THE PUCK

Like all video productions of staged opera, the cinecasts feature subtle adjustments in the audio mix to reflect the source of sound (e.g., an aria demands a different mix than does a full chorus). The audio engineer Richard King puts it this way: "A good analogy to balancing live opera is mixing audio for a televised ice hockey game—the audio mixer learns to 'follow the puck,' always favoring those microphones closest to the action, while keeping all other microphones lower and level in an effort to reduce comb filtering effects, background noise, and the buildup of diffuse sound in the mix."[47] Implied here too is the coordination of audio mix and image: that a wide shot of the stage, for example, will be balanced differently than a close-up (the former will be more reverberant, while the latter may favor the intimate sound of feeds placed close to the singer or even body-mounted radio microphones). As we discovered in chapter 2, however, "mixing for picture" is not a seismographic pairing in which cuts in the image edit are registered as sudden adjustments in audio balance.[48] The compromise Haigh et al. describe in their account of the sound-recording practices at the Royal Opera House are much in evidence at the Met. The practice, that is, blends the need to locate the sound in a way that is synchronized to the image (thus lending truth to the image) with a degree of sonic continuity modeled on the experience of the stationary auditor. This compromised blend between adjustment and consistency can be read as critical to licensing the virtual mobility of the visual edit: the sound neither completely conforms to what Sheppard calls the *disorienting* quality of the image edit (which would in effect reinforce its hypermediacy) nor contradicts and flattens out visually represented space with absolute sonic continuity (as though dedicated solely to transparency). Instead, it serves a mediating role, more beholden to the transparent ideal of virtual attendance than the frenetic visual edit, but nevertheless shaped to support and reinforce the (untheatrical but highly televisual) mobility of perspectives that the visuals imply.

As for the surround channels, their role in perspective audio suggests a cinematic genealogy in what Mark Kerins characterizes as the nuanced audio mix in which surround channels primarily carry ambient sound (cityscapes, nature, busy interiors, etc.).[49] Discreet sometimes to the point of inaudibility, Kerins adds, these "surround ambiences" draw no attention to the sound apparatus itself, in contrast to the kind of self-advertising effects associated with what Tony Grajeda has described as, paraphrasing Tom Gunning, the "audio of attractions."[50] They support rather than challenge orientation toward the front of the auditorium and audience focus on the two-dimensional screen. In its *Met: Live in HD* manifestation, surround sound reinforces the mediating role of the audio: no perspective realism from the walls, still less any spot effects. Instead, the surround speakers discreetly echo the balance between location and continuity already generated by the screen channels. But, with resources of the movie theater at their disposal, cinecasts promise more than that. Taking a cue from cinema's appeal to superlatives of scale, the rhetoric around the cinecasts promises more than mere presence.

CHAPTER FIVE

You Are More Than Here

An anticipation of the authenticity paradigm at work in *The Met: Live in HD* can be found in the observations of Nathan Halpern on the goals of the TNT transmissions from the Met. "Recreating" theater, Halpern claims, demands a theater, even if it is of the movie variety. Only the scale of the cinematic screen, he insists, can do justice to the stage of the Metropolitan Opera.[1] Recall, too, Taubman's *New York Times* review, which had identified in the transmission an optimal combination of televisual intimacy and cinematic scale. This trope of the happy marriage of movie theater to opera house resurfaces in the rhetoric associated with *The Met: Live in HD*. "These are live events on a giant screen," Gelb told *Musical America Worldwide*, "which is an appropriate forum for the larger-than-life art form that is opera."[2] Put another way, the scale of cinema is true to the scale of opera because both exceed a life-size measure. In part, this excess can be understood in terms specific to the Met: the physical scale of the stage and the auditorium is superlative and demands a superlative scale in remediation. And this remediation is a double process. It begins with image capture (how cameras are positioned, how the stage and its inhabitants are framed, camera resolution, decisions about lenses and depth of field, composition, cutting pace, and editing) but continues with image display (the size of the screen and the scale of projection, the spectator's position in relation to the screen). Wide shots, for example, favor wholeness at the expense of detail, miniaturizing the whole, and thus generating, at least according to the unified perspectivism favored by mainstream cinema and television, the impression of distance within the represented space.[3] But the impact of miniaturization on a given image when viewed on a television or a computer screen is not comparable to that on a given image when viewed on a large cinema screen, and this has historically been one determinant of the divergent aesthetics of the image in television and cinema.[4] This is more than a sequential relationship because the parameters of display can predetermine the process and composition of image capture: panoramic vistas for wide-screen projection, mid-shots and close-ups for the box in the living room or, more recently, the computer screen.

Televised opera encounters this problem in the form of the wide shot of the full stage. It is a shot type that, on the one hand, enjoys a privileged place in critical reception as the proper substitute for the in-house experience (an attitude itself encouraged and reinforced in the presentation and marketing of the productions as relays of the live experience). Often, its importance is noted in its absence: why, critics repeatedly ask, are video directors so unwilling to provide us with this important spatial context? (More on this criticism later.) On the other hand, as Senici points out, the presence of full-stage shots in televised opera has invited criticism of the legibility of the image, a historical problem addressed only in recent years with the improvement of image resolution and expanded screens. Haswell makes a similar point with respect to online streaming, recalling that, when he anticipated a particular scene gaining traction as an excerpt on YouTube, he avoided wide shots altogether.[5] Now the cinecast, with its big screen and HD resolution, offers a display experience with the potential, at least in principle, to address the problem of size and detail.

The touted correspondence of the larger-than-life Met stage with the larger-than-life medium of cinema gestures toward *actual size*, to borrow the terminology widely used in representations of scale in the marketing of consumer goods. The arrangement of spectators in the movie-theater auditorium in front of a screen mimics the arrangement of spectators in the Met auditorium in front of the proscenium, and, if the screen is filled with an image of the full stage shot from one of the camera positions in the Met auditorium, the effect is potentially that of an alignment of perspective and scale. Cinema audiences are invited to a screen replica of the Met. The problem is that, in keeping with the grammar of multicamera production in opera more generally, this is a shot type typically featured sparingly in *The Met: Live in HD*. The wide shot performs an establishing role (providing scenic context at the beginnings of acts and scenes) and a framing function in response to closing curtains and applause (its role in *Written on Skin* was, as we saw, exceptional). But it forms only part of a multicamera production grammar that features not only a range of other shot types from its complement of eight to ten auditorium cameras but also energetic cuts between these feeds, an emphasis on movement *within* each shot via slow zooms, and, in a practice atypical for multicamera opera, camera movement using cranes/jibs and robotically controlled track mounts. The cinecast spectator seeking a virtual Met encounters a screen with other ideas.

You Are More Than Here | 127

SUPERSIZE ME!

To crave the wide shot is, in other words, to invite disappointment. Those critics and observers of remediated opera who express the wish that this was the *only* shot articulate a desire utterly at odds with the grammar and aesthetics of multicamera production—which is to say, at odds with several decades of media practice in the broadcast and recording of staged opera. For at the heart of the multicamera production standards that have been the default for opera is precisely the multiplicity of shot types and the decoupage that assembles them into a sequence. If we can speak of a privileged shot within this multiplicity, a first among equals, it is not the wide shot but the close-up. Televised productions of staged opera have long followed this face-facing logic of multicamera production. Although close-ups of the set or props are not uncommon—a slow pan or zoom of details of the set will sometimes act as an establishing shot during an orchestral prelude—it is above all the face of the singer that attracts the camera's gaze. This is not the richly composed, risky composition associated with the extreme close-ups of cinema but the more cautiously framed medium close-up typical of live multicamera production practices. The close-up has, however, become more and more prominent in the grammar of opera on video, as it has in multicamera production more generally.

A lingering take of a full stage, then, is doubly peripheral within the conventions that have increasingly prevailed in video productions of staged opera: lingering when the norm is cutting between shots, wide when the favored shot is close. *The Met: Live in HD* follows these conventions of multiplicity and movement and then some. It, too, energetically interleaves feeds from its typical complement of eight to ten auditorium cameras and, in a further blow to the desire for a static image, emphasizes movement *within* the shot via slow zooms. And all this before we even consider the camera mobility that has become a Met signature. I begin, however, with the close-up, which in the cinecasts is at once familiar (nothing about the composition of the close-up differs from televisual practice) and strange (the scale of projection in the movie theater recasts the close-up in terms quite different from the small screens that have historically played host to televised opera).

In a corollary of the observation that the size of the television screen rendered it unsuitable for wide shots, John Ellis attributes the prominence of the close-up in televisual aesthetics to the capacity of the television screen to display a face on a human scale—to approximate, in other words, actual size measured in anthropomorphic terms.[6] Recall the references to the "intimacy" of television by Halpern and in the critical reception of

TNT. What they recognize is this anthropomorphic encounter with the human face on television; what they fail to register in their best-of-all-worlds reading of the encounter of television and cinema is the shock of rendering the intimate grand, the human face gigantic.

Cinema, of course, had long challenged the anthropomorphic measure of scale in the close-up on its own terms, a topic Mary Ann Doane has considered in depth. Yet, as Annie van den Oever points out, televisual norms would challenge the conventions of cinema, as, for example, when the New Hollywood directors of the 1970s brought to cinema the aesthetics of television, above all its foregrounding of sound and the close-up.[7] Here, blown up on the movie-theater screen, were the close-ups Ellis characterizes as life-size on the television screen.

The postmillennial introduction of cinecasts might be regarded as the next stage of this encounter. Now, however, it is not simply the aesthetics of television that are incorporated but its apparatus as a whole—the multicamera production, live feeds via satellite, video rather than film. Not an incorporation at all, then, and still less a convergence of media, but a sometimes awkward interface between technologies and conventions: cinema plays host to a medium it has admitted only in historical experiments like TNT; the televisual image is screened on a scale impossible in the home. If there is a point of reference, it is the giant screens that have adorned sports stadiums since the 1990s or the temporary outdoor screens set up in civic spaces, including relays outside opera houses.[8] Like the cinecasts, these screenings present the multicamera video production style of television but on the scale of cinema: that is to say, they render the intimacy of the televisual image gigantic.

This is not to claim, however, that they have somehow familiarized the encounter. Outdoor public screenings are rare enough to retain a festive quality, and the experience of attending a sports event at a stadium large enough to house a giant screen is still arguably *evental*—but, for most, not habitual. Granted, the longevity of the cinecast phenomenon might be understood to have normalized the idea of watching TV on a cinema screen, yet cinecasts do remain a niche market, one that has never quite gained the traction that might have been expected when they arrived on the scene. In this sense, they can be read as retaining a certain strangeness, still an exceptional experience for all but the most devoted patrons and the curious, and completely uncharted territory for many more. Brianna Wells likens the audience experience at *The Met: Live in HD* to the Freudian uncanny, a characterization that possibly bestows on the cinecasts a more radical disorientation than their safe packaging and presentation merits but that at least addresses the question of unfamiliarity.[9] The novelty of

You Are More Than Here | 129

the experience chimes with the possibility, proposed by Gunning, that adjustment to and familiarization with media forms can be countered by a "re-enchantment" when new forms and experiences disrupt habituation.[10]

GULLIVER AT THE OPERA

What happens, then, if the scale represented in and by the image begins to seem *dis*proportionate with life, with anthropomorphic scale—bigger, even, than the big of the Met. The media theorist Erkki Huhtamo notes in the proliferation of screens a double development toward ever-smaller and ever-larger screens. From the miniaturization of handheld devices to the gigantic displays in sports stadiums and IMAX theaters, we encounter what Huhtamo calls a *gulliverization* of screen media (see n. 7). Doane reminds us that classical narrative cinema developed a system of representation to incorporate and harness the close-up. The principle of continuity editing contributed to the formation of an apparently unified and homogeneous spatial field in which the perception of scale could be mapped onto represented space. What Doane calls the *threat* of disproportion and the *distortion of scale* posed especially by the close-up was displaced into and partially allayed by a perception of represented distance anchored in a carefully constructed economy of coherent space: in this context *large* equates to *near, small* to *far*. The very terminology in English is predicated on proximity, not the magnification suggested by the French *gros plan* (large shot) or the German *Großaufnahme*, used interchangeably with *Nahaufnahme*. Although it manufactures the continuity of continuity editing via the (uncinematic) assembly of simultaneously shot perspectives, multi-camera production typically seeks, like cinema, to preserve the coherence of represented space, carefully contextualizing the close-up within a grammar of shot types and sequences that situate it precisely as close. Thanks, as Ellis reminds us, to the scale of the television screen, this impression of proximity generates an intimacy with the face, here rendered at anthropomorphic scale. But now, in the cinecast, that scale is dramatically magnified. The shot grammar may be familiar from television; the scale is not. To return to Swift, does the cinecast close-up not locate the spectator in Brobdingnag, the land of giants?

"Partly it's the size of the screen," wrote John Wyver of *Tristan und Isolde* (video director, Barbara Willis Sweete, 2008). A multicamera director himself, Wyver wondered whether he was witnessing a new future for opera on screen, one quite different from its treatment in television "squeezed into the box in the corner."[11] Reviewing *The Barber of Seville* (video director, Gary Halvorson, 2007), Tim Ashley enthused: "The sheer enormity of a movie screen confers tremendous immediacy on the proceedings."[12] "Watching it in the cinema," wrote Peter Conrad of the same cinecast, "was like having not just the best seat at the Met but all the best seats simultaneously."[13] The movie theater comes across as pivotal here for Conrad, who had once written of the underwhelming domestic experience of televised opera "squeezed into the box and deposited in our houses as a small and undemanding piecemeal package."[14] On the scale of the movie theater, however, the impression of dispersal and fragmentation across a virtual auditorium becomes a form of superspectatorship: the cinematic scale not only returns screened opera to an operatic scale but exceeds it. This is opera remediated in quantum terms. The actual opera house might even come to seem diminished. "Will seeing the same production from the Family Circle at the Met," wrote Tommasini of *Hansel and Gretel* (Barbara Willis Sweete, 2008), "just make everything seem too flat and far away?"[15]

EYES ON POGO STICKS

Conrad's review of *The Met: Live in HD* also draws attention to the number of cameras set up in the Met auditorium and to the characteristically rapid cutting rate that edits the multiple feeds together: "My eyes felt as if they were attached to irrepressible pogo sticks."[16] If the number of cameras at the Met exceeds norms for opera telecasts (eight to ten as opposed to a typical complement of six), the pace of editing can be mapped, to some extent, onto broader trends. Wyver has remarked, for example, on what now appears to be the "funereally slow" practices of early broadcast history, and Will notes that the historical distinction between the styles of live broadcasts and edited recordings has narrowed as the former have increasingly incorporated the "kinetic manner" of the latter.[17] This is certainly the impression registered by Anthony Sheppard in his review of the Met's *The First Emperor* (Brian Large, 2007). Sheppard observes that the pace and number of cuts combined with contrasts of scale generated a "kinetic" effect bordering on disorientation, something he did not experience attending the same production in the opera house.[18]

Illustrative here is a comparison of a scene from the 1987 telecast of the premiere of *Nixon in China* (Houston Grand Opera, directed for stage by Peter Sellars) with the *Met: Live in HD* transmission of Sellars's 2011 revival. In the closing moments of act 1, scene 2, Mao Tse-tung, dutifully echoed by his chorus of three translators, utters a passage from his *Little Red Book* ("Founders come first, then profiteers"). In Brian Large's video direction of the 1987 telecast, the final forty-five seconds of the scene comprise a sequence of only three shots: a three-quarter-length body shot of Mao and his translators, followed by a medium close-up of Mao and a concluding static medium shot of the four characters during the brief curtain music as Mao slowly leaves the room. The *Met: Live in HD* transmission, directed (unusually for the Met) by the stage director (Sellars), features no fewer than eleven shots of the same scene, concluding with a rapid montage of close-ups of the three translators eyeing each other with suspicion. It is as though the cinecast were participating in the "media coverage" theme so central to the opera and famously realized in Nixon's solo "News has a kind of mystery," with its rapid repetitions and juxtapositions reminiscent of media cuts. The scene ends, not with a curtain this time, but with a (cinematic) blackout in the theater that plays well with the self-consciously mediatized presentation of the cinecast. If the risky, rapid cuts of the later production reflect the increasingly pacy editing of television and cinema more broadly, they also suggest what might be considered a Sellars signature. In his celebrated Mozart/da Ponte trilogy of 1990, Sellars had already demonstrated a distinctive editing style based on rapid montage of close-ups, and this scene in *Nixon in China* and many more like it suggest a stylistic consistency with his earlier practice: the multicamera director as auteur.

RIGHT INTO THE ACTION

The idea that such a style might be characterized by kineticism invites consideration of movement not just between camera feeds but within individual shots. Asked to identify his signature as a director, Halvorson singled out "movement." Examination of the camerawork under Halvorson's direction corroborates his self-analysis, not least in those shots that feature the perceived motion made possible by the zoom lens. To observe that the cinecasts make extensive use of zooming shots is rather like noting that the Met foregrounds singers or that strings are prominent in the orchestra. So consistent is the zoom motion that static shots become the exception. Occasionally, the direction of the zoom will be an outward one, slowly situating individual figures in crowds or the emptiness of a bare stage. But, overwhelmingly, it is the inward zoom that is in play in the cinecasts. This is familiar territory for multicamera production both in opera and beyond. Television began to capitalize on the potential of zoom lenses in the 1960s, when directors of multicamera production in televised sports and other live programming discovered the flexibility and range of shot types made possible by the availability of different focal lengths on one lens. While "offline" (i.e., not providing the live feed), camera operators could reposition the lens to reframe the shot.

132 | CHAPTER FIVE

Live manipulation of the zoom lens to close in gradually on a subject began to feature too, above all in drama, where the slow focal transition to a close-up (a technique that had not hitherto featured significantly in cinema) seemed to represent a journey or narrative of interiorization, all without the necessity to move the camera. To zoom slowly into the face was to reveal subjectivity, not by cutting instantly to the intimacy of the close-up, but by *traversing* the imaginary distance to the subject. The fit with televised opera is not difficult to imagine. In the opera house, a shooting location unsuitable for camera movement, productions could multiply the range of shot types and compositions available with fixed lenses. As for the slow forward zoom, here was a televisual counterpart to the interiority intimated by stage and music, not least in those many introspective numbers and scenes that foreground the individual subject. Depending on how they are sung and staged, solos and duets can flirt unsettlingly with voyeurism, and something about the stealth magnification of the zoom reinforces that intrusive gaze. But arias and other extended solos are sometimes prefaced with an appeal to listen to a confession, to behold a fate. Performance and stage production can reinforce the rhetoric of invitation with an isolated focus that commands attention, and here the zoom has a role to play in establishing and intensifying that attention. If the underlying exhortation is "draw closer," the zoom seems calculated to render the response in visual and spatial terms.

The Met's cinecast directors not only capitalize on this legacy but seem to take it to new lengths. Long zooms from distance feature repeatedly, but characteristic is a use of the zoom lens so slight that the movement in the image is almost imperceptible: not, in other words, an obvious closing in on a subject but a sense that the image is never quite still, that the camera is leaning in. Typical is the camerawork in *Samson et Dalila* (2018) directed for stage by Darko Tresnjak and for the cinecast by Halvorson. Samson's act 3 lament "Vois ma misère, hélas," delivered as the blind, imprisoned strongman labors at a mill wheel, is explicit in its exhortation to bear witness: "Behold my misery." Alexander Dodge's literalist set design (replete with fiberglass mill wheel) situates the tenor Roberto Alagna in classic dungeon gloom, torn robes and gray hair completing the picture of destitution. Halvorson's camerawork accepts the invitation to behold with cuts broadly synchronized to Saint-Saëns's long phrases and an almost perpetual zooming motion. Each shot, whether from a camera position near or far, zooms slowly toward Alagna, sometimes explicitly, sometimes almost imperceptibly, climaxing in a close-up as Samson, now prostrate on the floor, cries out in despair and urges God to free the imprisoned Israelites. In the ten-minute duration of the solo, the zoom lens is still for a total of seventy seconds. Not that the advance toward Samson is linear. Rather, in the looped form of multicamera production, offline cameras reset to a more distant focal length, ready to replay their inward zoom. The effect is of an infinite approach to the subject, not unlike the barber's pole or the auditory illusion of infinitely ascending or descending frequencies created by the phased introduction of layers in the Shepard tone. In this scene, however, the cyclic zooming arguably maps most explicitly onto the infinite circles of Samson's toil at the mill wheel. The act of drawing closer becomes a vortex, as if the act of witnessing participated in the dramaturgy—or, in the economy of presence, as if spectatorship were choreographed by the gestures witnessed.

Nor are the cameras themselves necessarily stationary. Like *NT Live*, *The Met: Live in HD* features jib-mounted cameras, here anchored in the loges above the orchestra pit and capable of extending to a position above midstage to capture a range of static, zooming, and boom shots. As Halvorson puts it: "[A camera] gives you all these different perspectives of looking down, but then can boom down and go right into the action, and you feel like you're always in it."[19] The result, then, is not only height perspectives but also the sense of penetrating the stage. And here again the virtual superspectator is invoked, someone who is drawn closer by the action and approaches the stage. It is an effect not unlike that observed in cinema when, as Tom Gunning points out, the camera generates the impression that the viewer is mobile *within* the space of the film. Although he stresses the virtual nature of this movement—the space of the viewer remains fixed; the ontological divide between viewer and image unchanged—Gunning seeks to account for something striking and even unsettling about the shifting frame line that alters orientation and perspective as it uncovers and conceals, penetrates and withdraws from the represented space. The effect, he concludes, is to draw the viewer into the image, to generate the sense of being—and here is that term again—"immersed."[20]

This imaginary mobile spectator is nowhere more clearly summoned than in the shots generated by one of the Met's prize assets. Halvorson explains that, as an avid sports fan, he was struck by the use of robotic cameras to track the movement of athletes, for example, in sprinting. On taking up directorial responsibilities for *The Met: Live in HD*, he recounts, he proposed the installation of a (discreet) camera track on the lip of the stage. This camera, in use ever since, has facilitated what is, in effect, a signature shot of *The Met: Live in HD*: an upward-facing medium shot in slow lateral motion across the stage. The camera is used extensively in the *Nixon in China* scene I discussed above. Rarely motionless, it captures all the full-body group shots with a slow tracking motion and adjustments in tilt, pan, and zoom to keep the subjects tightly framed. One of the results of this combination of movements is a fluid sense of perspectival space in which foregrounded bodies, even when actually still, appear to move in relation to the scenic background and to each other. The image is, in effect, animated beyond any movement generated on the stage itself, as though the static pose of the *tableau vivant* were set in motion by a mobile observer. This is an effect that recalls, as Halvorson claims, the camerawork of broadcast sports; it also summons, in its parallax effect, the mobile camera of cinema, all while generating a virtual theatrical spectator liberated from seated immobility. It is the same effect that Pascale Aebischer identifies in the *NT Live* cinecasts when she observes that the camerawork made possible by jibs and tracks generates an experience "not identifiable with a possible audience viewpoint within the theatre."[21]

On the other hand, although modeled on a staging, the Mozart trilogy was a studio-based recording. In the cinecast, Sellars brings this style to live editing, something that seems inconceivable without the experienced production personnel on which the Met relies, not to mention the developments in camera technology, broadcast image resolution, and lighting so formative in the cinecast initiative. And, as a corrective to any explanation rooted too firmly in the individual style of the director-auteur, we should note that the cinecast of *The Last Emperor*, the pace of which had seemed so striking to Sheppard, was directed by Brian Large. Similar pacing is evident, too, in the work of other directors at the Met: action sequences in productions directed by Halvorson, for example, feature some furious cut rates. Might this suggest a Met house style, shaped in part by individual directors, no doubt, but also by other elements of the apparatus at work there: the specific resources and technology available, not to mention the many in-house collaborators in the production process?

Although Halvorson claims it as a signature, movement is a characteristic much in evidence across the work of other directors for the series. I noted the stark contrast in cut rate in the two productions of the scene in *Nixon in China*, but in the minutes before the exchange of glances between translators, as the meeting between Mao and Nixon concludes and characters disperse, it is in fact the Large production that features the higher cut rate as different cameras lock on to moving characters with a series of panning mid-shots. What happens in the Sellars video is quite different: here it is one camera, the front-of-stage dolly, that performs the lion's share of registering movement. Combining its signature tracking motion with pans and zooms, it produces images that are never still. Movement, that is, comes not from the cut but from the pervasive and persistent mobility of the camera. And, while the Large production *responds* to movement on stage with panning shots, the dolly camera in Sellars's production is in ceaseless motion throughout the segment. It is as though the dolly camera demanded its signature role regardless of the specifics of the scene in question. As a key component of the Met's cinecast apparatus, it claims the camera equivalent of the roles taken by the singers at whose feet it scurries back and forth.

Perspective is critical here too. While the distant cameras of the Large production have the effect, even in mid-shots, of flattening depth of field, the close range of the dolly camera generates deep focus, while its constant motion creates the effect of shifting patterns of relief between foreground character and background scenery. Finally, while Large's cameras view characters from waist height, the dolly camera looks up from a position level with the stage floor so that they appear to tower over the viewer: truly Swift's land of giants. For Sheppard, the effect in *The Last Emperor* was to supplant the intimacy of close camerawork with an impression of the "monumental."[22] Again, my point here is not to single Halvorson out; it is, rather, that the scene illustrates what has become a *house* style for the Met. Together with the jib camera, the dolly shot offers movement and perspective that lends *The Met: Live in HD* a defining look and defines its articulation of space. It is, in other words, the signature shot of the series, one that the cinecasts feature consistently.

ACCESS ALL AREAS

Far less coy about its supplemental value and clearly foregrounded as exclusive to the cinecast is a feature that generates as much conversation as the operatic performances: backstage access during intermissions. In part, as I suggested in chapter 3, a practical solution to the problem of lengthy intermissions for cinema patrons, the interviews with artists that form the core of this content represent the Met's equivalent of the many modes of privileged access offered to patrons of screened live events: the virtual VIP and backstage pass for popular-music and theater events, the exclusive interviews associated with subscriber and pay-per-view telecasts and live streams, the behind-the-scenes glimpses offered by almost all the cinecast content providers. Often presented in reality-TV form as revealing encounters with singers still breathless from the stage or nervously waiting in dressing rooms, the Met interviews assume and then satisfy a voyeuristic curiosity. Is this not, Sam O'Connell asks, an equivalent to the making-of features and other bonus paratexts offered on DVDs, and does it not effectively offer the cinecast audience more content and experience for less money than their opera-house equivalents?[23] More than compensation for the remoteness of the cinecasts, in this view, the backstage features offer a substantial supplement to the performance. This is certainly how Gelb characterizes them when he notes, in an article for the *New York Times*, that only cinema audiences for *Lucia di Lammermoor* (2011) were privy to Natalie Dessay's announcement during an interview that her performance of the title role that day would likely be her last.[24]

The interviews offer other insights. One of the questions directed at singers during the interviews is whether the cinecast brings additional pressure. This is a topic the mezzo-soprano Susan Graham addressed in an interview for the making-of documentary *Live at the Met*. "For the performers it's all heightened," she explains. "The stakes are very high because you want to be perfect. Because (*a*) it's going out to a worldwide audience, (*b*) it's preserved."[25] Gelb put it in starker terms in an interview during the intermission of the *Parsifal* transmission of 2013: "All these stars in this dream cast of *Parsifal* have their adrenaline pumping at a greater level than usual, and the result is I think that they're giving—even though they're great every day they perform—today may be the best performance of this run, and that's a great treat not only for them but also for the audiences in the movie theaters." Contrary to the promoted notion that the cinecast is a representative sample, that we in the movie theater drop in virtually on one performance of a run, Gelb here suggests that the performance is altered—intensified—in the act of filming it.[26] Speaking on a panel on cinecasts, the soprano Corinne Winters (featured in a number of Royal Opera House cinecasts) concurred with the view that nerves are heightened by the cinecasts. Her acting style, she adds, is more intimate, and her makeup may be more lightly applied for the camera's gaze. This is not an admission director and fellow panelist Haswell had expected: "When we come in to do these shows, we try to be as 'backed off' as possible, because as far as I was concerned, all we're doing is putting cameras in the auditorium, and they [the performers] are just doing the same thing they do every time they go on stage. So I was actually quite surprised it was different for the performers because I'd made this assumption."[27] That even an experienced professional had not realized what might be different about these performances suggests just how ingrained and successful the characterization of the cinecast as immediate has been. It is hardly surprising, then, that patrons would make similar assumptions, understanding the cinecast as a transparent relay of something happening anyway. Instead, we learn that the performance has a supercharged quality, that even its materials and gestural language might be altered to accommodate the cameras. You are more than here because the here you witness has been transformed by the knowledge of your spectatorship.

CHAPTER SIX

You Are Not Here

As we have seen, Nathan Halpern's observations on the TNT telecasts carefully balanced promotional claims on behalf of the initiative with deference to the in-the-house experience. What we could do, Halpern argues, is not necessarily what we should do: "Working with cameras and sound reproducers we are, of course, in the position to go backstage, under the stage, into the throats of the singers—all of which is exactly what we want to avoid. Our purpose is to give opera-lovers all over the country the same effects enjoyed by those seated in the Met. We try neither to improve on grand opera nor to make it less grand and more intimate; we wish simply to recreate the form as it is, essentially in terms of the theater."[1] Despite the historical and technological gulf, Halpern here sets the scene for the critical reception of *The Met: Live in HD*. If the as-it-is rhetoric anticipates the promotional language of *The Met: Live in HD* and other cinecast series, the careful privileging of the master venue brings to mind the persistent caveat from *Live in HD* hosts that nothing compares to being at the Met. Out of this contradictory discursive space—this unresolved conflict between here and elsewhere—comes the critical flip side of all the praise for the audiovisual impact, all the astonishment at the larger-than-life experience. A calculated commercial tactic designed to avoid what Gelb once provocatively called *cannibalization*, the cautious delimitation of the opera house as authentic nevertheless sits uncomfortably with the cinecast's pretense of presence, with the message "you are here."[2] At the same time, as Halpern's warnings about close-ups and backstage access foreshadow, the attempt to supercharge presence—to generate a more than here—risks drawing attention to the means of production. In this way, the cinecast invites scrutiny of what seems to exceed—and thus also fall short of—the experience of in-person attendance. Much criticism of *The Met: Live in HD* implies that the cinecasts have undermined their own message of immediacy by going precisely where Halpern feared to tread. In what follows, I

138 | CHAPTER SIX

revisit the signature backstage interviews and the reception of close-ups and other production techniques to consider the critical reservations they provoke. What, I ask, might the evident resistance to the presence effects of the cinecasts tell us about the limits of the appeal to virtual attendance? And is there room—discursively, phenomenologically—for the cinecasts not as ersatz theater but on televisual and cinematic terms? Is there space, that is, for other spaces?

CURLING TOES

"Please don't subject us to live artist interviews," wrote a critic in response to *La traviata* (2017), "they're toe-curling."[3] Representative of a wider critical response to the backstage interviews, the plea taps into a perception that the format is contrived and awkward. While intermissions in the Royal Opera House's *Live Cinema Season* feature a mixture of prerecorded features, the Met focuses on live interviews by the hosts (almost always singers) of creative personnel (predominantly singers). The result, critics complain, is not so much insight into the craft of performance, still less a forbidden glimpse, as clichéd exchanges, at once stilted and superficially self-regarding. As James Steichen's autoethnography illustrates, however, none of this is accidental or improvised. Part of a carefully scripted institutional dramaturgy that both defines the Met (in this case, as the ultimate "singer's house") and commodifies it, the choreographed interviews, in Steichen's words, "monetize the backstage," revealing precisely what they want us to see, how they want us to see it.[4] Cautioning against a naive belief in voyeuristic access behind the scenes, Nicolò Palazzetti adds that the actual backstage—that which we cannot be permitted to see, including the *Met: Live in HD* camera crew itself—retreats further from sight.[5]

Not that the mask does not drop occasionally. In the cinecast of *La damnation de Faust* (2008), the mezzo-soprano Susan Graham is interviewed by Thomas Hampson immediately before she assumes her stage position, seventy-four steps up a scaffold, for part 3. A handheld camera follows her up the steps, and an understandably self-conscious Graham fills the silence with a comment to the assistant accompanying her: "Now I'm completely dried out from all that talking. It's funny to talk and then go on to sing." It is an uncomfortably intrusive moment as a singer prepares to perform—or, rather, transition from one performance (the interview) to another—and it suggests that the heightened quality Graham herself associates with the cinecast performance may not be rooted solely in positive experience.

It is also a reflexive commentary on the discomfort the intermission interviews so often seem to generate when they transform the backstage into a space of sometimes awkward encounters with handheld cameras. Gelb once likened *The Met: Live in HD* to Monday night football, and it is perhaps in the interviews that the resemblance to sports broadcasting is clearest. Just as athletes are followed by camera crews and interviewed on the field of play immediately before and after the action, so the host at the Met becomes a stand-in for the audience's imaginary access backstage, intercepting singers as they enter and exit the stage. In this televisual space, the roving interviewers and camera teams backstage are not so different from those waiting on the sidelines of the big game, and dressing rooms are not so far from locker rooms. Sports interviews of this kind promise to capture the white heat of an immediate pre- or postperformance exchange, the authenticity of which is supposedly guaranteed by its temporal proximity to the act. Part of what is on display here is emotion and the body: this is not about the composed anticipation of a future event but about the nervous energy of immanent action, not mature reflection but residual affect. The latter was certainly on show in *Tosca* (2019) when the host, Susan Graham, met a breathless Karita Mattila, still clearly exuding stage energy after act 2, and remarked on her current disposition, asking (unscripted, as she later pointed out) how she "recovers" from performing.

The interviews, however, are just as likely to provoke nervous energy of a more awkward kind, not to mention distraction and (understandable) impatience, all cloaked in the flamboyant mannerisms native to the backstage area. That the actual conversations are so often banal is hardly surprising given that the scripts for the singer-hosts tend to couch the interviews as expressions of admiration or collegial sympathy for the challenge of the role.[6] This is where the parallels with sports broadcasting seem to break down. Unlike professional broadcasters, the Met's interviewers are not charged with the task of subjecting a performance to critical scrutiny or asking difficult questions on behalf of disappointed fans: success in opera, as in the performing arts more broadly, is not mapped onto a win-lose binary as it is in sports, and critical commentary is not broadcast from backstage or the dressing room.

Yet even here there are parallels. Tough questions or not, sports interviews are notorious for the often-clichéd language of the answers ("We have to come together as a team," "I gave 110 percent"). The journalist Mihir Bose argues that this tendency has been exacerbated by a trend for broadcasters and print media to rely increasingly on ex-athletes as hosts and pundits. Tapping into what he calls a "show me your medal" mentality, this trend subordinates media expertise and training to the popular and celebrity-centered notion that only those who have competed are in a position to comment or ask the right questions. Although he concedes that this can lead to revealing insight, he concludes that a loss of independence and objectivity threatens rigor and compromises professionalism: now the platitudes uttered by interview subjects are often heard from those who ask the questions.[7] The practice of filming singers interviewing singers seems likewise to rest on the principle that fellow practitioners have the insider knowledge that best positions them to ask the right questions. The flattering tenor (or tenor flattering) of those questions—in essence, what does it take to be like you?—takes a cue from the most solipsistic and facile tendencies of sports broadcasting, awkwardly importing its observational frames and spaces to the operatic backstage. Presented in this way, behind-the-scenes access unmasks the artifice of theater only to reinforce the self-regarding myths of performance. The backstage, that is, turns out to be just another stage. Yet the visit contributes to the mythology of the event precisely because it is framed not as a performance but as a privileged glimpse beneath the mask. In what Cachopo characterizes as Brechtian distantiation in reverse, exposure of the spectacle becomes "a spectacle in itself."[8]

TOO CLOSE FOR COMFORT

But it is the close-up—"into the throats of singers"—that has attracted some of the most strident criticism. Singers should never be seen in this detail, observers complain, in part because the image magnifies, literally, the problem of the unsightly production of voice—what Melina Esse dubs the "tongue-and-teeth problem" already prevalent in reactions to singer close-ups on screen long before the cinecasts.[9] Now, in the movie theater, the problem is writ large. Reviewing the Met's *Otello* cinecast (2012), one critic expressed (justifiable) astonishment that blackface could still feature in an opera production while at the same time complaining that Renée Fleming was now rather too "matronly" to play Desdemona. The focus of his concern? That these visual characteristics of the production are now "hugely magnified" in the movie theater.[10]

Critics also identify an issue of craft. Reporting on the 1954 gala TNT telecast, *Variety* noted reservations about "the appearance and acting ability of many of the Metop principals."[11] It is a theme that has returned in responses to *The Met: Live in HD*. "Live opera acting," writes Zachary Woolfe, "depends more on posture and physical fearlessness than on the kinds of details—a quiver of the mouth, a quick turn of the eyes—that convey emotion in cinematic close-up."[12] The natural domain of opera singers, in other words, is a space that demands extrovert gestures unsuited to the screen close-up. And note how Woolfe presents the *cinematic* close-up as the comparison: having entered the movie theater, opera singers will now be judged according to the techniques and values native to a space in which the scale of the image renders legible the tiniest of details. At work in the cinematic close-up, writes Doane, is the logic of the microscope, with its impression of "moving ever closer" to the object, rendering the miniature gigantic.[13] Applied to staged opera, this means that the singer's body is subject to the scrutiny of an enhanced gaze: powerful lenses focus microscopically on the face to capture intimate expressive detail, which is in turn projected onto a large screen. Revealing much, these optical devices of magnification and projection seem to bridge distance and bring the object close—closer, certainly, than opera glasses, repeatedly cited by critics and observers as a weak form of magnification that the cinecasts surpass.[14]

As we have seen, Doane reads the constructed impression of proximity (near/far) in represented space as one of the conventions mobilized by classical narrative cinema to address the problem of disproportion (large/small). With the cinecasts, however, it is not the represented space of narrative cinema—or of television—that is typically invoked by observers and critics but the representational compact of the theater. To the extent that the close-up of an opera singer on stage presents a problem of disproportionate scale or excessive detail—and the reception of *The Met: Live in HD* suggests that it often is—it is not a problem easily solved by imagining proximity within the represented space because proximity is itself regarded as a problem. By bridging the distance to the stage, the close-up is understood to threaten the theatrical abyss of representation, what Herbert Blau identifies as "the experience of fracture" so foundational to theater.[15] If video once troubled practitioners and scholars of theater concerned about inauthenticity and misrepresentation—Jonathan Miller referred to the "surreptitious" editing that transformed the theatrical event—the field, as I suggested in the book's introduction, now seems much less guarded and defensive about screen remediation, perhaps precisely because of the kind of integration of screen media into and onto the stage that is the focus of part 1.[16] Yet the old debates about authenticity have found fresh soil in the cinecasts, which, as public events, seem to generate more commentary than the private/domestic encounters with opera on DVD or television ever did. It helps, of course, that the arrival of the cinecasts coincided with the rise of social media, the explosion of the blogosphere, and the wider online dissemination of print media.

Indicative of an inability or unwillingness to escape the discursive orbit of mimesis and relay, this reinvigorated critical focus on the untheatrical quality of the cinecasts is symptomatic of the logic the cinecasts encourage in the first place—the same "deceptively self-effacing attitude" that Senici detects in opera videos more widely.[17] According to this logic, the magnifying capacity of the camera lens relocates the virtual spectator to a place too close for theatrical spectatorship, not so much an even more here as a thoroughly untheatrical experience. Conrad reconciled these conflicted spaces by invoking a kind of superspectatorship modeled on virtual attendance at the Met, while Wyver accepted the video production on its own terms, describing the close-up of Isolde in the "Liebestod" of *Tristan und Isolde* (2008) as "right and true and thrilling."[18] Other observers have been more resistant.

Although dedicated, as its name suggests, to appreciation of the cinecasts, the Facebook group "Met Opera Live in HD Fans" attracts frequent critical comments about close-ups at the expense of full-stage shots. One group member wrote: "I usually do not see opera in HD exactly because of the camera always focusing on the singer in close up rather than allowing us to see the whole stage as we would in the theater."[19] During the transmission of *Akhnaten* (2019), another posted a graphic with the words "I want to see all the stage all the time . . . ok a few closeups," then followed up with a qualification directed at a member of the group who happened to be one of the camera operators: "Jay Millard, I just want to say I think you and your crew ROCK—sorry for the instant flip-out at Act I when I was crazy to see THE WHOLE THING. This opera is a powerful argument for viewing IN THE HOUSE."[20] It is an attitude echoed in published reviews. Reporting on *La damnation de Faust* (2008) for Montreal's *Le devoir*, Christophe Huss complained: "The poetry of this production in the auditorium is predicated on an overall view, the exact opposite of the aesthetic of the movie-theater screening, which uses and abuses magnifying-glass effects."[21] To opera glasses and microscopes we can add another optical device for magnification, this one clearly unwelcome.[22] Is the problem with the zoom lens not precisely this resemblance to these devices, this "mechanical" quality, as Will puts it?[23]

UNDER THE MICROSCOPE

Nor, it seems, is the idea of being the subject of these magnifying instruments necessarily appealing. Corinne Winters relates the anxiety that attends the prospect of being viewed in such detail, noting in particular the not always camera-friendly sight of vocal production. But she also identifies as challenging the need to play to two spectatorial spaces at once: "In opera, I occasionally in my performance try to be subtle and they say, well it's great for the front row but it doesn't really reach the back of the hall. But in this medium I can aim for a more realistic performance. But it is a balance, because it has to work for both sides [the stage and the screen audience.]" At stake for Winters is a balance, but this also suggests the need to compromise both spaces of performance. Playing to the camera imagines a spectator in a place closer to the singer than many or all of those in the opera house occupy; projecting to the back of the hall caters to the audience in person but generates adverse reactions from critics in the movie theater. Addressing those reactions, Winters concludes that cinecast audiences are equally situated in a space somewhere between television sports and scripted programming. Audiences, she adds, need to be realistic in their expectations: "For people who want to see that up close, I think it's for you. But if you want to see pristine, that's not opera: opera is bloody!"[24] In this reading, the question of proximity is a question of contested spaces both in front of the camera and in front of the screen.

MOVING TOO MUCH

Critical unease with close-ups tends to go hand in hand with concerns about the other signature characteristics of *The Met: Live in HD*: cutting rate and camera movement. In part, this is a reflection of the wider and long-standing problem of the perceived disparity between theater and screen media, opera house and video. As Lawrence Kramer puts it: "Not only do we get too close, but we move too much; in reading the camera we must so to speak read around or through the convention that demands changes in angle and distance regardless of the subject matter of the scene."[25] The problem is a recurrent topic in the "Fans of Live in HD" Facebook group. One member posted: "When we see opera in theater—we see from one angle and one only. I think the multiple camera angles are unnecessary. Plant one camera somewhere in mid orchestra and that's plenty, and it would be a good opera seat."[26] One camera, not several; planted, not mobile. In a critical assessment of recent practice posted on *Operawire*, David Salazar acknowledges the need for cuts and multiple angles but wonders why video directors seem increasingly unable to exercise restraint: "The modern HD era," writes Salazar, "is one dominated by rampant edits, strange camera choices, and a general lack of storytelling vision and cohesion."[27]

Similar concerns surface in criticism published in traditional media, as vividly illustrated in the reviews of *The Met: Live in HD* by Christophe Huss in Montreal's *Le devoir*. "This is not the first time we have spoken to you about this Gary Halvorson," writes Huss of *Carmen* (2019). "Only the writing of this article kept us in a cinema that we would normally have left after twenty minutes of supercharged cutting and erratic tracking shots."[28] Struck by critical observations that stretch back to Halvorson's earliest work with *The Met: Live in HD*, Gaudréault and Marion read Huss's criticism as the epitome of a misunderstanding of the video director's role. The video production is not and cannot be a mere "copy" or "recording," they argue, and the director should not be berated for coming between the cinecast spectator and the fantasy of virtual presence in the opera house.[29]

If there is a misunderstanding, it may stem from expectations generated by conventions that have long attended the shooting of staged opera. As with cinema and other forms of multicamera production, the filming of stage productions has historically observed the so-called 180-degree rule, which stipulates that camera perspectives and shot sequences should preserve coherent spatial mapping by avoiding a reversal of the perceived position of characters in a narrative or teams in sports (left stays left, right stays right). In the remediation of staged opera, this amounts not simply to an imposition but to the *preservation* of an axis already embedded in the framing of the stage. The vast majority of the venues featured in these productions are traditional opera houses that limit the range of perspectives on the stage thanks to a proscenium: video remediation honors and reinforces this limitation. As Will puts it: "Notwithstanding the cuts, which imply instantaneous seat changes, or the close-ups, which suggest improbably good seats (or opera glasses), an ironclad convention of showing everything from in front of the stage fosters the illusion that the viewer is sitting in the theater."[30] Glimpses from the wings or the fly tower are possible but rare, shots from behind or within the action even rarer. Now come the cinecasts to put these conventions to the test.

Writing on spoken-theater cinecasts, Ann Martinez wonders whether the value of the format lies in its potential to reconfigure, in spectatorial experience, the very architecture of theater. "There is no longer a front, back, or a side to the stage," she writes, "because the camera can take the viewer anywhere. . . . Instead, there are degrees of distance."[31] Erin Sullivan picks up on this argument to identify a paradoxical transformation in which the camera's division of the performance space into zones (close-up, wide shot) dismantles the hierarchical zoning of the auditorium into good and bad seats.[32] Crucial here is the arrangement put in place to shoot the production. *NT Live*, the subject of the observations by Martinez and Sullivan, makes special arrangements for the cinecast, installing cameras in positions that may distract live audiences (reduced ticket prices compensate audiences for the intrusion at that performance). Seats are even removed to allow for installation of a crane mount and dolly tracks.

To illustrate the possibilities opened up by this configuration, Sullivan singles out the use of crane shots to effect powerful and absorbing transitions between the context and perspective offered by broader views of the stage and the intimate detail and insight made possible by the camera's approaches to the stage. She analyzes, for example, the camerawork in *NT Live*'s *King Lear* (2011). Here, Gloucester's attempted suicide on Dover cliff was shot from the crane-mounted camera, which slowly advanced toward him during his final prayer, then paused and slowly reversed, "creating the space into which the broken earl would soon jump." Critically, for Sullivan, this "delicately sweeping" camerawork presented the scene in terms quite different from those of the stage production, inviting, in its articulation of the space around Gloucester, a greater sense of his cruel isolation and the physical and psychological void into which he felt compelled to leap. More than a spotlighting or mechanical magnification that merely distorts or enhances in-house spectatorship, these shots model, for Sullivan, "a new and more poetic way of seeing."[33] The reflexive implications of this reading—that camerawork might inflect the very act of seeing—recalls Kramer's observation that "with videos the problem of how to look, how to show, is itself always literally on view."[34] In Sullivan's reading, the camerawork in *NT Live* successfully negotiates the kind of tension Kramer identifies, compellingly articulating space on its own terms. Like Martinez, Sullivan identifies what she sees as novel spatial implications in the camerawork of *NT Live* productions, implications that challenge the paradigm of transparent immediacy so insistently invoked in the promotion of event cinema generally.

Might similar conclusions be drawn from observation of *The Met: Live in HD*? Unlike the National Theatre, the Met prides itself on filming with minimal distraction to in-house patrons. Anchored in loges above the very front of the orchestra seats, the jib arms position cameras in a range of vertical positions in front of the stage, but they do not move forward or backward in relation to the stage, which would amount to hovering over the orchestra pit and even penetrating the imaginary fourth wall framed by the proscenium (with a thrust stage and no pit, the Olivier Theatre, the venue for many *NT Live* cinecasts, is arguably more conducive to forward tracking from a crane-mounted camera). This capacity to boom, however, opens possibilities of its own. Consider Willis Sweete's video direction in *Lucia di Lammermoor* (stage director, Mary Zimmerman, 2011). As though tracing the verticality of Daniel Ostling's split-level set for the wedding scene in act 3, the jib-mounted camera repeatedly booms down from an upper landing to a large hall beneath. It is from the landing, site of the unseen matrimonial chamber, that the chaplain, Raimondo, re-

146 | CHAPTER SIX

lays to stunned wedding guests in the hall below the news that Lucia has killed her bridegroom, and it is from there that he will descend the spiral staircase linking the two floors. Armatage singles out this series of shots, noting how the camera's downward trajectory mirrors the production and performance in multiple ways: Raimondo's descent of the stairs, the octave descent with which his announcement opens, Lucia's plunge into madness.[35] As in *Samson et Dalila*, the camera resets its position unseen, only to repeat the downward journey. Yet, unlike the perpetual zoom motion toward Samson, this descent resists both the invitation to draw near embedded in the rhetoric of the operatic solo and the impulse to look more closely embedded in the grammar of multicamera production. It is as though the camera's descent registered physically—*embodied*—the gestures and affects of text and production. Visible in the shifts of perspective and parallax made possible by actual camera movement, the movement seems to embody that articulation of a "visual architecture" that Armatage identifies in Willis Sweete's direction.

A more poetic way of seeing? Possibly. Certainly, a challenge to consider again how we look at opera. That challenge is implicit too in the handling of the Met's other prized asset: the robotic dolly-mounted camera at the lip of the stage. In Willis Sweete's production of *Parsifal* (stage director, François Girard, 2013), the camera is featured at a number of pivotal moments. In act 2, for example, Kundry's revelation that she laughed at Christ on the cross ("Und lachte!") is staged as a moment of sudden stasis: the silence following the outburst is matched by Kundry's frozen posture, hand across mouth, while zombified flower maidens behind her pivot to adopt a stance suggestive of crucifixion. Everything is still except for the dolly-mounted camera, which now begins a slow track from right to left, beginning with a full-body shot of Kundry and gently zooming to a three-quarter shot, all while panning to keep Kundry centered as flower maidens are revealed and concealed behind her in parallax. A still camera might have been the obvious response, yet the camera's motion seems to register the stillness and emptiness of the stage space precisely by moving slowly across the front of it, just as it does in the act 1 transformation scene, when all the bodies on stage are immobile, the only movement registered by a projected image at the back of the stage (images of northern lights) and the slowly tracking camera at the front.

In these examples from *Parsifal*, the subjects of the shot are positioned some distance upstage. The effect is rather different when, as often happens, the singer is near the lip of the stage and effectively directly above the dolly camera. In the mad scene of *Lucia di Lammermoor*, Dessay repeatedly occupies the space at or near the prompter's box at the very front of the stage, and it is there that the dolly camera captures her, scanning back and forth while gazing upward in a series of shots that frame her against the uppermost reaches of the set. It is a shot type repeated time and again in the Met cinecasts, often triggered by scenes in which characters lie prostrate (as though the camera wanted to adopt their perspective) or assume positions near the lip of the stage (as though the camera could not resist the proximity and immediacy). Rarely still, these tracking shots at times resemble footage of an accident shot from a vehicle passing slowly by; at other times, the upward angle transforms singers' bodies into towering forms, generating the "monumental" effect noted by Sheppard.

Willis Sweete's use of the dolly camera, however, is restrained in comparison with Halvorson's 2009 cinecast of the same production. From the beginning of the wedding scene, the upward gaze and restless motion of the dolly camera is the favored shot in Halvorson's production: it captures the guests from the floor on which their feet dance, its movement seeming to register their energy, and it adopts their view of Raimondo on the landing above, doubling the already-monumental effect of his elevated position. As it tracks back and forth, the camera seems to pace uncomfortably at the news. But it really comes into its own when Lucia (here sung by Anna Netrebko) takes up her position at the front of the stage. Here, too, Halvorson's production features a more prominent and sustained use of the dolly camera than does Willis Sweete's, but it is the framing that sets the 2009 production apart.[36] As it glides beneath Netrebko, Halvorson's camera at several points zooms in so tightly as it looks up at Netrebko's face that the movement generates distorting and disorienting shifts in perspective and depth of field, and the shot comes to resemble something between reality TV, surveillance footage, and a video selfie (figs. 6.1 and 6.2).

Nor is this combination of tracking and lens movement confined to the dolly camera. Insofar as the jib-camera shots I highlighted in Willis Sweete's production of *Lucia di Lammermoor* boom down without zooming, they are exceptional. More representative of this production—and of the Met cinecasts more broadly—is a boom and zoom combination in which zoom lens manipulation morphs with and mimics actual movement. When Halvorson observes that the jib-mounted cameras can "boom down and go right into the action," he means that they can boom and *simulate* forward movement via the zoom. The jib cameras, in other words, construct horizontal depth via that "mechanical" effect Will associates with the zoom lens. It is a movement, as John Belton stresses, that lacks the shifts in perspective and parallax so crucial to the illusion of depth in a tracking shot: "Though the zoom, like the track, preserves the sense of space as an unbroken, temporal continuum, it also, unlike the track,

FIGURE 6.1. Lucia (Anna Netrebko). *Lucia di Lammermoor*, director, Mary Zimmerman, 2009. Met Opera on Demand, 2009.

FIGURE 6.2. Lucia (Anna Netrebko). *Lucia di Lammermoor*, director, Mary Zimmerman, 2009. Met Opera on Demand, 2009.

abstracts that space by flattening or elongating it. In effect, zoom produces an ellipsis of space by both traversing and not traversing it."[37] And is one of the effects of this abstraction, Gunning asks, not a curious sense of disembodiment "as if our eyes moved forward without the orientations of our body following?"[38]

Not so much a superspectator, then (to return to the notion of virtual attendance in the opera house), as a fragmented or impossible one. As Lucia descends the circular staircase in a state of delirium, Willis Sweete's jib camera tracks her by booming down slowly, yet it cannot resist combining this movement with a zoom toward her. Here, as in so many similar shots in this production and in the cinecasts more broadly, the vertigo of the downward movement seems submerged by the magnifying motion of the zoom, the vertiginous descent of the camera displaced by a synthetic swoop. It is as though the camera's embodiment of the affect and architecture of the stage now competed with the familiar voyeuristic gaze of multicamera production—a reminder, perhaps, not to be blinded by the exceptional, what Martin Barker has called the *bravura moments* of cinecasts.[39] In their default mode, the poetic (to use Sullivan's term) gives way to a (prosaic) documentary impulse predicated on news gathering, monitoring, and coverage.

ARTIFICIALLY NATURAL

Recall Jay Saks's articulation of the goal of his sound recordings as generating the impression of "a really good seat." The mimetic impulse that underpins this goal does not mean, however, that microphone placement imitates or maps onto actual seats. Saks points out that, if the recording were to depend solely on a microphone located in a given seat, the result "would sound dreadful."[40] What the movie-theater audience hears, in other words, is a composite; it is sound recorded from no one seat, no one location. Noting, too, that recordings from the Met make the acoustic seem drier than that experienced in the auditorium, Saks acknowledges in an interview that this manipulation includes adding artificial reverb to the recorded sound: "I try to make reverb sound like it isn't artificial. I also use compression, filtering and EQ—anything to re-create in someone's mind the sense that they're experiencing an excellent live performance. The irony is, to do that I have to use these processing tools!"[41] A careful manipulation, then, one calculated to enhance the sense of being there by recombining, filtering out, and supplementing the sounds registered there.

That audio production in the cinecasts involves artifice would hardly make it an anomaly. On the contrary, pure, unfiltered capture is itself the fiction. A common practice in live sports broadcasting, for example, is the "sweetening" of the audio with stock sounds to add ambience (crowd noises, environmental sounds) in settings that pose challenges for recording.[42] Artificial reverb in music is arguably nothing more than a form of sweetening. What is significant in this case is the contradiction between these production practices and the claims of transparency and authenticity so evident in the promotional rhetoric of *The Met: Live in HD*, not least in the touted capacity of surround sound to immerse the audience in a duplicated Met. I noted earlier the tensions evident in responses to video cut rate and moving cameras, but sound seems to trigger critical sensitivities that video does not, and this may reveal something of the weight of matters musical in opera, especially at the Met. Sound, music, voice—this is sacrosanct territory, something not lost on Saks's interviewer: "Wait, did Saks just say that the Met uses reverb in its broadcasts?"[43]

The same sensitivities surface when, as we saw in chapter 2, the *New York Times* critic Anthony Tommasini goes in search of evidence that the Met uses body microphones, as though he were uncovering a state secret.[44] Unlike the debates on video direction, which focus on interventions that are quite literally there for all to see, concerns about audio manipulation seem, like a quietly circulating conspiracy theory, to hinge on the anxiety that something is happening undetected and that the establishment—in this case the Met—is happy to leave it that way. Unexpected revelations and prying journalists aside, discussion of audio processing in the cinecasts is rare.[45] Among the best kept of these secrets is the Met's handling of the multichannel mix. As Saks explains, *Met: Live in HD* performances are simultaneously recorded and broadcast, in stereo, for the live Saturday matinee season on radio. Rather than attempt separate stereo and multichannel mixes live, the Met's practice is to mix in stereo and "up-convert" via a processor to the 5.1 stream that is fed to cinemas.[46] One of the effects of this processing, as David Trippett points out, is an overlap in which the supposedly discrete feeds of the 5.1 mix include ambient sound from the stereo mix. The result, Trippett concludes, is the erasure of any coherent point of sonic orientation for audiences of *The Met: Live in HD*.[47] Like the applied reverb, surround sound is a sonic fiction that depends on the effectiveness of manipulation human and nonhuman.

What does it mean for claims of immersion if the so-called surround sound is in fact a technologically processed phantom? Sonic immersion, as Lisa Coulthard observes, is nothing short of an obsession in the film industry, which increasingly associates it not merely with emotive or narrative engagement but with the impression of being physically submerged in or enveloped by the sound field.[48] As we have seen, however, the ambient surround sound of *The Met: Live in HD* is not the visceral, effects-laden sonic environment with which Dolby promotes itself in cinematic trailers; nor does it resemble the elaborate sound design characteristic, as Gorbman and Richardson observe, of the new "cinema of the senses."[49] Sound in the cinecasts is not, in other words, attuned to the practices associated in the marketing and promotion of cinema with immersive experience.

Nor is it even considered immersive according to the standards now adopted by audio engineers and producers in the field of music recording. Jonathan Allen, an audio producer at the Royal Opera House, defines immersive sound as surround sound that integrates additional height channels, such as those featured in the Dolby Atmos format now widely installed in cinemas and available, in necessarily compromised form, for home cinema configurations and headphones.[50] Immersion here hinges on release of the speaker configuration from confinement to the horizontal plane of traditional surround-sound configurations into a third axis. If this opens up possibilities in cinema for sound effects, in opera, Allen contends, it relieves the front and center speakers from some of the burden of carrying sonic information, particularly in loud passages with complex ensembles: "These same moments in immersive audio feel much more satisfying as the density and intensity of the loudness is spread over more speakers, bringing enough space to accommodate and control the power of the ensemble with clarity."[51] What these new configurations purport to offer, then, is a less saturated, less compressed sonic delivery and a greater sense of space. But why is this considered immersive? Or, rather, why is this suddenly considered immersive in a way that the previous generation of surround sound is not? Coulthard's observation about the obsessive use of the term in the film industry offers one answer, shifting the focus of inquiry away from the ontology or even the phenomenology of media to discourse *about* media. Immersion, in other words, is defined by a marketing and technological arms race as much as by any agreed-on standards or coherent conceptualization. That the industry brands new developments such as Dolby Atmos immersive depends on promotional hype, not meaningful definition.

As a project based on an earlier generation of technology, *The Met: Live in HD* is in one sense isolated from the question of immersion. The lack of height channels means that the cinecasts are *not*, according to Allen's definition, immersive. Even their capacity to encourage cognitive immersion is put into question because, in Powell's reading, this kind of investment is enhanced by spatial immersion: "With the advent of immersive sound technology, I feel we have a fresh opportunity for opera and ballet to deliver a listening and viewing experience that draws the listener further into the music."[52] If, however, we understand immersive sound as rhetoric and ideal, the argument shifts. Allen's claims echo the language of presence that had already underpinned the launch press release of *The Met: Live in HD*, which linked the promise of immersion to what was then state-of-the-art: 5.1 surround sound.[53] Anticipating the current marketing focus on technologies like Dolby Atmos, the Met demonstrated a capacity to cloak its offering in the glow of the language of immersion, language that was and is all the more marketable for being so vaguely understood. It was far from alone in making the link between surround sound and immersion. A 2002 research report on behalf of the European Broadcast Union considered the immersive effects of 5.1 surround sound, and, as Paul Grainge has argued, as early as the 1980s "Dolby Stereo" branding of cinemas was in part a means of promoting the "immersive potential" of cinematic sound as distinct from television.[54]

Even critical and scholarly definitions of immersion register the impact of inflated industry rhetoric. In the forward to a recent title published under the aegis of the Audio Engineering Society, we are told that immersive sound not only is "strategically aligned with the future of communication and entertainment" but also carries with it the "potential to improve the quality of life."[55] In this consumerist dream, immersive sound maps onto a model of commodification rooted in an appealing (i.e., strategic) loss or dissolving of the self in cinematic space. Surveying media and film studies accounts of the term in what amounts to an arguably futile attempt to establish a more disciplined taxonomy, Nilsson et al. note that immersion, associated with presence or telepresence in accounts of virtual reality environments, has been widely applied in literature on noninteractive screen media, where it connotes impressions ranging from envelopment, to submersion, to absorption, to transport.[56] Doane traces the scholarly investment in elsewheres to what she characterizes as a "symptomatic crisis of location" in contemporary culture. Even if these accounts concede that audiences remain aware of their actual location—that they are not naively duped—immersion is put forward, she adds, as a desirable release from spatial bounds, "an elsewhere designed as a lure."[57] It is a perspective that echoes wider warnings about the impact of globalization (the loss of community and rootedness) and the digitization of media and communication (the dissolution of indexicality, materiality, and the body into ethereal binary code).

As digitized spectacle disseminated on a global scale, *The Met: Live in HD* seems, like cinecasts more broadly, to epitomize the erosion of place by virtual space, of locality by digital evanescence. Accessed in remote and multiple locations, the cinecast offers an audiovisual environment that purports to collapse distances and bind separate locations into one. Is this immersive encounter with the Met not predicated on the lure of the virtual? And does this lure not threaten with homogeny and hegemony? That is, in the cybermarket of virtual attendance fashioned on global recognition, what is the fate of the smaller company, the in-house performance, the local or regional theater? Torn between anxiety about monopolies and the enabling potential of participating in digital dissemination, the opera industry continues to grapple with these questions.[58] But, if the association of *The Met: Live in HD* with the forces of globalization is understandable, it needs to be balanced by a consideration of the actual locations of the cinecast audiences. Attending to satellites and global networks of cinemas is not unjustified, but the cinecasts too have their localities, their places, and it is to them that I now turn.

NOT QUITE RIGHT

Let me begin with the sound of locality. Large recalls attending a *Met: Live in HD* screening and finding the audio "not quite right."[59] The remark might suggest a failure of fidelity, where "right" equates to the sonic experience in the Met auditorium. But Large points in a different direction when he speculates that the problem may have been local, a result not of recording or mixing but of audio playback in that particular cinema. Considered in this way, the audio mix—and its processing—is only one layer of its dissemination, so that the "mix itself," to paraphrase language historically applied to music, is in fact an abstraction subject to delivery in specific and material terms. Although audio systems in cinemas are designed and installed according to shared specifications, in practice the actual delivery of sound can vary significantly, depending on equipment variations, acoustic qualities of particular cinemas, and the relative unfamiliarity (still) of running live audiovisual feeds. The Met, for example, sends test signals before the simulcast to allow operators to calibrate and balance sound, but this is a matter of trial and error, dependent on installations and the individual decisions and tastes of technical staff charged with assessing the results. Allen notes the problem of reliance on local expertise: "There have always been good, average and bad-sounding cinemas, and cinema sound has suffered for too long from being solely reliant on a cinema manager or chain who care about audio and can actually hear when speakers get broken or other problems arise."[60] Even assuming that local or chain management is attentive to audio, the kind of sound delivery appropriate for cinema—with its layered sound design comprising spoken dialogue, music, and precisely rendered and located sound effects—is not necessarily a strong match for *The Met: Live in HD* and its front-focused blend of voices and orchestra complemented by discreet ambience in the surround speakers.[61]

In the context of this messy encounter between localities, genres, and sonic imaginaries, I take Large's concern about getting the sound right to mean not a naive desire for replication of Met acoustics—whatever that might mean—but a realistic desire for a playback balance and blend that at least avoid distortion and frustration and possibly even align with expectations based on a pleasurable sonic experience of opera live and recorded. My own experience of cinecast audio in multiple cinemas in several countries has not always been pleasurable. In some cinemas the sound has been unbearably loud, in some muddy or bass heavy.[62] I appear not to be alone. Published reviews and posts on social media and review blogs repeatedly flag the problem of sound in local cinemas. "In outsourcing opera to cinemas," wrote one critic in *The Independent*, "we leave a demanding art-form at the mercy of second-rate sound-systems."[63] Threads on opera cinecasts on forums such as talkclassical.com and Reddit repeatedly identify problems with sound that is too loud or too soft, and, in response to a post on muted sound on the "Met Opera Live in HD Fans" Facebook page, several posters complained of poor audio quality in their own cinema.[64] These admittedly isolated observations may not be broadly representative of experience, but they may equally highlight the problem of making meaningful general observations about sound quality in the cinecasts, which are always mitigated by local practices and conditions.

More difficult to assess are those experiences in which the surround speakers have been silent or virtually inaudible, leaving all the sound, apparently, to the front speakers behind the screen. If the latter seems a long way from the plenitude of the promised surround sound, it may be the case that a very subtle use of surround speakers is in fact the point, as Kerins notes of ambient surround sound in cinema. My observation here is not about the validity of a particular balance (although I have preferred more generous use of the surrounds) but about the inconsistency of that balance across venues. In one case, for example, I was able to compare the strikingly different balance in one cinecast when I attended the original and encore performances at different venues. To speak of the cinecast as a consistent entity would be, in my experience, a misrepresentation of what was in fact a mutable encounter contingent on local conditions.

NONPLACES?

Sound is not the only local variable. When the Met flags its global network of two thousand cinemas or boasts, as it does in the opening promo sequence of cinecasts, of 350,000 patrons watching simultaneously, the temptation is to imagine this network in homogenized terms—a globalized mass audience. It is a temptation reinforced by the scholarly consensus that the anonymous, corporate multiplex, with its apparently identikit interiors and amenities, has come to epitomize contemporary cinemagoing, as though we all now belong to what one author calls *generation multiplex*.[65] The range of venues screening *The Met: Live in HD* complicates this picture. True, the multiplex dominates the network, but other types of venue are well represented too, from restored classic theaters like the Hayden Orpheum Picture Palace in Sydney to university arts centers like the Roxy Theater, SUNY Potsdam, and from urban art houses like Atelier in Düsseldorf to civic arts venues like the Lensic Performing Arts Center, Santa Fe. These spaces—some devoted to cinema, others multipurpose venues that double up as cinemas—house diverse textures of experience with the potential to channel varied modes of encounter with the cinecast. And are those textures not woven into the fabric of the venue, stored in the memories of audiences who have occupied these seats for other spectacles? Reflecting on her experience of cinecasts in the opera house in Watertown, Maine, Laurie E. Osborne remembers those other events—music performances, amateur theater—that color her experience of the venue as well as her experience of a wider community investment in and association with that stage as an institution and a site of events artistic and political.[66]

But what about the multiplex venues? Is there not some justification in associating these ubiquitous boxes with a globalized nowhere, another venue to add to the airports, leisure parks, and hotel chains that Marc Augé associated with the *nonplaces* of capitalism?[67] Part of the problem with this characterization, as Paul Grainge argues, is that it denies to the multiplex cinema the kind of integration into the fabric of the community that Osborne associates with a venue like the Watertown Opera House. Is it not possible, Grainge asks, that multiplex cinemas too store collective memories and channel something of their place? Besides, he adds, this charge of bland anonymity seems increasingly dated in the face of a pivot in the industry over the last two decades away from conformity and toward the cultivation of forms of individuation that present cinema complexes as "destinations" with a distinct and often localized character rather than mere outlets or franchises. Although potentially rooted, Grainge adds, in "spatial fantasies" of locality and urban renewal, this trend has nevertheless generated considerably greater variety than the model of the placeless, faceless multiplex allows.[68]

This kind of individuation is arguably reinforced in the case of cinecasts by the diversity of their presentation and packaging. That a university arts center on a remote campus might offer different amenities or represent a different vibe than a plush downtown megaplex is hardly unexpected, but even among the supposedly cookie-cutter venues, presentation can vary considerably. Some cinemas integrate the cinecasts seamlessly into their regular operations, as though they were just another movie offering, while others set them apart by packaging them in ways distinct from the practices typical of the venue: assigned seating even where general seating is the norm, patrons being shown to their seats by ushers, promotional and informational literature, customized catering distinct from the standard lobby offerings. These practices distinguish the cinecast presentation not only from the standard movie fare but from cinecast presentations in other venues. Presented regularly, cinecasts arguably even form and reinforce what Keir Elam has called a *microcommunity* with its own conventions accumulated from shared experience and a learned competence in engaging with a form of spectacle that combines characteristics of different media and genres. More than just an interloper from the domain of theater and television, the cinecast becomes, in this reading, a subgenre predicated on a different mode of engagement with those same screens and speakers that play host to feature films. It becomes, too, a fixture embedded *within* its cinematic setting, capable of drawing from and contributing to a collective memory of that place.

Similar questions about encounters between the local and the global, the familiar and the novel, have informed readings of so-called live cinema, an increasingly popular event type that supplements screenings, typically of cult films, with audience participation, including sing-alongs and role-play.[69] Elsaesser wonders whether the participatory character of these events transforms the role of the screen, which becomes "a map to be navigated, an environment to be entered rather than a window to be viewed or a text to be read."[70] Watched in silence (except for possible applause), cinecasts are not live cinema in this sense, but perhaps the perceived need to negotiate appropriate modes of spectatorship in the cinecast invokes what Elsaesser characterizes as *navigation*, while the invitation to be virtually present suggests entry into an environment, an entry mediated by participation in a separate, local audience. This is something Sheppard highlights when he recalls that the initial "presence envy" invoked by the sight and sound of the Met audience had, over the course of the event, given way to a collective sense of independence from that audience.[71]

Gaudréault and Marion concur. What, they ask, are we to make of this audience gathered to watch *together* the kind of live transmission traditionally screened in domestic settings? Drawing on the Greek for *gather-*

ing place, they propose the emergence in the movie theater of what they term the *tele-agora*. A reversal of the equally paradoxical *home theater*, they argue, the tele-agora, with its predetermined content and (almost) unrepeated schedule, robs its audience of control, "as if the freedom that viewers had just won in their living rooms thanks to the digital were, at the same time, lost in the 'movie' theater." But, they add, the tele-agora compensates for that loss of freedom when it introduces an evental quality lacking in the home. And that event registers not only as a point in time but also as a spatial encounter that makes public what had been private, opening up to shared spectatorship what has for decades been consumed in isolation.[72]

There is a parallel here with another transformation from private to public. As Martin Barker notes, the formation of multiple remote audiences in cinecasts resembles the practices of sports fans who treat remote screening venues such as bars/pubs as proxy event spaces in their own right.[73] Barker cites a study of soccer spectatorship in pubs by Mike Weed, who summarizes sociological research on the value placed by fans on "physical proximity" to the sports event, adding that ethnographies of the phenomenon of viewing sports communally and remotely suggests that this desire for proximity is not necessarily directed at the sports event itself "but to others sharing in the experience of watching the event."[74] Applied to the cinecasts, this observation would mean that the question of proximity, of being there, is in part a question of proximity to other fans/spectatorships. Quite what that will mean may depend not just on the character or texture of the location but on the numbers in attendance. Cinemas located in densely populated urban areas and those that have established a loyal audience will often have capacity audiences; just as common, if reports on social media are to be believed, some are almost empty venues.

True, as Barker concedes, equating pubs with cinemas and sports fans with opera audiences raises questions about differences in class, socioeconomic status, and cultural capital. But he is right, I think, to insist that these questions should not invalidate the comparison completely.[75] The overlaps in practice and personnel between the cinecasts and television genres suggest that investigating cinecasts in isolation risks invoking an exceptionalism that is both unhelpful and misleading. As Gelb puts it, *The Met: Live in HD* is "the performing arts equivalent of what sports teams do, to keep the bond strong between teams and their fanbase."[76] Sociologies of opera have rightly identified parallels between its devotees and the intense and passionate devotion demonstrated by sports fans. In both cases, that devotion now manifests itself in part in the formation of remote fan communities, both online and as satellite audiences, and in both cases the spectatorship is mediated by a screen.

Screens to be navigated, microcommunities of the movie theater, proximities in proxy audiences, cinema as the gathering place for the televisual—what these constructs register is a tension, even contradiction, lodged in the in-betweenness not only of encounters of media and genres but of the places that play host to these encounters. Elsewhere than the event the cinecasts transmit, this place is also elsewhere than the movie theater as we have come to know it. Yet the cinecasts are textured by those places and embedded in those localities, their appeal to the immediacy of media technology always in tension with immediate surroundings. That opera has been one of the primary vehicles mapping out these elsewheres is no surprise given its history of willingness, through trial and error, to swap one technology for another, one materiality for another, even to allow itself to lose its sight altogether (phonograph, radio), only to be reunited with vision in a strengthened embrace (television, cinema, web). If, for now, the way opera is pictured and heard in the movie theater invites as much frustration as pleasure, it will have been one of its boldest trans-formations yet to invite, in the twenty-first century, a reconsideration of the last century's signature venue by populating it with forms and media hitherto unknown there.

Part 3

CHAPTER SEVEN

Hosts and Ghosts

Attracted to locations outside the norm, site-specific theater occupies a strange place conceptually as well as physically. Tailoring productions to locations outside traditional theater spaces has never been more in vogue or more contested. It is a tension evident in Joanne Tompkins's introduction to *Performing Site-Specific Theatre*.[1] On the one hand, Tompkins can write enthusiastically about "the form's current popularity," citing as evidence not only the profusion of practice and theory but also the publication of a survey of the field aimed at an undergraduate readership (always a sign that a field has arrived). On the other, she repeatedly qualifies her remarks with reference to the "instability" and "mutability" of the term *site-specific* and of the practices it signifies.[2] She reminds readers, too, that several essays in the collection voice concerns about the proliferation of site-specific theater and call for a critical reevaluation in practical and theoretical terms. The book echoes a wider disquiet among theater critics. "These days," writes Andy Field in *The Guardian*, "'site-specific' can be just about anything that doesn't happen in a theatre. . . . At best these productions—regardless of their merits—borrow the atmosphere and aesthetic of their new homes in a relatively superficial and inorganic manner, all take and no give."[3]

Anticipating this debate, Gay McAuley called in 2005 for a critical distinction between *site-based* and *site-specific* performance. If the former term implies a nontraditional setting or backdrop chosen on the basis of certain formal or aesthetic qualities and potential, the latter, McAuley writes, should be reserved for projects that engage with the history and politics of their location and seek dialogue between that location and thematic strands in the work performed.[4] Only this most embedded form of practice, she adds, lives up to the name and the claims made on its behalf. And this understanding of the term accords with the widely cited definition of *site-specific performance* articulated by Mike Pearson and Mike Shanks as a *reciprocal* engagement between site and performance, one in which performance draws something from the site while in turn transforming that site by shifting perceptions and representations, engaging communities in ways that affect their understanding of space, and even contributing to the ongoing *production* of that space (to borrow the language of Henri Lefebvre, whose 1974 *La production de l'espace* assumes something of the role of master text in theories of site-specific performance).[5] "Performance," according to Pearson and Shanks, "is the latest occupation of a location at which other occupations—their material traces and histories—are still apparent: site is not just an interesting, and disinterested, backdrop."[6]

Vague and idealistic as much of this language is, it at least constitutes an attempt to wrestle with definitions, while the creative output of the more critically engaged practitioners—many of whom are also academics—offers to explore, reflexively, the nature and limits of the exchange between site and performance. The broader tendency, however, has been to ignore finer critical distinctions and define and promote a broad range of unconventionally situated performances (many featuring little more than exotic locales) as site specific. The appeal? A desire for innovation (or to be seen as innovative) perhaps, but clearly also a response to calls from government agencies, funding bodies, and the wider community for access and engagement, buzzwords with particular implications for traditional art forms branded elitist.

GETTING OUT OF THE HOUSE

Cue opera, the archvillain of elitist culture. Though slow to pick up on the broader theatrical trend toward site-specific performance, opera companies are showing signs of embracing it with enthusiasm. Opera outside the traditional opera house hardly represents a recent breakthrough: performances in outdoor venues and temporary theatrical spaces (especially during festivals or carnival season) have been a historical feature of operatic production, while nontraditional spaces—the lakeside venue of the Bregenzer Festspiele, the outdoor courtyard theater of the Théâtre de l'Archevêché in Aix-en-Provence, or the spectaculars performed on the water's edge in Sydney Harbor—are familiar in contemporary practice. These, however, are all repeatedly used and custom-designed venues. Equipped with an infrastructure capable of emulating the conditions of the traditional opera house, they are effectively opera houses in themselves. We might think of this, in McAuley's terms, as site-*based* opera.

What has distinguished some of the more recent production trends is a move toward a much riskier utilization of sites—lacking any obvious performance infrastructure. If avant-garde music theater celebrated its utilization of unusual spaces as a mark of its break from opera and its conventions, the more canonical repertoire of the major companies tended to remain firmly housebound. Given opera's technical and resource requirements, the reticence is perhaps understandable. In a sense, opera is and always has been site specific in its dependence on a particular configuration of space within a carefully designed and precisely mobilized environment. Thought of this way, moving opera out of the house is tantamount to diluting the specificity of medium, even while purporting to situate and site its narrative contents with more precision. And abandoning these customized facilities in favor of ad hoc spaces brings with it formidable logistic challenges.

Nontraditional venues (and nontraditional utilization of theaters) have long featured in the programming of avant-garde music theater and experimental groups. What we now call *site-specific performance* can be understood in part as a legacy of the experimental practices, cultivated from the 1960s on, of environmental theater, itself a legacy of early twentieth-century open-air productions (in 1920, Max Reinhardt famously staged Hugo von Hofmannsthal's *Jedermann* on the steps of Salzburg Cathedral, and Nikolai Evreinov directed an on-site reenactment of the storming of the Winter Palace) and reconfigurations of the proscenium stage in the work of directors like Adolphe Appia and Vsevolod Meyerhold.[7] Immersive performance, often associated with factory and warehouse settings and presented as nonlinear narrative, is increasingly familiar in operatic practice too. For example, Punchdrunk Theatre, a company specializing in immersive theater, collaborated in 2010 with the English National Opera to commission an adaptation of Webster's *The Duchess of Malfi* (music by Torsten Rasch) for performances in an unoccupied office block in the London docklands. Contemporary music theater has also embraced digital technology to experiment with multisite, networked performances, immersive experiences such as sound walks, and other forms of "locative performance."[8] If these modes of music theater have historically cultivated a genre identity separate from opera, there has been a partial rapprochement in recent years, at least with the term *opera*, if not with its traditions.[9] The Los Angeles–based company The Industry defines its site-specific practices within a broader mandate to expand "the definition of opera (whom opera is for, who is involved and where opera takes place)."[10] As we saw in chapter 2, The Industry's *Invisible Cities* (2013) equipped audiences with wireless headphones, inviting them to roam Union Station in Los Angeles while listening, silent-disco-style, to a newly commissioned work.

What has emerged parallel to this body of new work is a proliferation, challenges notwithstanding, of performances in nontraditional locations of works from the established operatic repertoire. Several alternative or fringe opera companies have formed with a mandate to do just that. London's Silent Opera mobilizes wireless headphones in a manner similar to that employed in *Invisible Cities*, presenting promenade performances of canonic operas in the city's vaults and tunnels. New York City's On Site Opera defines its mission thus: "By staging each opera in an environment specific to the piece, OSO surrounds the audience and artists in the music and drama of the story, amplifying the connection between the world of the opera and the reality of the audience."[11] This foregrounding of venues explicitly motivated by the operatic text has been a theme of much site-specific opera. With what might be characterized as an overdetermined realism, two small companies each staged *Fidelio* in disused prisons (Philadelphia's The Other Company in 2005 and the Dublin-based Opera Theatre Company in 2006). Larger, more mainstream opera companies and festivals followed suit. The Aldeburgh Festival, for example, presented *Peter Grimes* (2013) on the pebbled Suffolk shores that feature in the opera, and the southern Italian city of Matera, a European "City of Culture" in 2019, stood in for small-town Sicily in a staging of *Cavalleria rusticana* presented as part of the civic engagement project "Abitare l'opera" (Inhabit the opera).[12]

But the charge of superficiality continues to haunt productions of this kind. On Site Opera's 2014 staging of Rameau's *Pygmalion* in the New York Madame Tussaud's Wax Museum prompted David Patrick Stearns, a music critic for the *Philadelphia Inquirer*, to reflect on the "increasingly fashionable endeavor" of liberating opera from its traditional performance settings.[13] In a largely unfavorable review, Stearns echoes the problem identified by Gardiner: that the engagement with the venue is superficial, the choice actually quite random. Worse, opera has been accused of exploiting nontraditional venues in what amounts to "location washing" designed to clean up opera's elitist image. The Industry, for example, attracted considerable criticism with *Hopscotch: An Opera for 24 Cars* (2015), a project accused of occupying public spaces in ways insensitive to local communities.[14]

HAUNTS OLD AND NEW

With these discursive tensions in mind, I want to return to the series of productions Andermann collectively entitled *La via della musica—Tosca: In the Settings and at the Times of Tosca* (1992), *La traviata in Paris* (2000), and *Rigoletto in Mantua* (2010)—and consider especially the last of these. I also investigate *La bohème im Hochhaus* (A High-Rise *La bohème*, 2009), one of a set of Swiss site-specific opera telecasts that also included *La traviata im*

Hauptbahnhof (*La traviata* in the Central Station, 2008) and *Aïda am Rhein* (*Aïda* on the Rhine, 2010).[15] What the two trilogies have in common—and what distinguishes them from the site-specific productions I outlined thus far—is their origin in and as television. Andermann dubs his productions *live films*, stressing their novel harnessing of several constituent media forms within a televisual framework: "Various forms of the entertainment arts—lyrical theater, cinema, television—had their cards reshuffled to fulfil a need for expression fueled by a dream: the desire to broaden the horizons of television."[16] Meanwhile, the Swiss productions, conceived by the television producers Thomas Beck and Christian Eggenberger as a project for the Swiss channel Schweizer Fernsehen, are couched in a rhetoric that credits television with a unique capacity to bridge high-low cultural divides and reimagine traditional art forms like opera. In both cases, the televisual is associated in part with a capacity to connect a performance and an audience in real time: key to the overdetermined mimesis of the Andermann project is its unfolding at the times specified in the libretto (as we saw in chap. 3 in relation to *La traviata in Paris*), while the Swiss productions foreground their evental quality as performances that attract a real-time audience of bystanders as well as inviting a live television audience to contribute feedback in the manner of a current affairs program or reality TV. But this is also about television *on location*, about its mobility and its facility with space and place. What I want to stress in this chapter is the locative dimension of these productions: how they negotiate the space in which they unfold and how this space registers on screen. The productions foreground a titular formula based on place: opera *x* in location *y*. I take this as a cue to consider how, as screen-media projects, they mobilize image and sound with the intention of (re)fashioning the spaces in which the performances unfold and to ask what this might say about ways opera physically and discursively occupies sites, including its familiar haunts.

TRICKS FOR THE EYE

Already in *Tosca in Rome* we can observe some of the characteristics and parameters that will characterize the *Via della musica* productions: the staggered broadcast times, a remotely located orchestra linked by monitors and microphones, the absence of an on-site audience, actual singing rather than dubbed performances. Camerawork, supervised by Vittorio Storaro, draws on idioms ranging from art cinema to what resembles soap opera and news gathering. Thanks to mobile cameras and long takes, we move with and among characters in a space that is represented as three-dimensional, unconfined by a proscenium or wings. With close-ups and intrusive footage shot in the thick of the action, cameras closely follow the singers, as though they were disgraced politicians being followed on the street or the subjects of a reality-TV series. Evident too—and all the more so thanks to this close camerawork—is a gestural grammar that combines theatrical stock mannerisms with a more intimate, screen-focused presentation. The singers, clearly well rehearsed by experienced film/theater directors (Giuseppe Patroni Griffi for *Tosca* and *La traviata*, Marco Bellocchio for *Rigoletto*) yet expected to harness their bodies to produce operatic sound, negotiate two spaces of performance. The challenge, as the tenor Vittorio Grigolo put it in an interview during rehearsals for *Rigoletto in Mantua*, is how to contain conventional and familiar gestures and play to the camera.[17] That is, the conventions of opera present themselves as problematic in this setting, as though the catch-you-in-the-act gaze of handheld cameras caught singers in the act of repeating entrenched practices shaped by a very different performance environment.

Still, there are marked differences within the series. *Tosca in Rome* conveys an excitement at the very possibility of the project. Introduced with scrolling text proclaiming the global reach of the telecast, it seems to ask whether this can really be happening. And, despite the liberating potential of the steadicam, the production's gaze repeatedly "lingers," as Andrea Malvano puts it, on the sheer spectacle of the surroundings, like an awestruck tourist.[18] By comparison, *La traviata in Paris* seems emboldened by experience and harnesses the movement of the steadicam with long takes defined by gliding movement around singers, through spaces, and across thresholds from one room to another, from interior to exterior. "In *Tosca*, we were just amateurs," the cinematographer Vittorio Storaro is quoted as saying. "Now the camera is even freer because the Steadycam can be used emotionally. The Steadycam is now part of the style."[19] Free to explore the still-sumptuous but no longer monumental surroundings that stand in for the domestic interiors of the opera, the steadicam dwells not on the particulars of the location but on the very act of circulating through space. And if there is an element of self-referentiality to this—as though celebrating the medium and the technology—there is also, as Malvano argues, a dramaturgical insistence, at times extreme, on the "collective and morally insensitive background" to Violetta's individual struggle.[20]

The monumental and touristic returns with a vengeance in *Rigoletto in Mantua*. Like some historical reenactment performed for tourists—but without the tourists—*Rigoletto in Mantua* unfolds amid the famed frescoes and marbled columns of the city's Palazzo Ducale. Inhabited by the living bodies of performers, and remediated in the flickering images of Andermann's production, the site is a monument "brought to life," as the marketing rhetoric puts it when sites are appropriated for spectacle.[21] Just as the emotive, theatrical expressions of Tosca and Scarpia had been photographed against the backdrop of the lavishly painted walls in the Palazzo Farnese, the agitated inhabitants of Mantua appear against the deep-focus backdrop of frozen interiors: flesh against stone and marble, melodrama against monument. It is a juxtaposition starkly illustrated in the act 2 duet "Piangi, fanciulla," when a close-up reveals tears rolling down Domingo's face. If the tears are fleeting moments, no sooner glimpsed than gone, the backdrop that frames the close-up never seems more solid, more fixed and frozen. What we encounter in the composition of this shot, simultaneously distanced and close up, is a juxtaposition between the enduring, historic, rooted-to-site architecture and the seemingly unpredictable, contingent moment of performance in the foreground—between the monumental permanence of a Renaissance palazzo and the performative ephemeral (Live! Now!) of Domingo's tears.

But the production, alive to the potential of exchange between an actual place and its own fictional representation, unsettles this flesh-stone binary. In the overdetermined economy of the *Via della musica* productions, the site substitutes its own referent for the theatrical double. It is as though the flats and props of classic illusionist staging have finally traversed and collapsed the representative compact they had once sustained but at the price of their own erasure. The conceptual hook? The Palazzo Ducale, shaped by the Gonzagas as a mirror of the family's embrace of art and pleasure, is famously adorned with murals, themed rooms, and trompe l'oeil effects. The ducal complex is itself already theater, as the production seeks to demonstrate.[22] The steadicam is still here, and the close-ups at times seem more intrusive than ever. When in act 2 Rigoletto confronts the courtiers about their abduction of Gilda, the camera comes so close to the faces of the assembled performers that it seems about to collide with them (fig. 7.1).[23]

Elsewhere, however, the mobility of the camera seems much curtailed compared to that seen in *La traviata in Paris*. The nocturnal scenes of acts 1 and 3 are shot with multiple cameras positioned to capture the high-contrast lighting and moody, monochromatic color palette characteristic of Storaro's "painterly" style. Meanwhile, the shots of the backdrop of *actual* painting in the frescoes of the palace interiors are carefully composed and call into question the mobility of the cast itself. The duke and his courtiers are first pictured in a frozen pose, a *tableau vivant* set against the carefully lit scenes of pleasure painted on the walls of the Palazzo del Te (part of the ducal palace complex), as though the one were an extension of the other (fig. 7.2).

FIGURE 7.1. Rigoletto (Plácido Domingo) and Marullo (Giorgio Caoduro). *Rigoletto in Mantua*, director, Marco Bellocchio, 2010. Blu-ray Naxos NBD0052–54, 2016.

FIGURE 7.2. *Rigoletto in Mantua*, director, Marco Bellocchio, 2010. Blu-ray Naxos NBD0052–54, 2016.

When Rigoletto arrives, he leaves his cloak in the Camera dei Giganti (Hall of the giants) beneath Giulio Romano's fresco depicting the struggle between the gods in Olympus and the race of giants who had battled them for supremacy. In one shot, gathered courtiers behind Rigoletto stand motionless, their conversation frozen beneath the fresco. Later, the deformed hand of one of the giants seems to reach out and touch Rigoletto (fig. 7.3). Here, where walls seem to become extensions of scenes and animate and inanimate are placed in dialogue, the *tableau vivant* becomes a trompe l'oeil. In fact, when Rigoletto returns, having been cursed by Monterrone, to collect his cloak, a televisual trompe l'oeil will take place against the backdrop of the ceiling, itself already a trompe l'oeil effect. Shot from beneath, Rigoletto's anguished face is foregrounded against the room's false ceiling; the gods in Olympus look down while he, the hunchbacked jester, remains earthbound (fig. 7.4).

Tableau vivant and trompe l'oeil, then, become conduits: between production and site and between the media of theater, painting, and cinema/television. The interiors of the Palazzo Ducale, which once cast imaginary shadows on the flats of illusionist operatic scenography, now recover their mass and form in the actual interiors they once represented, only to return to the flatness of screen media. That these two effects also traverse the space between reality and illusion is, as Brigitte Peucker argues,

FIGURE 7.3. Rigoletto (Plácido Domingo). *Rigoletto in Mantua*, director, Marco Bellocchio, 2010. Blu-ray Naxos NBD0052–54, 2016.

FIGURE 7.4. Rigoletto (Plácido Domingo). *Rigoletto in Mantua*, director, Marco Bellocchio, 2010. Blu-ray Naxos NBD0052–54, 2016.

emblematic of the cinematic play with reality: both *tableau vivant* and trompe l'oeil stage the very problem of representation, inviting a playful and pleasurable oscillation between belief and knowing resistance, between absorption and distance.[24] The play on the animate and inanimate characteristic of the *tableau vivant* is central to the effect of the production. Live performers may play against and among inanimate backdrops, but that is not the scene of performance because *both* are remediated in the fluid visual representation that is the telecast. If Storaro's cinematography is painterly—modeled in part on the Renaissance imagery that adorns the Mantuan interiors—then this is painting charged with movement, brought to life. And the whole production pivots on a trompe l'oeil in that the gap between the scene of representation and its referent becomes ambiguous. How telling that one of the press reactions to *Rigoletto in Mantua* was the observation that Storaro's lighting had made these locations resemble a stage set for *Rigoletto*.[25]

But perhaps this resemblance becomes all too obvious. The clever play on illusion that characterizes the interior scenes from the Palazzo Ducale evaporates when the action shifts in act 3 to Sparafucile's tavern, here represented by the ruins of a fourteenth-century fortress known since the late nineteenth century as the "Rocca di Sparafucile." Transforming this ruin into a tavern required scenic intervention, and what better guide, the

DVD booklet suggests, than the designs sketched by Giuseppe Bertoja for the opera's premiere?[26] In keeping with Bertoja's scenography (an exterior with an arched opening to reveal the interior) and Verdi's musical-scenic configuration of the act as both single and divided (not unlike the split-screen stagings we encountered in chap. 2), the production positions protagonists and cameras on either side of the tavern's windows, repeatedly alternating between exterior and interior, between looking in and looking out. In scenes like this, Malvano argues, fidelity to the score's scenic imagination surfaces as the guiding principle, the bold articulations of space evident in the camerawork of *La traviata in Paris* now contained in a reassertion of the conventional underpinnings of the series.[27] In place of the mobile camera and long take, the production turns to a multicamera configuration and an edited montage of contrasting perspectives. The final location of this site-specific production turns out to be the illusionist opera stage, and, in a reversal of the indexical doubling of actual and represented location, the production models itself on the very mediality—the video of a staged production—from which it might have escaped.

This sense of a return to the theater is reinforced in the way the production presents the orchestra. One of the recurring features of the Andermann production is the inclusion, during orchestral preludes, of cutaway shots of the conductor, Zubin Mehta, and the orchestra performing. Despite their remote location (in *Tosca*, e.g., the orchestra performed from RAI studios in Rome) and their function in these productions as session musicians, they are presented in full concert dress. Here is another nod to tradition and to the evental quality of the project. It is also a nod to the grammar of video productions of staged opera, which typically train cameras on the orchestra in overtures, preludes, and interludes, provided nothing is happening on the stage. As for the remote locations, the darkened studio of *Tosca* gives way to the belle epoque interior of the Salle Wagram in *La traviata* and, in *Rigoletto*, to an actual theater. Surrounded by the ornate, artfully illuminated boxes of the eighteenth-century Teatro Scientifico di Bibiena, the orchestra appears to have come home. Unlike the earlier productions, *Rigoletto in Mantua* even features one of the rituals of live operatic performance: at the beginning of act 2, Mehta enters and gestures to the orchestra to stand, as though taking the interim applause customary in the opera house. This is no studio, the choreography seems to say, even if the orchestra has the theater to itself and no applause greets the gesture.

As for the recorded sound, the mix reconciles the remote locations, balancing, synchronizing, and controlling what one of the engineers characterized as the "very reverberant" acoustics of "some of the rooms" to emulate the stereo soundscape familiar from opera telecasts and DVDs and, by extension, from the hi-fi era of opera recordings.[28] Although ambient sounds (crickets, distant dogs barking) are incorporated into the opening moments of each act, the most important ambience is arguably shaped by the acoustics of the production's imaginary opera house, that "theatre of the mind" proposed by the Decca producer John Culshaw.[29] Invoking what Jonathan Sterne describes as the "Euclidean fantasies of stereo," the audio mix offers the listener an apparently unified audio perspective, healing the spatial divide of the production while carefully concealing its work beneath a mask of fidelity to a familiar original. Despite the disparity of the locations represented visually, perspective audio—that mapping of sound to image that we encountered in chapter 2—is carefully contained, with only the most subtle shifts evident. The audio in this production is specific not to its pictured sites but to an imaginary sonic theater.[30]

RESONATING HIGH-RISE

If the Andermann productions dress historic locations as period settings linked to the libretto, the Swiss television trilogy of site-specific performances stresses the interface between historical narrative and contemporary environments: the central train station in *La traviata im Hauptbahnhof* and riverbank locations in central Basel in *Aïda am Rhein*. Broadcast live in September 2009 on the Franco-German Arte channel, *La bohème im Hochhaus* adapted a stage production of *La bohème* from Stadttheater Bern and relocated it to the Gäbelbachquartier, a social housing project in western Bern built in the 1960s to accommodate the influx of workers to the rapidly expanding city (see fig. 7.5).[31] While the two flanking Verdi productions would seem to qualify as site based only in McAuley's terminology (their settings, quite arbitrary, seem merely to provide a colorful contemporary backdrop), *La bohème im Hochhaus* at least gestures to overlaps between libretto and setting: social class, economic disadvantage, high-density urban dwelling.

The winner of Eurovision's Rose d'Or prize for arts programming, the production utilizes the various spaces in the complex—apartment interiors, the main concourse of the shopping center, a bus stop, a laundry room (see fig. 7.6), concrete precincts—and mobilizes remote video feeds, radio microphones, and earpieces to connect the singers with a conductor and orchestra performing in the shopping center. The orchestra occupies its traditionally operatic, concealed location (even if the pit is now an electronic one), while period costumes reveal the origins of the event in a relatively conventional, midbudget stage production. The performance is interrupted after most scenes for interviews with cast members, documentary features on the neighborhood, and feedback via text and email from viewers.

FIGURE 7.5. *La bohème im Hochhaus*, director, Anja Horst, 2009. DVD Schweizer Fernsehen 7640117266185, 2009.

FIGURE 7.6. *La bohème im Hochhaus*, director, Anja Horst, 2009. DVD Schweizer Fernsehen 7640117266185, 2009.

174 | CHAPTER SEVEN

La bohème im Hochhaus demonstrates some awareness of the sensitivities involved in basing the production in a particular community—a community chosen in part because it was seen as socially deprived (although this needs to be understood in its Swiss context: by the standards of many European cities, the Gäbelbachquartier appears to offer relatively comfortable and well-maintained accommodation). There was, for example, an attempt to involve and inform the community during planning by offering information sessions and recruiting extras for the production.[32] There is, too, a transparent effort to meld the urban, quasi-realist quality of *La bohème* with the everyday experience of the community in this housing project: interviews with residents during the telecast, an emphasis on functional living spaces. At the same time, there is a sense in which the everyday becomes a prop in an aesthetic project: for example, in act 1, set in the building's laundry room, two residents were evidently co-opted and instructed to do their washing as they would normally, and, in the bohemians' apartment, the building superintendent prepares a meal in his kitchen, as he normally would, while intercut shots show residents watching the production on television. More pointed are the extras recruited to flesh out the setting with stereotypes: the idle young man hanging around a precinct, vacantly nodding to the music in his headphones, or the drunk at the local establishment that stands in for Café Momus. Not to mention the intermission interviews with local real-life bohemians and a making-of feature that flirts with the more racial connotation of *bohemian* by emphasizing the diverse ethnicity of the building's residents.

Equally telling, however, is an undercurrent of aestheticization as social improvement and even sublimation of the debased. Echoing the promotional rhetoric characteristic of so much site-specific performance, the producers affirm the power of art to redeem broken communities. The narrator of the making-of documentary (briefly available on the Schweizer Fernsehen website but also included on the commercially released DVD) registers this transformative potential at its crudest: "The neighborhood derided in local parlance as the ghetto of Bern becomes a stage for high culture."[33] And might this transformative potential transcend the performance itself? The question, the narrator continues, is whether the "operatic glamour will endure through time, on and within the walls of the Gäbelbachquartier," something the residents "secretly wish for."[34] Thomas Beck, the project manager, recounts, in terms reminiscent of E. T. A. Hoffmann, his founding vision of a "klingende Hochhaus" (resonating high-rise).[35] And, as though to illustrate the idea, a CGI promo sequence depicts the apartment building breaking away from its foundations as it resonates with Puccini's music. Meanwhile, the video director,

Christian Eggenberger, is quite taken by the spectacle of the neighborhood: "At night the three apartment blocks are illuminated wonderfully in the landscape. They even have the right proportions: 16:9 (the ratio of widescreen television)."[36]

Here, the producers resemble the opera's bohemians in their blending of art and everyday reality—Eggenberger could be the romantic idealist Rodolfo surveying the rooftops of Paris—though, I fear, without the irony and self-mockery that characterizes the bohemians sketched by Puccini's librettists.[37] Not even the striking juxtaposition of contemporary setting with classic period costume—of CCTV with bonnets and shawls—triggers any irony or playfulness. Admittedly, the double quality of the opera, which juggles irony with sentimental melodrama, might not easily lend itself to a mere locational adaptation without a more thorough and inventive intervention, while the stage history of La bohème will not have inspired a lightness of touch, anchored as it is in—one might say smothered by—an illusionist tradition for which the work stands as something of a touchstone.[38]

Part of the problem here might also lie in the characteristic baggage of opera more widely—not least its paradoxical combination of liberal, democratic sentiment with the trappings of elitist, establishment culture. But what about television? In one publicity piece published on the Swiss government website swissinfo.ch, La bohème im Hochhaus is praised for presenting "high culture in the democratic medium of television."[39] Yet the project's clumsy juxtaposition of high and low seems, if anything, to accentuate the gap, as though, like so much cultural programming, the telecast relishes the opportunity to elevate television with reverential language and bow ties as much as much it attempts to demystify and desublimate high art. Meanwhile, the interviews with residents seem, like the production's journalistic cousins on television news, to be looking for a story: deprived neighborhood gets dose of high culture. One reviewer was struck by the "talk-down" attitude of the presenters, who, he observed, seemed too eager to remind audiences how happy the residents must be to host the "big wide world of television and opera."[40]

And how this dynamic plays out is tellingly illustrated in the promotional sequence that opens the production. In this CGI video, which is far more playful and ironic than the production it introduces, sound—operatic sound—resonates in and through one of the apartment blocks. It begins with a shot of a distant block to the accompaniment of a quiet suburban soundscape of birds chirping and distant, faintly heard music. A close-up of foundations shows cracks forming as the building begins to elevate to the swelling climax of the duet "O soave fanciulla." As the duet reaches its climax, foundations begin to crack, and windows shatter, the music now reinforced with sound effects suggesting a rocket launch. Day turns immediately to night, the duet fades, and the building hovers, suspended above its surroundings in the nocturnal ambient sounds of crickets. It is as though musical force had elevated the high-rise above its environment, the high-density neighborhood of the Gäbelbachquartier. Like the impoverished Rodolfo, who tells us that he has "the soul of a millionaire" when it comes to "dreams and reveries and castles in the air," the sequence imagines a space transcended through the power of art.[41]

Two qualities of the sound of this promo sequence are worth considering in more detail. The first is that the sound of opera—voices and orchestra—is represented here as possessing immense power, enough force to crack foundations and move buildings. Like the phonograph blaring Caruso's voice across the Amazon in Werner Herzog's *Fitzcarraldo*, music powerfully resounds across its environment and rends the air (or, in this case, concrete). Or is this perhaps a particularly powerful manifestation of the "intermaterial vibration" that Nina Sun Eidsheim links with the singing voice?[42] The second is that the sound is very precisely rendered—to use Michel Chion's term—so as to spatialize and situate it.[43] Each cut in the video is synchronized with a precise sonic cut to a new sound quality: now immediate, now distant, now muffled, now tinny. At last we have the kind of perspective audio that engineers seems so keen to contain in multicamera production in the name of a unified perspective. Should we imagine that there is a tenant somewhere in the block with a very powerful stereo system? Is an amplified performance of "O soave fanciulla" taking place somewhere in the building? Or does the building itself produce and resonate with music (the *klingende Hochhaus*)? And note the carefully textured silence that follows when the duet quickly fades from earshot—not silence at all, of course, but crickets and distant church bells, two cinematic tropes of the peaceful, idyllic landscape. It is the calm after the storm, a sudden repose that frames and accentuates the rapid sequence of cuts that preceded it. The field of sound studies has increasingly drawn attention to these virtual sound fields and especially to the question of the situatedness of the auditor. How, it asks, do engineered sound fields—filters, effects, surround channels—locate the listener and construct or fragment the spaces they occupy? The listening subject is here imagined not as a stationary beholder immersed in a fluid soundscape but as a subject in motion, dispersed and repositioned repeatedly and rapidly to different points of audition within that field. This is sound on the run, sound that relinquishes the notion of a stable and centered subject in favor of one spread across and constituted by cuts and splices.[44]

But this representation in the promo sequence of a soundscape that is both powerful and fragmented/fragmenting does not tally with the sound of the actual production. What we get once the opera begins is business as usual: sound that is the result of a carefully controlled combination of networked input and balanced output, offering the listener the same front-and-center perspective engineered in *Rigoletto in Mantua*. It is sound produced via a network inaudible to the audience in attendance and realized publicly only in the mixed, engineered form of the broadcast audio. For those on-site, whether the singers linked to the network or the audience cut off from it, the sound might be likened to the "secret theater" Hosokawa associated with the emergence of the Walkman and elaborated in Michael Bull's work on the private, immersive sonic environment of the iPod.[45] Except, of course, that a network of sound being assembled for television broadcast is hardly secret or private. It is, however, isolated and diverted away from its acoustic counterpart, as though one site were being layered on top of another. The difference between these layers is vividly demonstrated by comparing a scene in its broadcast form with the same scene as shot on location by an individual in the audience and uploaded to YouTube.[46]

The scene in question (the departure of Rodolfo's friends for the Café Momus while he and Mimì remain at home alone) may not quite match the sonic complexity of Puccini's late operas, but it is a soundscape nonetheless: accompanied in the score by carefully gradated dynamics, the friends' gradual retreat is marked in the score *allontanandosi* (walking away), then *perdendosi* (dying away).[47] But the effect registers in strikingly differently ways in each of these recordings. The friends, departing via a concrete concourse elevated and distanced from Rodolfo and Mimì, head for and board a bus. What interests me here is just how fragile and vulnerable the soundscape of Puccini's opera is when transplanted from the operatic stage to a busy semiurban location that, first, does not allow the orchestra to participate acoustically (only through headphones), second, situates the voices in spaces that they cannot effectively negotiate as dialogue, even dialogue delivered with operatic voice, and, third, threatens to drown the Puccini soundscape with ambient sound. For all its purported power, opera turns out to have a weak and fragile sonic field that perishes in this alien space. If the apartment building resounds, it is less with opera than with its everyday acoustic environment: voices, traffic, ambient noise. Yet what we hear on television registers almost nothing of this environment: the broadcast filters out almost every trace of the sonic environment and replaces it with a soundtrack synthesized according to the conventional and generic virtual soundstage familiar from opera recordings. Were it not for the prominent head microphones, we might imagine that the whole performance is lip-synched, like so many of the classic opera films. To speak of specificity in a scene like this is really to speak of the visual: *sight*-specific opera. Sonically, *La bohème im Hochhaus* is another recording of *La bohème* in the late twentieth-century stereo tradition, just as *Rigoletto in Mantua* is another recording of *Rigoletto* in the late twentieth-century stereo tradition.

BIG BROTHER AND THE BOHEMIANS

Other sights in the production deserve consideration too, not least the insistence on some of the visual modes we have already encountered in this book: one is video surveillance, the other a documentary style of camerawork. The production, that is, draws on what we might call the *aesthetics* of reality TV: a cable-mounted spider cam offering establishing shots of the complex; cuts to CCTV-style footage (see fig. 7.7); extensive use of the steadicam, here seemingly back on home turf; interrogative camerawork resembling news gathering; interpolated narrations (the scenes are interrupted with plot synopses); and behind-the-scenes interviews and reporting of viewer feedback via text and email. If the production is specific about a site, it is not a housing complex in Bern but an episode of a reality-TV series: the site is, as it were, the televisual itself, here imagined

FIGURE 7.7. *La bohème im Hochhaus*, director, Anja Horst, 2009. DVD Schweizer Fernsehen 7640117266185, 2009.

FIGURE 7.8. *La bohème im Hochhaus*, director, Anja Horst, 2009. DVD Schweizer Fernsehen 7640117266185, 2009.

as a mise en abyme of self-regard. That the 16:9 building ratio noted by Eggenberger is itself composed of multiple illuminated apartments in the same ratio gives the impression of a giant bank of television monitors (see fig. 7.8: note the solitary figure of the telecast host, Sandra Studer, in the center). And in several of those apartments we glimpse the characteristic white glow of television screens.

Looking at the production in this way leads to a number of possible interpretative trajectories and conclusions. What to make, for example, of the very unreality-like period costumes in this otherwise twenty-first-century contemporary setting? Pearson's vision of the traces left by the various events and lives that have occupied a place suggests a kind of haunting, and this is a trope that Pearson elsewhere employs more explicitly when he characterizes the creative work as a *ghost* at large on a site.[48] It is an image, as Cathy Turner points out, that has endured in the discourse of site-specific performance but in ways that leave open the question of who and what haunts, "whether the site haunts the work or vice versa."[49] Haunting is foregrounded in *La bohème im Hochhaus* when a figure in the costume of a nineteenth-century seamstress (Mimì) walks the corridors of a contemporary high-rise. That some of these scenes should be presented in the form of CCTV footage only heightens the anachrony, the sense of dislocation. Or perhaps this an allusion to found-footage representations of the supernatural used in contemporary cinema and television (although this may give the production more credit than it deserves—the costumes probably have more to do with the origins of the production in a staging of the opera for Konzert Theater Bern than any critical take on period and history)? The charge that the ghost in this production might be opera itself—a genre, after all, often reputed to have died with Puccini—is perhaps harsh but not completely unwarranted, given the clumsy encounter of art and the everyday staged by the production.

Another perspective forms when we attend to the audience assembled on site and what that audience hears. Surveillance is exhibit 1 in Baudrillard's dystopian vision of media technology. Not all will share his anxiety about the loss of the real in the infinitely receding mirror images of mediatization, but he makes a telling point about reality TV when he argues that it is merely a side effect of something that is happening anyway. Baudrillard argues that complaints about reality TV and virtual reality miss the point because we are now living in the midst of total media saturation anyway. We have lost the relation to the spectacle now because we are in it; we are, in short, starring in our own reality show. Critics further obfuscate the issue, he adds, by implying that there is an external reality that the reality shows somehow miss. If the original critics of Puccini's opera complained that it had collapsed the necessary distance between art and reality, Baudrillard laments that we have collapsed the necessary distance between spectating and living: "The virtual camera is in our head, and our whole life has taken on a video dimension. . . . We have swallowed our microphones and headsets."[50]

This *Bohème*, in effect, stages Baudrillard's observation: the microphones and headsets are physically present—had Rodolfo's friends not interrupted their intimate scene, Rodolfo and Mimì were about to experience, we imagine, an embarrassing case of mic bumping (see fig. 7.9), yet representationally absent, conceptually swallowed as though invisible. It also casts the on-site audience in its own reality show. Occupying a strange, liminal diegetic space, this is at once an actual audience and a set of figures within the dramaturgy of the production, gathered on the street like curious passersby to witness . . . what? A performance, the filming of a television show, or the dramatic collapse of a gravely ill lover on the street outside their building? Their spectatorship is itself a pretense: they *seem* to be hearing what we in front of the screen hear, but that sound is available only to the performers they watch. Just as local extras are called on to play locals, so the spectators play themselves as opera spectators: not only is the spectacle virtual, but so is the spectating (see fig. 7.10). The circle is completed by those spectators who fail to go along with the pretense of

FIGURE 7.9. Rodolfo (Saimir Pirgu) and Mimì (Maya Boog). *La bohème im Hochhaus*, director, Anja Horst, 2009. DVD Schweizer Fernsehen 7640117266185, 2009.

FIGURE 7.10. Rodolfo (Saimir Pirgu) and Mimì (Maya Boog). *La bohème im Hochhaus*, director, Anja Horst, 2009. DVD Schweizer Fernsehen 7640117266185, 2009.

FIGURE 7.11. Musetta (Eva Liebau) and Marcello (Robin Adams). *La bohème im Hochhaus*, director, Anja Horst, 2009. DVD Schweizer Fernsehen 7640117266185, 2009.

attending a live performance and instead enact the contemporary ritual of watching themselves watching (see fig 7.11). To the right of the frame, two spectators, illuminated by the glow of a monitor, watch the mediatized version of the action unfolding in front of them. Like Baudrillard's contemporary subject, whose life is a reality-TV show, these spectators occupy multiple layers, traversing reality and its mediatized representations.

CONCLUSION

Let me try to escape the orbit of these circular transactions and offer some conclusions. The first emerges from the contradiction in these site-specific television productions between, on the one hand, an investment in the reflexive potential of media technology and, on the other, a desire to, as it were, step out of the chain of reflections, to become transparent and present themselves as grounded in—a natural extension of—the values of the chosen work and the traditions of its performance. Cachopo notes the caveat in Andermann's articulation of the aims of the *Via della musica* project: new forms of communication and new ways of thinking about opera, yes, but all with what Andermann, sounding like Brian Large, describes as "total respect for the original."[51] The Via della musica turns out to lead, as the title might have foretold, precisely to the score and to the opera house. As for *La bohème im Hochhaus*, a proliferation of screens and one or two attempts at irony and self-mockery notwithstanding—Mimì's death is staged not as an exhausted collapse on her bed but as a journey on board a bus marked "Endstation" (Terminus)—the production takes itself all too seriously, clothing itself in the language of community improvement and the ennobling power of art embodied, as the hosts repeatedly remind us, in Puccini's *Meisterwerk*.

My second conclusion arises from my point about the fragility of operatic sound in the *Hochhaus* project. On the operatic soundscape, Alessandra Campana writes: "Opera studies' sophisticated ears, increasingly trained nowadays to attend to mediation and performance, are often deaf to the design choices that always shape in advance the very experience of sound, voice, and orchestra, both live and recorded."[52] Campana's observation, part of an introduction to an essay by an acoustic engineer, addresses the opera house and its acoustic qualities. Here, the opera house is already a site, understood both as materiality and as a set of practices and configurations conditioned by and conditioning that materiality. Site-specific indeed, but not one-off projects. That is, even if we worry about the superficiality and novelty factor of site-specific productions—about the politics of these practices—more familiar sites continually shape opera and demand our critical attention precisely because, as Eidsheim puts it, they emerge from a "naturalized notion of acoustic-spatial relations."[53] Campana's reference to *recorded* sound reminds us, too, that mediatized forms now and increasingly represent one of opera's sites. And, if, as Eidsheim argues of *Invisible Cities*, there is value in attending to practices that mobilize recorded sound in ways that destabilize assumptions about what is natural, there is equally value, I want to suggest, in considering how these assumptions might manifest themselves in contexts more reflective of mainstream values. Predicated on a desire to get out of the house, *Rigoletto in Mantua* and *La bohème im Hochhaus* sonically overlay visual representations of spatial freedom and fluidity with a centered and unified perspective. It is the generic, not the specific, sites that are most telling.

I end with one more site, this one a truly secret theater. Although both these productions were broadcast in stereo, their DVD releases include a 5.1 surround-sound mix. Multichannel sound was included in the specification of the DVD format from its launch in the late 1990s. Targeted in particular toward the home release of feature films, these multichannel mixes promised the consumer the possibility of a cinematic experience in a home equipped with appropriate receiver and speakers.[54] Something equivalent was soon to be offered to opera devotees when recordings of telecasts of staged opera, already well established as a niche market in the VHS catalog, began to feature on DVD. Initially stereo only, by the early years of the new millennium many of these titles included both stereo and surround-sound tracks (the latter typically processed "up-conversions" of the stereo recordings, not unlike the Met cinecasts, as we discovered in chap. 3).[55] Although productions have more recently been recorded in dedicated 5.1 multichannel audio, the sound mix has tended to retain the pattern already established in the earlier up-converted recordings: the vocal and orchestral sound, sourced in the microphone array in front and around the stage, is panned across the front speakers, with the center speaker filling out the space between the front left and right speakers. Rear channels, meanwhile, are all about ambient sound sourced in microphones placed in the auditorium, while the low-frequency effects channel (the .1 associated with cinematic rumbles and booms) is typically silent in the music-centered environment of operatic sound. This focus on ambience is in part, as we saw in chapter 2, a form of sonic design rooted in fidelity to the opera house as an acoustic space, but it is equally an effect of the acoustic conditions of recording: unlike cinematic sound, which can be recorded and processed in isolation, microphones in an opera house occupy overlapping sonic spaces. The sound that one microphone records will register on other microphones.

This is where *Rigoletto in Mantua* and *La bohème im Hochhaus* differ from standard practice. Although they offer stereo tracks that blend voices and orchestra into a sonic image indistinguishable from the norm, their surround-sound tracks actually isolate solo voices in the center channel and direct orchestra and chorus to the left and right channels (rear channels continue to offer ambience). That is, because the spaces of recording are physically remote, the audio channels are separate, and this is harnessed to create playback that is unblended—or, rather, that becomes blended only as a combination of sound from separate speakers.[56] There is a model here, and it is not a musical or an acoustic one. Isolating voices to the center channel is exactly what multichannel soundtracks do in home cinema: dialogue is isolated in the speaker closest to the screen, leaving music and sound effects to the remaining channels. What these DVD releases offer, then, is a rare opportunity to hear opera in this cinematic form, unbeholden to the standard acoustic soundstage, and shaped by the sonic paradigms of another site: home theater. Few, I suspect, have ever heard it. This location, seated just so, in the middle of a carefully placed array of speakers, may be the most specific site of all.

Conclusion

One of the recurring themes in the press coverage of and online conversations about the filmed version of the Lin-Manuel Miranda musical *Hamilton* (director, Thomas Kail, 2015) is whether it is in fact a film. Shot at live performances in 2016, the filmed version (directed by the stage director Thomas Kail) was acquired by Disney and released on its streaming platform in 2020. "The 'what is and isn't a movie' talk can get really tedious," wrote the *Vulture* columnist Mark Harris, but apparently not tedious enough to prevent him from going on to explain how this version of *Hamilton* was shot at live performances using an array of cameras and edited in such a way as to embrace the live "stage show" quality of the musical. "It is not," he concludes, "an attempt to turn *Hamilton* into something it isn't; it's an attempt to share with you what *Hamilton* is."[1] Interviewed about the production, the editor Jonah Moran elaborates on the importance of generating a sense of the live event, including framing it with introductory audience noise and a request by one of the actors, in character, that the audience turn off mobile phones: "Having that in was an important part of saying, 'This is the theater, we're watching what happened on these nights.'" Kail, meanwhile, stresses the need to find a "grammar" for the production, and he goes on to explain that, while the nine cameras afford a range of perspectives, these must be deployed and edited judiciously, with a calculated, narrative-driven use of close-ups.[2]

If this language has a familiar ring, it is because it articulates the syntax and aesthetic that have long informed remediated stage productions—including the occasional DVD release of staged musicals on video but, above all, opera.[3] For it is opera—on television, on video, in cinecasts, streamed—that has done the most to cultivate these conventions and, as I have shown, the rhetoric of fidelity that attends them. Yet Kail and Moran present the production as though it were something novel, and the press lazily endorses the claim. Certainly, this "discovery" may remind us of the niche audience reached by remediated opera, despite its decades of dissemination and its accumulated archive. My point, however, is not simply to protest this ignorance, real or feigned, of long-established practices but simply to ask whether this is the moment when the conventions of the remediated stage and its televisual apparatus went mainstream. The remediated *Hamilton* immediately became a streaming sensation, generating record-breaking viewing statistics.[4] Now plans are afoot for more video productions of staged musicals. Is this how captures or relays finally find some kind of genre identity in wider discourse? Or will the rhetoric of respect, to use Brian Large's term, continue to confine this televisual apparatus to the role of dutiful servant to an in-the-flesh original?

Admittedly, the success of the streamed *Hamilton* owed something to extraordinary circumstances. Originally scheduled for theatrical release, it was instead debuted as a stream when, like theaters of all kinds, movie theaters were forced to close their doors. The lockdowns imposed in response to a global pandemic all but suspended public gatherings, and any cultural form predicated on the assembly of an audience was drastically affected. Catapulted into crisis-management mode, opera companies reached for alternatives to live performance and found one via remediation. Planned stage productions were hastily adapted to social-distancing guidelines and live streamed; companies with archives of transmissions made the content accessible without charge on a rotating basis; new projects were developed with cameras and microphones in mind. Was this not, one friend and colleague asked me, a moment when opera on video became a thing?

At the time, I answered with a qualified yes. On the one hand, it seemed to me that creative thinking was being channeled with unprecedented intensity toward projects that either were conceived specifically for screen or seemed to break out of the old mold of multicamera production based on virtual audience perspectives of the opera-house stage. So, for example, the Irish National Opera commissioned a film version of Peter Maxwell Davies's *The Lighthouse* (director, Edwina Casey, 2021) and screened it at outdoor locations, the Met refashioned its gala in Zoom form, the Berwaldhallen in Stockholm streamed a *Don Giovanni* (director, Andrew Staples, 2020) without audience but with freely roving cameras, and Yuval Sharon's *Götterdämmerung* adaptation *Twilight: Gods* (Michigan Opera Theatre, 2020; Lyric Opera of Chicago, 2021) doubly responded to restrictions with a site-based "drive-through" production that was itself filmed and streamed (director, Raphael Nash, 2021). I began to wonder whether success with these innovations might embolden opera producers and raise the bar for audiences typically fed a diet of unadventurous productions content with the notion of capture. "At a time of profound crisis," reads the introductory text in the *Twilight: Gods* stream, "the gods' destruction brings a new day." Would these words prove prophetic?

On the other hand, it seemed possible that all this was going to last only as long as the lockdowns, that it would be a case of business as usual once theaters reopened. Some of the initiatives—certainly the split-screen Zoom-style collages from performers' homes—came across as "the best we can do, under the circumstances," as a *New York Times* critic put it.[5] That some of the larger institutions fell back on the virtual safety net of their video repository exposed the limitations of the traditional model of transmitting or streaming stage productions. What happens when the supply from the stage dries up? Even a substantial back catalog was quickly exhausted when the Met offered its nightly streams. Its response was simply to keep cycling back through the list, as though the looped form so characteristic of twenty-first-century audiovisual media realized itself on a horrible metalevel. Here, surely, were the perfect hothouse conditions to germinate nostalgia for the opera house predicated on resentment toward all these screens, which might now be tainted by association with dark days.

One production, in particular, illustrated for me the anxiety generated by the pandemic, but also a tension that I think pre- and postdates the crisis. Faced with the prospect of canceled public performances of its new production of *Falstaff* in December 2020, the Bayerische Staatsoper opted to present it instead on its Staatsoper.tv streaming platform. No audience was in attendance, but this hardly registers when the Staatsoper's in-house cameras capture the stage. After all, the convention, as we know, is that the audience—or anything other than the stage—does not figure once the performance is under way. As it has been doing for over a decade, Staatsoper.tv models its undistracted gaze on the imaginary of the always-attentive spectator, the same spectator for which the now-empty opera house was designed. The show must go on, and on Staatsoper.tv it did. Yet this insistence on *normality*—to use a term much in evidence during the pandemic—was framed by something else. As I argued in chapter 4, the introductory sequence of remediated stage productions has its own conventions: shots of the opera-house exterior with arriving patrons, the buzz of the assembling audience inside the auditorium, a close-up of the conductor entering the pit. The *Falstaff* stream instead greets us with an eerily empty piazza and a wistful panning shot of unoccupied seats. When the conductor, Michele Mariotti, enters the pit, it is to the applause of the orchestra alone.

And what of the other side of the frame, the closing moments of the production and the conventional spectacle of stage bows and applause?

Here, the video production was not left to its own devices. The stage director, Mateja Koležnik, adapted the closing scene of the production expressly for the stream; for once, stage direction and video direction worked in partnership. At the moment Falstaff (Wolfgang Koch) protests that the world would be a dull place without comedians like him, the music comes to a sudden halt. Falstaff (or is it Koch?) glances wistfully to the auditorium and walks silently offstage. Only then does the music resume, the cast for now hidden backstage. When the singers do reappear, it is not in person but on a large monitor. They have swapped their costumes and wigs for their street clothes and now appear in split screen as though participating in a Zoom meeting. There they will remain for the remainder of the performance. But as the fugal finale "Tutto nel mondo è burla" (Everything in the world is a jest) begins, figures assemble on stage and stand motionless, their faces covered by protective masks. They are members of the production team. Soon they are joined by the chorus and the cast in costume, all silent and masked while their on-screen doubles continue to perform. Finally, the conductor emerges to stand in front of the screen, and a camera positioned at the side of the orchestra pit slowly pans from the stage across the orchestra and out to the auditorium. The orchestra, in full dress and holding instruments, is not playing but standing silently, and the auditorium is empty save for a few cameras and their operators. The opera ends and a wide shot of stage and orchestra pit shows the cast and personnel slowly leaving while the orchestra sits. Fade to black.

It is an eloquent and moving cry of protest at a moment when the reopening of theaters was still only a dream, when life and livelihoods were threatened and institutions brought to their knees. And Koležnik bemoans not simply biology but what she characterizes in an interview as a "stupid" and "dangerous" politics of lockdown that silences art when it is most needed. What is clear, too, is the critique of media technology. The need for art, Koležnik argues, is a need for "something other than our mobile phones."[6] When in-person performance gives way to mediated performance—when voices become ventriloquized and performers start dialing in—we, watching and listening to the video production, do not necessarily register what has happened. Only slowly, as clues begin to emerge, do we become aware that, like Falstaff, we have been duped. What is the difference between a copy and a copy of a copy? The message of the stage production, reinforced by its video remediation, is that, with media technology, you never really know. It is as though the production were invested in a reestrangement of what has come to seem too ordinary. Is its ventriloquized sound an instance of what Connor called the *vocalic uncanny*, when sound detaches itself from its sources?[7] Or is it, rather, an instance of what Connor has in mind when he later rethinks that uncanny as a reaction summoned to compensate for having played along with the deception? Is this really unease, he asks, or in fact a "reparative unease, evoked in order to make up for our apparent willingness to allow the voice to be so easily replicated, redoubled and impersonated"?[8] Yet, for all the suspicion and critique and resentment, the *Falstaff* stream opens a door usually locked: it is an invitation, however begrudging, to the cameras and microphones to participate instead of observing, to perform instead of monitoring. A pity that it took these circumstances to unlock the door, and that the door seems to have closed again.

I began my investigation of remediated opera some years ago with an article that opened with this question: "What is it about video recording that brings out the purist in theater practitioners and theorists?"[9] I sense that attitudes have shifted markedly since I wrote these words. Certainly, the fields of theater and performance studies now seem to me much less defensive than this question implies, and there is no better illustration of this than the scholarship on theater cinecasts. As for practitioners, one need look only at the number of sessions and workshops devoted to media technology in the recent conferences of the umbrella bodies Opera America and Opera Europa to understand the level of commitment among producers to realizing the potential of video production. Granted, the anxiety about restoring attendance postpandemic means that media technology seems, more than ever, placed in the service of audience development. At the same time, there is evidence of a desire to rethink priorities. One contributor to an Opera America panel discussion urged delegates to think of "digital distribution" as a mission of equal importance to the traditional one of performing to "in-person" audiences.[10]

But this *Falstaff* reveals the durability of a certain suspicion, and the reliance on media technology during the pandemic may indeed, as I suspected at the time, have worked in two directions. While we may in some ways have become habituated to certain forms of (re)mediation—being made into a Zoom window to meet with other Zoom windows is surely no longer as strange as it was—the lifting of restrictions and, thus, of reliance on media technologies generated, I think, a backlash born of a new desire for in-person contact, for an older form of presence. During the pandemic, the cultural status of the remediated stage seemed to me to hang in the balance. Now that opera houses have reopened, it still does. Pivotal, I think, is the question of how video is to be deployed, of the nature of the apparatus at work: its means of production, its visual and sonic forms, its sites of spectatorship. Addressing the Opera America conference of 2020, the *ArtsJournal* editor Douglas McLennan urged delegates to embrace the language of screen media and avoid what he called the *facsimile* approach, according to which video remediation would dutifully copy the staged original.[11] In an article for *Opera*, Nicholas Payne, then the director of Opera Europa, read the enforced reliance on media technology during the pandemic as an anticipation of the forms of dissemination that opera producers will increasingly need to embrace. He urged companies not to return to prepandemic "habits" but to "be open to partnerships with broadcasters, film producers and other digital media."[12] Opera providers show evidence of taking this advice seriously, drawing inspiration from some of the innovation on show during the pandemic, innovation that itself owed something to prepandemic experimentation with opera-film hybrids and digital shorts. Perhaps, as Jane Forner has recently argued, this is a moment for optimism about opera's embrace of what she calls the *streaming age*—at least with respect to specially commissioned and contemporary work.[13]

But what about the operatic canon? What about those grand stages on which the canon plays? Here, the facsimile model endures. More than that, I fear that initiatives based on in-house production—something streaming has facilitated—are actually turning the clock back to a video language once prevalent in multicamera production for broadcast: static mid-shots, a turgid editing pace, a lack of distinguishing or challenging perspectives. Three decades have passed since, in his introduction to *A Night in at the Opera*, Jeremy Tambling confronted what he presented as the contradiction embedded in video productions of staged opera. Watched on television screens, these productions encouraged what Tambling characterized as a Benjaminian state of distracted spectatorship: opera as MTV. Yet, in its conservative homage to the event, opera on screen remained beholden, he countered, to the enduring ideal of contemplative spectatorship associated with the opera house.[14] What we encounter in the signature operatic media of our time—the cinecast, the live stream—is at once a retreat from, and an intensification of, this contradiction. The cinecast offers its patrons the convenience and creature comforts of the local multiplex, but it also duplicates the darkened auditorium of the opera house and demands the same attentive viewing and listening as the master venue. Live streams, with their limited availability, recover the ephemerality and aura of the unrepeatable operatic performance in the theater, yet they are surely the epitome of distracted spectatorship: opera as YouTube clip, opera as a glance available to the dual-screening spectator.

Illustrative of this trend is much of the content produced by Staatsoper .tv, including the 2020 *Falstaff*. Here is the epitome of that aesthetic of "self-obliteration" that Davis had once associated with "perfection" in

CONCLUSION | 191

multicamera production. Now harnessed to live and on-demand streaming, this old-school language of televisual perfection shows how suited it is to the distracted spectatorship that Casetti associates with the *logic of the display*. This is not, it has to be said, the kind of pointed invocation of surveillance I identified in *Written on Skin*. Rather, we seem to encounter here, as with much streamed content, something less reflexive, more transparent, determined not to intervene. In these streams, being there and not being there collide with new contradictory force. Never has the staged performance seemed more fugitive, dispersed, and homeless than it does in its windowed display on computer screens and phones. Yet nothing in this radical remediation of the stage challenges the expectations and conventions embedded in the darkened and reverent opera house since the nineteenth century. Unless opera is ready to rethink that too.

Acknowledgments

Long in the making, this project owes much to colleagues, friends, and family. My thanks, first of all, to the supportive staff at the University of Chicago Press, above all Marta Tonegutti for her patience and words of encouragement. David Levin and Mary Ann Smart, editors of the Opera Lab series, offered crucial guidance, as did the anonymous readers of the manuscript.

Much of the writing took place during a sabbatical year from Maynooth University. I am grateful for support from the university for research travel and materials. The National University of Ireland Publications Scheme awarded a generous grant in support of publication costs.

I have been sharing versions of the book's material in seminars and conferences for a decade, and I thank all those who offered feedback and pointed me in new and fruitful directions. Participating in research events organized on behalf of the *Opera Quarterly* has been a great privilege; I am grateful for the opportunity they afforded to think about and through opera, on stage and on screen. My thanks to Nicholas Till, Joseph Attard, João Pedro Cachopo, and Nicolò Palazzetti for invitations to participate in symposia that offered valuable feedback. I am indebted to Antonio Cascelli, not only for his guidance and support, but for his commitment to collaboration on research projects.

Special thanks are due to Emanuele Senici, Clemens Risi, Bonnie Gordon, Francesca Placanica, Laura Anderson, and John O'Flynn for sharing their expertise and insight; to Áine Sheil for many enjoyable conversations about opera on stage and on screen; and to my valued friend and collaborator Alessandra Campana, who always asks the right questions.

Above all I thank Cindy, on whose support and patience this project relied the most.

This book is dedicated to the memory of my mother.

Portions of chapter 7 appeared in "The Mute Stones Sing: *Rigoletto* Live from Mantua," *TDR: The Drama Review* 59 (2015): 51–66 (reprinted by permission of MIT Press); and in "The Deadness of Live Opera," in *Performing Arts in Transition: Moving between Media*, ed. Susanne Foellmer, Maria Katharina Schmidt, and Cornelia Schmitz (Oxford: Routledge, 2018), 126–39 (reprinted by permission of Routledge).

Notes

Unless otherwise indicated, all translations from non-English-language sources are mine.

INTRODUCTION

1. Peter Conrad, *Television: The Medium and Its Manners* (Abingdon: Routledge, 1982), 13, 14.

2. OperaVision, "This might be your first time," Facebook, October 18, 2017, https://www.facebook.com/OperaVisionEU/photos/pb.100063555009952 .-2207520000./153209645283549.

3. Luke O'Shaughnessy, "Audience Development: Introducing the Opera Europa Streaming Platform," presentation at the European Theatre Convention, October 27, 2017, https://youtu.be/5gNESI3CL2g. In response to a delegate who raises concerns about streaming video replacing in-person attendance, O'Shaughnessy argues that the two forms of spectatorship can coexist.

4. The article states the case in the simplest terms: "The goal is to develop new audiences for opera." John O'Connor, "TV: 'Gioconda' Week Begins on Channel 13," *New York Times*, April 14, 1980, C18, https://www.nytimes.com/1980/04/14/archives/tv-gioconda-week-begins-on-channel-13.html.

5. Conrad, *Television*, 14.

6. The front cover of one Warner NVC Arts series of VHS releases from the 1990s featured an inset production still against a flowing texture resembling silk or satin.

7. For the laptop image, see OperaVision, "Do you know?," Facebook, August 28, 2018, https://www.facebook.com/OperaVisionEU/photos/pb.100063555009952 .-2207520000./281103955827450.

8. Erika Fischer-Lichte, *Routledge Introduction to Theatre and Performance Studies*, ed. Minou Arjomand and Ramona Mosse, trans. Minou Arjomand (London: Routledge, 2014), 18. For one account of the *metaphysics of presence* (the term is Heidegger's), see Jacques Derrida, *Speech and Phenomena and Other Essays on Husserl's Theory of Signs*, trans. and ed. David B. Allison (Evanston, IL: Northwestern University Press, 1973), 74. As Michelle Duncan points out, the critique of the

metaphysics of presence is a critique not of presence per se but of "the founding of *metaphysics* on the illusion of presence." Michelle Duncan, "The Operatic Scandal of the Singing Body: Voice, Presence, Performativity," *Cambridge Opera Journal* 16, no. 3 (2004): 283–306, 295. See also Marvin Minsky, "Telepresence," *Omni*, June 1980, 45–51; and Hans-Ulrich Gumbrecht, *The Production of Presence: What Meaning Cannot Convey* (Stanford, CA: Stanford University Press, 2004). For more on the problematic of presence in opera, see my "The Deadness of Live Opera," in *Performing Arts in Transition: Moving between Media*, ed. Susanne Foellmer, Maria Katharina Schmidt, and Cornelia Schmitz (Oxford: Routledge, 2018), 126–39.

9. Matthew Lombard and Theresa Ditton, "At the Heart of It All: The Concept of Presence," *Journal of Computer-Mediated Communication* 13, no. 3 (September 1997), https://academic.oup.com/jcmc/article/3/2/JCMC321/4080403.

10. Jay David Bolter and Richard Grusin, *Remediation: Understanding New Media* (Cambridge, MA: MIT Press, 1999), 19, 53.

11. Steve Wurtzler, "She Sang Live, but the Microphone Was Turned Off: The Live, the Recorded, and the Subject of Representation," in *Sound Theory, Sound Practice*, ed. Rick Altman (New York: Routledge, 1992); 87–103, 92. Philip Auslander cites Wurtzler in support of his argument that ontological claims on behalf of live performance mask their retroactive conceit: that it is only with the rise of mediated performance that the concept of the liveness assumes importance. Philip Auslander, *Liveness: Performance in a Mediatized Culture* (1999), 2nd ed. (London: Routledge, 2008).

12. Bolter and Grusin, *Remediation*, 73.

13. Danielle Ward-Griffin argues that Kirk Browning, the director of the *Live from the Met* telecasts from 1977 on, incorporated some of the televisual techniques he had learned and developed as a director of studio telecasts of operas at NBC during the 1950s and 1960s. Danielle Ward-Griffin, "As Seen on TV: Putting the NBC Opera on Stage," *Journal of the Society for American Music* 13, no. 2 (2019): 216–31, 228.

14. That these transmissions, well into their second decade, still lack an agreed-on term is perhaps telling in itself. I return to this question in chap. 4.

15. Wagner Society of New York, "Opera in HD: A Panel Discussion," pt. 1, March 27, 2012, https://youtu.be/MMxTtz_sDZY.

16. John Ellis, *Visible Fictions: Cinema, Television, Video* (London: Routledge & Kegan Paul, 1982), 131.

17. Stanley Cavell, "The Fact of Television," *Daedalus* 111, no. 4 (Fall 1982): 75–96, 90.

18. "'Opera Cinema, the Modern *Gesamtkunstwerk?*': Jonathan Haswell, John Fulljames, and Corinne Winters in Conversation with Eleonora Sammartino," in "Opera at the Multiplex," ed. Joseph Attard and Christopher Morris, special issue, *Opera Quarterly* 34, no. 4 (Autumn 2018): 343–54, 347.

19. Wagner Society of New York, "Opera in HD," pt. 1.

20. Desmond Davis, *The Grammar of Television Production* (London: Barrie & Rockliff, 1960), 9.

21. The *Guardian* theater critic Michael Billington argued that the time had come for the theater community to stop treating live theater as "an unreproduc-

ible event." See Michael Billington, "Let's Stop Pretending That Theatre Can't Be Captured on Screen," *The Guardian*, June 18, 2014, https://www.theguardian.com/stage/2014/jun/18/ghosts-digital-theatre-richard-eyre-almeida. On the emerging scholarship on live transmissions in the field of theater studies, see n. 46.

22. Matt Trueman, "The Surprise Success of NT Live," *The Guardian*, June 9, 2013, https://www.theguardian.com/stage/2013/jun/09/nt-live-success.

23. John Wyver, *Screening the Royal Shakespeare Company: A Critical History* (London: Bloomsbury/The Arden Shakespeare, 2019), 293.

24. Nancy Groves, "Arts Head: David Sabel, Head of Digital, National Theatre," *The Guardian*, April 10, 2012, https://www.theguardian.com/culture-professionals-network/culture-professionals-blog/2012/apr/10/david-sabel-digital-national-theatre.

25. François van den Anker, "Gary Halvorson: De Man Achter Live in HD," Place de l'Opéra, May 26, 2020, https://www.operamagazine.nl/achtergrond/52214/gary-halvorson-de-man-achter-live-in-hd.

26. "'Opera Cinema, the Modern *Gesamtkunstwerk?*,'" 350.

27. André Gaudréault and Philippe Marion, *The End of Cinema? A Medium in Crisis in the Digital Age*, trans. Timothy Barnard (New York: Columbia University Press, 2015), 92.

28. Martin Barker, *Live to Your Local Cinema: The Remarkable Rise of Livecasting* (London: Palgrave Macmillan, 2013), 21.

29. Kenneth A. Wright, "Television and Opera," *Tempo* 45 (Autumn 1957): 8–14, 12. Wright refers here to a telecast of *The Decembrists* from the Kirov Theater in June 1954. He adds: "The mysterious effect of the gloomy setting was entirely destroyed. My film turned out well, but what the producer of the opera and the public thought, I dared not ask." Ibid., 12.

30. João Pedro Cachopo addresses this issue of perceived fidelity to the original in remediated opera. Drawing on Deleuze, he identifies as pivotal in this discourse not the distinction between original and copy but the distinction between supposedly "good" and "bad" copy, the former characterized by its faithful adherence to the original, the latter by "deviations and detours." João Pedro Cachopo, "The Aura of Opera Reproduced: Fantasies and Traps in the Age of the Cinecast," *Opera Quarterly* 34, no. 4 (Autumn 2018): 266–83, 267.

31. Studio-shot opera, including operas commissioned for television, represented an alternative production method, albeit without the aura of the "live." More suited to the limitations of television camera technology in the 1950s and 1960s, studio production became a relative rarity by the end of the century, perhaps in part owing to cost. With advances in lighting technology, camera light sensitivity, and sound-recording technology, not to mention the introduction of high-definition cameras and televisions, many of the challenges associated with live transmission from the opera house were overcome or at least mitigated. On the decline of commissions for television, see Jennifer Barnes, *Television Opera: The Fall of Opera Commissioned for Television* (London: Boydell, 2003). For more on the technical history of live telecasts from the theater, see Wyver, *Screening the Royal Shakespeare Company*.

32. The term *posttelevision* had already been proposed as long ago as the mid-

198 | NOTES TO PAGES 12-13

1990s, but the concept developed real traction in the following decade. See Peter d'Agostino and David Tafler, eds., *Transmission: Toward a Post-television Culture* (Thousand Oaks, CA: Sage, 1994). For a more recent account, see Michael Strangelove, *Post-TV: Piracy, Cord-Cutting, and the Future of Television* (Toronto: University of Toronto Press, 2015). For a discussion of these developments in the context of music broadcasting, see Christina L. Baade and James Deaville, "Introduction," in *Music and the Broadcast Experience: Performance, Production, and Audiences*, ed. Christina L. Baade and James Deaville (Oxford: Oxford University Press, 2016), 1–35.

33. This has not escaped the attention opera companies, which, like so many content providers, have seized on the potential of the smart TV by releasing apps capable of playing live and on-demand streams on these typically large, ultra-high-definition screens. The Metropolitan Opera and the Wiener Staatsoper, e.g., offer apps for streaming devices that connect to TVs. Recall that OperaVision specifically cites casting to a TV as one of the possibilities for viewing its content.

34. "What the televisual names," Tony Fry wrote in 1993, "is the end of the medium, in a context, and the arrival of television as the context. . . . Television has acquired its own legs and walks where it will." Tony Fry, "Introduction," in *R U A TV? Heidegger and the Televisual*, ed. Tony Fry (Sydney: Power, 1993), 11–23, 13. This bold claim for an expanded understanding of the reach of television coincides with the emergence of the notion of posttelevision. It certainly seems dated in the current digital-media environment. In the preface to the second edition of his *Liveness* (2008), Auslander wondered whether his characterization of the televisual in the first edition (1999) as the "cultural dominant" was now justified. Auslander, *Liveness*, xxii. I use the term *televisual* in a limited sense, to connote the persistence of the grammar and techniques of opera telecasts beyond television. This, I think, properly reflects the conservative values and modest aims that characterize multicamera production in the context of the remediation of opera.

35. On this history, see Barnes, *Television Opera*.

36. On opera films, see Marcia Citron, *Opera on Screen* (New Haven, CT: Yale University Press, 2000), and "Opera-Film as Television: Remediation in Tony Britten's *Falstaff*," *Journal of the American Musicological Society* 70, no. 2 (Summer 2017): 475–522. On opera's engagements with and representation within cinema, see Jeongwon Joe and Rose Theresa, eds., *Between Opera and Cinema* (London: Routledge, 2002); Michal Grover-Friedlander, *Vocal Apparitions: The Attraction of Cinema to Opera* (Princeton, NJ: Princeton University Press, 2005); Sander Gilman and Jeongwon Joe, eds., *Wagner and Cinema* (Bloomington: Indiana University Press, 2010); Marcia Citron, *When Opera Meets Film* (Cambridge: Cambridge University Press, 2010); Jeongwon Joe, *Opera as Soundtrack* (Farnham: Ashgate, 2013); and Karen Henson, ed., *Technology and the Diva: Sopranos, Opera, and Media from Romanticism to the Digital Age* (Cambridge: Cambridge University Press, 2016). Case studies in the history of televised opera include Danielle Ward-Griffin, "Realism Redux: Staging *Billy Budd* in the Age of Television," *Music and Letters* 100, no. 3 (August 2019): 447–80, and "As Seen on TV."

37. I offer here a selection (certainly not exhaustive) of this scholarship: Jeremy Tambling, ed., *A Night in at the Opera: Media Representations of Opera* (London:

NOTES TO PAGES 13–15 | 199

John Libby, 1994); Melina Esse, "Don't Look Now: Opera, Liveness, and the Televisual," *Opera Quarterly* 26, no. 1 (Winter 2010): 81–95; Christopher Morris, "Digital Diva: Opera on Video," *Opera Quarterly* 26, no. 1 (Winter 2010): 96–119; Emanuele Senici, "Porn Style? Space and Time in Live Opera Videos," *Opera Quarterly* 26, no. 1 (2010): 63–80; Richard Will, "Zooming in, Gazing Back: *Don Giovanni* on Television," *Opera Quarterly* 27, no. 1 (2011): 32–65; Héctor J. Pérez, ed., *Opera and Video: Technology and Spectatorship* (Bern: Peter Lang, 2012); Nicholas Ridout, "Opera and the Technologies of Theatrical Reproduction," in *The Cambridge Companion to Opera Studies*, ed. Nicholas Till (Cambridge: Cambridge University Press, 2012), 159–78; Paul Fryer, ed., *Opera in the Media Age: Essays on Art, Technology and Popular Culture* (Jefferson, NC: McFarland, 2014); Julia Sirmons, "'Guarda un po': Seductive Visuality in Remediated Opera," *Opera Quarterly* 35, no. 4 (Autumn 2019): 297–322; Richard Will, *Don Giovanni Captured: Performance, Media, Myth* (Chicago: University of Chicago Press, 2022).

38. See, e.g., Clemens Risi, *Opera in Performance: Analyzing the Performative Dimension of Opera Productions* (Abingdon: Routledge, 2021); and Caitlin Vincent, *Digital Scenography in Opera in the Twenty-First Century* (New York: Routledge, 2021). Helpful in this context, too, is recent scholarship on intermedial opera. See esp. Tereza Havelková, *Opera as Hypermedium: Meaning-Making, Immediacy, and the Politics of Perception* (New York: Oxford University Press, 2021).

39. For an approach that mobilizes empirical research to investigate audience attitudes to opera cinecasts, see Joseph Attard, *Opera Cinema: A New Cultural Experience* (New York: Bloomsbury, 2022).

40. Jean-Louis Comolli, "Notes sur le nouveau spectateur," *Cahiers du cinéma*, no. 177 (April 1966): 66–67, 66. The classic essay is Jean-Louis Baudry, "Ideological Effects of the Basic Cinematographic Apparatus," trans. Alan Williams, *Film Quarterly* 28, no. 2 (Winter 1974–75): 39–47.

41. One issue devoted to television has this to say about its relationship to cinema: "Les deux appareils (cinéma et TV) se soutiennent et s'entretiennent, reproduisant l'un pour l'autre les conditions idéologiques de leur fonctionnement reconduisant les systèmes de reconnaissance idéologique qui les programment et qu'en retour ils confirment." (The two apparatuses [cinema and TV] support and maintain each other, reproducing for each other the ideological conditions of their operation, renewing the systems of ideological recognition that program them and that they in turn confirm.) Groupe Lou Sin d'intervention idéologique, "À armes égales: Analyse d'une émission télévisée," *Cahiers du cinéma*, nos. 236–37 (March–April 1972): 4–29, 4.

42. Comolli, "Notes sur le nouveau spectateur," 66.

43. Francesco Casetti, *The Lumière Galaxy: Seven Key Words for the Cinema to Come* (New York: Columbia University Press, 2015), 12–13.

44. See, e.g., James Steichen, "HD Opera: A Love/Hate Story," *Opera Quarterly* 27, no. 4 (2012): 443–59; Brianna Wells, "'Secret Mechanism': *Les contes d'Hoffmann* and the Intermedial Uncanny in the Metropolitan Opera's Live in HD Series," *19th-Century Music* 36, no. 2 (Fall 2012): 191–203; David Trippett, "Facing Digital Realities: Where Media Do Not Mix," *Cambridge Opera Journal* 26, no. 1 (2014): 41–64; Bernhard Kuhn, "Live at the Cinema: The Metropolitan Opera's

Cinecast of *La traviata*," in *Verdi on Screen*, ed. Delphine Vincent (Lausanne: L'age d'homme, 2016), 210–25; Attard and Morris, eds., "Opera at the Multiplex"; and Attard, *Opera Cinema*.

45. For a summary of attendance statistics of a range of cinecast series, see Susan Bennett, "Shakespeare's New Marketplace: The Places of Event Cinema," in *Shakespeare and the "Live" Theatre Broadcast Experience*, ed. Pascale Aebischer, Susanne Greenhalgh, and Laurie Osborne (London: Bloomsbury, 2018), 41–58.

46. See Barker, *Live to Your Local Cinema*; Aebischer, Greenhalgh, and Osborne, eds., *Shakespeare and the "Live" Theatre Broadcast Experience*; and Pascale Aebischer, *Shakespeare, Spectatorship and the Technologies of Performance* (Cambridge: Cambridge University Press, 2020).

47. Steven Connor, "Sounding Out Film," in *The Oxford Handbook of New Audiovisual Aesthetics*, ed. John Richardson, Claudia Gorbman, and Carol Vernallis (Oxford: Oxford University Press, 2013), 107–24, 120.

48. Connor, "Sounding Out Film," 112.

49. Lloyd Schwartz, "Opera on Television," *The Atlantic*, January 1983, 84–90, 86.

50. "Home Video Goes Hi-Fi and Auto-Reverse," *New Scientist*, February 17, 1983, 445.

51. Emanuele Senici, "'In the Score': Music and Media in the Discourse of Operatic *Mise-en-Scène*," *Opera Quarterly* 35, no. 3 (Summer 2019): 207–23.

52. Samuel Chotzinoff, "Opera on Radio," in *Music in Radio Broadcasting*, ed. Gilbert Chase (New York: McGraw-Hill, 1946), 1–17, 7. Chotzinoff would go on to produce opera for NBC television but in studio-based form. He remained a critic of grand opera as practiced by companies like the Metropolitan Opera. For more on Chotzinoff, see Ward-Griffin, "As Seen on TV."

53. Andrew Porter, Review of *Das Rheingold*, *Gramophone* 36, no. 430 (March 1959): 472–73, 472.

54. Herbert Graf, "Opera in Television," in *Music in Radio Broadcasting*, ed. Gilbert Chase (New York: McGraw-Hill, 1946), 138–45, 138, 140. For more on this debate, see Shawn VanCour, "Spectacular Sound: Classical Music Programming and the Problem of 'Visual Interest' in Early US Television," in Baade and Deaville, eds., *Music and the Broadcast Experience*, 91–108.

CHAPTER ONE

1. Bayreuther Festspiele, "*Tannhäuser* im Roadmovie," August 14, 2019, https://youtu.be/CI2GMG3teqk.

2. Lyn Gardner, "Waves Sets a High-Water Mark for Multimedia Theater," *The Guardian*, December 4, 2006, https://www.theguardian.com/stage/theatreblog/2006/dec/04/wavessetsahighwatermarkfo.

3. Diedrich Diederichsen, "Theater ist kein Medium—aber was bewirkt es, wenn der Mann mit der Videokamera auf der Bühne arbeitet?," *Dramaturg: Zeitschrift der Dramaturgischen Gesellschaft* 1 (2004): 3–7, 3.

4. Peter Goddard, "A Reaction to Opera's Video Projection Fetish," *Toronto*

Star, February 14, 2008, https://www.thestar.com/discard/2008/02/14/a_reaction
_to_operas_video_projection_fetish.html.

5. Royal Opera House, News, https://www.roh.org.uk/news/debate-what-do
-you-think-of-the-use-of-video-projections-in-opera-and-ballet (accessed May 4,
2020; link no longer active).

6. This embrace is of course part of a set of contested possibilities, not an
inevitable tide, no matter how alarmed some critics might be. Most recent opera
production, innovative or conventional, features no projected video.

7. Greg Giesekam, *Staging the Screen: The Use of Film and Video in Theatre* (London: Palgrave Macmillan, 2007), 8.

8. Havelková, *Opera as Hypermedium*, 5–9. Havelková's focus is on case studies (Andriessen/Greenaway, Glass/Wilson) that are the operatic equivalent of
what Lehmann has termed *postdramatic* theater. See Hans-Thies Lehmann, *Postdramatic Theatre*, trans. Karen Jürs-Munby (London: Routledge, 2006). But she
nevertheless suggests that these examples may raise issues applicable to opera
more widely. See esp. Havelková, *Opera as Hypermedium*, 2–3.

9. David J. Levin, *Unsettling Opera: Staging Mozart, Verdi, Wagner, and Zemlinsky*
(Chicago: University of Chicago Press, 2007), 165.

10. Francesco Casetti, "Primal Screens," in *Screen Genealogies: From Optical Device to Environmental Medium*, ed. Craig Buckley, Rüdiger Campe, and Francesco
Casetti (Amsterdam: Amsterdam University Press, 2019), 27–50, 46.

11. Of course, productions that incorporate video need not be remediated.
There is much to be said about these practices as witnessed in the opera house
alone, something I have considered elsewhere. For a discussion of the Viola/
Sellars *Tristan und Isolde*, arguably the mother ship of video/live performance
practices in opera but a production never recorded for release on video, see my
"Wagnervideo," *Opera Quarterly* 26, no. 4 (Summer 2011): 235–55. See also Lawrence Kramer, "'The Threshold of the Visible World': Wagner, Bill Viola, and
Tristan," in Gilman and Joe, eds., *Wagner and Cinema*, 381–407. Another noteworthy combination of live performance and film, Philip Glass's adaptation of
Cocteau's *La belle et la bête* (1994), has also never been officially recorded for
video. For more on the work, see Jeongwon Joe, "The Cinematic Body in the Operatic Theater: Philip Glass's *La belle et la bête*," in Joe and Theresa, eds., *Between
Opera and Cinema*, 59–74.

12. Marvin Carlson, "Has Video Killed the Theater Star? Some German Responses," *Contemporary Theatre Review* 18, no. 1 (2008): 20–29, 22. Carlson characterizes the most innovative uses of video in contemporary German theater in
terms "of a codependence of the live and the mediatized, interpenetrating each
other in an ongoing feedback." Ibid., 29. See also Marvin Carlson, "Video and
Stage Perspectives: Some European Perspectives," *Modern Drama* 46, no. 4 (Winter 2003): 614–28.

13. Birgit E. Wiens, "Introduction," in *Contemporary Scenography: Practices
and Aesthetics in German Theater, Arts and Design*, ed. Birgit E. Wiens (London:
Methuen, 2019), 1–30, 11.

14. Andreas Englhart, *Das Theater der Gegenwart* (Berlin: C. H. Beck, 2013), 86.

15. Jan Speckenbach, "Der Einbruch der Fernsehntechnologie," in *Einbruch*

der Realität: Politik und Verbrechen, ed. Carl Hegemann (Berlin: Alexander Verlag/ Volksbühne am Rosa-Luxemburg-Platz, 2002), 80–84 (quote 82).

16. Peter Boenisch, "Frank Castorf and the Berlin Volksbühne, *The Humiliated and Insulted* (2001)," in *Mapping Intermediality in Performance*, ed. Sarah Bay-Cheng, Chiel Kattenbelt, Andy Lavender, and Robin Nelson (Amsterdam: Amsterdam University Press, 2010), 198–203, 203.

17. Moritz von Uslar, "99 Fragen an Frank Castorf," *Die Zeit*, July 11, 2013, https://www.zeit.de/2013/29/99-fragen-frank-castorf.

18. Martin Kettle, review of *Die Walküre*, Bayreuth Festival, *The Guardian*, July 28, 2013, https://www.theguardian.com/music/2013/jul/28/das-rheingold -die-walkure-review.

19. Anthony Tommasini, "The Real Rhinemaidens of Route 66," *New York Times*, July 28, 2013, https://www.nytimes.com/2013/07/29/arts/music/wagners -ring-opens-at-bayreuth-with-reality-cam-touch.html.

20. Daniel Ender, "Die Ölkrise des multimedialen Theaters," *Der Standard*, July 29, 2013, https://www.derstandard.at/story/1373513958167/die-oelkrise-des -multimedialen-theaters.

21. Werner Theurich, "Wie man aus Trash Gold macht," *Der Spiegel*, July 26, 2013, https://www.spiegel.de/kultur/gesellschaft/bayreuther-festspiele-premiere -rheingold-castorf-a-913318.html.

22. Peter Hagmann, "Auf der Spur des Öls," *Neue Zürcher Zeitung*, July 29, 2013, https://www.nzz.ch/feuilleton/auf-der-spur-des-oels-1.18124338.

23. Peter Hagmann, "Dekonstruiert und virtuos sinnlich," *Neue Zürcher Zeitung*, August 1, 2013, https://www.nzz.ch/feuilleton/buehne/dekonstruiert-und -virtuos-sinnlich-1.18126272. For more on the taboo quality of the backstage, see Nicolò Palazzetti, "Backstage Live: Opera and the Obscene in the Visual Age," in "Re-Envisaging Music: Listening in the Visual Age," ed. Antonio Cascelli and Christopher Morris, special issue, *Chigiana: Journal of Musicological Studies*, ser. 3, 3 (2021): 43–60.

24. Mark Berry, "Opera and the Politics of Postdramatic Theatre: Frank Castorf's Bayreuth *Ring*," *Cambridge Opera Journal* 33, nos. 1–2 (March 2021): 24–49, 34.

25. Video director, Myriam Hoyer; set designer, Aleksandar Denić; lighting, Rainer Casper; videography, Andreas Deinert and Jens Crull. All four evenings were telecast live in Germany and Austria; elsewhere only *Götterdämmerung* was telecast live. See https://mebucom.de/produktion/einzigartiges-erlebnis-11072 .html. In 2020 Deutsche Grammophon acquired the streaming rights to the production for its Stage+ platform.

26. Berry, "Opera and the Politics of Postdramatic Theatre," 32.

27. Dirk Buhrmann, "Interview: Myriam Hoyer," July 4, 2016, https://www.sky .at/musik-kultur/live-von-den-bayreuther-festspielen/interview-myriam-hoyer -104263 (accessed May 4, 2022; link no longer active). Hoyer also cites the cooperation with Castorf's production team on access to direct feeds of the onstage video projection. I will further explore these feeds below.

28. Thomas Oberender interprets *lived cubism* as the juxtaposition of scenic elements and screens to generate irreconcilable perspectives. Thomas Oberender,

"Das Drama des Sehens: Live-Video auf der Bühne oder die Politik des Blicks," *Dramaturg* 1 (2004): 15–21, 19–20. On the cubist effect of the layered and overlapping windows on a computer screen, see Anne Friedberg, *The Virtual Window: From Alberti to Microsoft* (Cambridge, MA: MIT Press, 2009), 3.

29. Buhrmann, "Interview: Myriam Hoyer."

30. Oberender, "Das Drama des Sehens," 15–21.

31. Jacques Derrida, *The Truth in Painting*, trans. Geoffrey Bennington and Ian McLeod (Chicago: University of Chicago Press, 1987).

32. For Derrida, the parergon serves as a metaphor for reflection on theory and philosophy. As Friedberg points out, however, there is value in redirecting Derrida's observations back to what appear to be more literal applications, not least because doing so facilitates reflection on the continual adaptation of the language of frames to new media. Friedberg, *The Virtual Window*, 13–15.

33. Later, during the "Entry of the Guests," prerecorded footage will feature a parallel narrative that takes place not in the past but in an imaginary present: in a reverse metanarrative, "Venus" attempts to disrupt the performance by breaking into the Festspielhaus.

34. That the backstage shot pans slowly adds another layer of signification, positioning the music almost like a soundtrack to a cinematic/televisual exploration of an interior.

35. Alain Perroux, "Entretien avec Christophe Honoré, metteur en scène," in the program booklet accompanying the January 2020 Opéra de Lyon performance of *Tosca*, n.p. "Here I have the opportunity," Honoré is quoted as saying, "to use the video as a counterpoint to what is happening on stage and to provide an additional perspective. Video allows me to converse with the past through the archives." Ibid., n.p.

36. I will have more to say in the next chapter about sound in this sequence.

37. Although long available for streaming on demand, the video has never been emended to correct the disparity. Like a blooper clip, it now preserves a technical failure for the archive.

38. Slavoj Žižek, *The Abyss of Freedom* (Ann Arbor: University of Michigan Press, 1997), 24. Žižek elsewhere considers camerawork in these terms, likening the close-up in David Lynch's films, as a penetration beneath the surface of reality, to the uncanny and repulsive substance of the Real. Slavoj Žižek, "David Lynch; or, The Feminine Depression," in *The Metastases of Enjoyment: Six Essays on Women and Causality* (London: Verso, 1994), 113–36, 114. In his reading of the Viola/Sellers *Tristan und Isolde*, Kramer similarly relates the question of the "over-proximity" of images to the Lacanian Real. For Kramer, however, part of what defines the production is its moves to resist this "debasement" of desire. Kramer, "The Threshold of the Visible World," 396.

39. Slavoj Žižek, *The Parallax View* (Cambridge, MA: MIT Press, 2006), 17.

40. Jesse Simon, "Countdown to Ecstasy," Mundoclasico.com, February 23, 2018, https://www.mundoclasico.com/articulo/30583/Countdown-to-Ecstasy.

41. Not all scrims, of course, double as projection screens for video. The blurring effect can also be seen in telecasts of productions in which the scrim serves more broadly as a means of diffusing light. See, e.g., Tcherniakov's *Dialogues des*

Carmélites (Munich, 2010; video director, Andy Sommer) and Romeo Castellucci's *Die Zauberflöte* (Brussels, 2018; video director, Myriam Hoyer). In Heiner Müller's *Tristan und Isolde* (Bayreuth, 1995; video director, Horant H. Hohlfeld), a scrim hosts projections of abstract light shapes, and, in Castellucci's *Moses und Aron* (Paris, 2016; video director, François-René Martin), text is projected onto a scrim.

42. For more on the Wagner curtain, see Gundula Kreuzer, *Curtain, Gong, Steam: Wagnerian Technologies of Nineteenth-Century Opera* (Berkeley and Los Angeles: University of California Press, 2018), 91–97. The performance of the orchestral preludes to *Die Walküre* and *Siegfried* in front of a close curtain introduces some slight differences in the sequence of shots. Following familiar practice for opera telecasts, Hoyer's production begins to zoom in on the stage but quickly cuts to a fixed-camera shot of the conductor, Marek Janowski, where it will remain for the duration of the prelude. As the prelude ends, the establishing zoom resumes as though it had merely been interrupted by the prelude.

43. The Bayreuth stage, Kreuzer writes, "implied an invisible scrim or screen at the front of the stage through which the production was viewed and to which its multiple material elements adhered." Kreuzer, *Curtain, Gong, Steam*, 259.

44. It is an effect reminiscent of Béziat's video production of the Corsetti/Sorin *La pietra del paragone* (2007), which juxtaposed projected blue-screen effects with live action. For more, see Senici, "Porn Style?"

45. The production, Tcherniakov's staging of *Der Freischütz* at the Bayerische Staatsoper (2021), splits the proscenium in the same manner as Kratzer's *Tannhäuser*. Joshua Barone, "When Opera Livestreams Became Live Performances," *New York Times*, October 28, 2021, https://www.nytimes.com/2021/09/03/arts/music/opera-livestreams.html.

46. Boenisch, "Frank Castorf and the Berlin Volksbühne," 203. As Boenisch points out, Speckenbach cites Bazin's concept of the *cache*, that which the camera conceals. Ibid.

47. Davis, *The Grammar of Television Production*, 9. Reporting on her observation of the production process in a cinecast for the Royal Shakespeare Company, Lindsay Brandon Hunter notes that the multicamera director Robin Lough recommended the Davis book to students. Lindsay Brandon Hunter, *Playing Real: Mimesis, Media, and Mischief* (Evanston, IL: Northwestern University Press, 2021), 9.

48. Havelková, *Opera as Hypermedium*, 70–71.

49. Morris, "Digital Diva," 109. The production is *Tristan und Isolde* (stage director, Olivier Py; video director, Andy Sommer), Bel Air Classiques, 2005.

CHAPTER TWO

1. Cavell, "The Fact of Television," 89. Cavell defines this "fact" of television as the recognition, in the face of scholarly neglect, of its role in "contemporary life" when it might be taken for granted and remain concealed by its quotidian function. This might have been true when the essay was published in 1982, but by the turn of the millennium the rise of television studies—and particularly the sociology of television—had done much to address the lacuna.

NOTES TO PAGES 57–60 | 205

2. Cavell, "The Fact of Television," 89.

3. Wagner Society of New York, "Opera in HD," pt. 1.

4. Cavell, "The Fact of Television," 86.

5. Heidi Waleson, "'Written on Skin' Review," *Wall Street Journal*, August 12, 2015, https://www.wsj.com/articles/written-on-skin-review-1439417190; Claire Seymour, "*Written on Skin*: Royal Opera House," *Opera Today*, January 15, 2017, http://www.operatoday.com/content/2017/01/written_on_skin.php; Robert Hugill, "Written on Skin at Covent Garden," Planethugill.com, March 17, 2013, https://www.planethugill.com/2013/03/written-on-skin-at-covent-garden.html; Owen Davies, "Written on Skin," Plays to See: International Theatre Reviews, January 14, 2017, https://playstosee.com/written-on-skin.

6. This was not the first time a Mitchell production had divided the stage into separate fictional spaces and times, although these spaces had typically included video projections, something absent from *Written on Skin*. Examples include *The Waves* (2006), *Wunschkonzert* (2008), *After Dido* (2009), and *Kristin, nach Fräulein Julie* (2011).

7. Andrew Clements, "Written on Skin—review," *The Guardian*, July 8, 2012, https://www.theguardian.com/music/2012/jul/08/written-on-skin-review.

8. Lehmann, *Postdramatic Theatre*, 87–88.

9. Boenisch, e.g., contrasts Castorf's adaptation of Dostoevsky's *The Idiot* (2006) with Mitchell's live cinema production . . . *some trace of her* (2008), based on the same novel. While Castorf's parallax theater had, in Boenisch's view, radically decentered spectatorial perspective in postdramatic fashion, the spectators in Mitchell's production "were ultimately confirmed in their traditional position watching a perfectly timed and choreographed theatrical spectacle." Peter M. Boenisch, "Towards a Theatre of Encounter and Experience: Reflexive Dramaturgies and Classic Texts," *Contemporary Theatre Review* 20, no. 2 (2010): 162–72, 167. On contested accounts of Mitchell's work vis-à-vis the notion of postdramatic theater, see also Benjamin Fowler, *Katie Mitchell: Beautiful Illogical Acts* (New York: Routledge, 2020), 136–41. Lehmann does, however, consider the critical potential of what he calls the *hypernaturalistic* character of scenes modeled on film and television, which effect a kind of "derealization" when presented on the theatrical stage. Lehmann, *Postdramatic Theatre*, 116–18.

10. See, e.g., *La damnation de Faust* (director, Lepage, Metropolitan Opera, 2008), *Wozzeck* (director, Tcherniakov, Bolshoi Theater, 2010), *Cavalleria rusticana/Pagliacci* (director, Stöltzl, Salzburg Festival, 2015), *Tristan und Isolde* (director, Trelinski, 2016), *Rodelinda* (director, Jones, English National Opera, 2017), and *Innocence* (director, Simon Stone, Aix-en-Provence, 2021).

11. Michael Billington and Tim Ashley, "After Dido," *The Guardian*, April 17, 2009, https://www.theguardian.com/stage/2009/apr/17/theatre-review-after-dido -young-vic. On *Lucia di Lammermoor*, see, e.g., Fiona Maddocks: "Attention was drawn constantly to another part of the stage, tearing us from the singer, usually poor Castronovo, who has a powerful, alluring voice but had to battle with compulsive distractions." Fiona Maddocks, "Lucia di Lammermoor Review— Flawed but Full of Provocative Thought," *The Observer*, April 10, 2016, https://www .theguardian.com/music/2016/apr/10/lucia-di-lammermoor-review-royal-opera

-katie-mitchell-diana-damrau. "While the main action is on one side," wrote Michael Tanner, "plenty of distracting business is being executed on the other, much of it the invention of Mitchell." Michael Tanner, "Tame and Drowning in Detail: Royal Opera's *Lucia di Lammermoor* Reviewed," *The Spectator*, April 16, 2016, https://www.spectator.com.au/2016/04/tame-and-drowning-in-detail-royal -operas-lucia-di-lammermoor-reviewed.

12. Ruth Ellis Haworth, "The Met's HD Transmission Fails Tristan und Isolde," Yappa Ding, March 24, 2008, http://yappadingding.blogspot.com/2008/ 03/mets-hd-transmission-fails-tristan-und.html. For a follow-up blog on Willis Sweete's direction of the transmission of *La damnation de Faust*, see "Is Barbara Willis Sweete Destroying the Met HD Program?," Yappa Ding, January 18, 2009, http://yappadingding.blogspot.com/2009/01/is-barbara-willis-sweete-destroying -met.html; and "One Giant Leap for Opera Video," http://therehearsalstudio .blogspot.com/2008/03/one-giant-leap-for-opera-video.html. For more on these complaints, see Senici, "Porn Style"; and Esse, "Don't Look Now."

13. For more on the question of using video to document theatrical performance, see my "Digital Diva."

14. Lehmann credits Robert Wilson for demonstrating the potential of a theater modeled on an imagistic, cinematic conception of the stage. See Lehmann, *Postdramatic Theatre*, 77–81, 114. Revisiting this claim, Arman Schwartz considers the implications for opera studies of what he argues is the antitheatrical impetus of these cinematic aspirations. Arman Schwartz, "Opera and Objecthood: Sedimentation, Spectatorship, and *Einstein on the Beach*," *Opera Quarterly* 35, nos. 1–2 (Winter–Spring 2019): 40–62.

15. Paul Taylor, "The Waves, National Theatre Cottesloe, London," November 20, 2006, https://www.independent.co.uk/arts-entertainment/theatre-dance/ reviews/the-waves-national-theatre-cottesloe-london-424996.html.

16. "Katie Mitchell on Lucia di Lammermoor," Royal Opera House, March 21, 2016, https://youtu.be/O7vpkZHoXRM.

17. Noting how the Williams production capitalizes on the cinematic qualities of the stage production and of the opera itself, Carolyn Abbate and Roger Parker wonder if "DVD [. . .] becomes the work's truest, best home." Carolyn Abbate and Roger Parker, *A History of Opera: The Last Four Hundred Years* (New York: Penguin Group, 2015), 1072.

18. Richard Will is no doubt right when he observes that the gap between live and postproduction editing has gradually narrowed so that the former now features the "kinetic manner" of the latter. Here, however, the gap remains sizable. I will return to the question of kineticism in chapter 5. Will, "Zooming in, Gazing Back," 36.

19. Paul Théberge, Kyle Devine, and Tom Everrett, "Introduction: Living Stereo," in *Living Stereo: Histories and Cultures of Multichannel Sound*, ed. Paul Théberge, Kyle Devine, and Tom Everrett (London: Bloomsbury, 2015), 1–34, 5–6.

20. William Moylan, *The Art of Recording* (New York: Springer, 1992). The stage metaphor is not without competitors. Allan Moore, e.g., proposes the term *sound box* as a means of conceiving the "virtual textural space" encountered by the listener in recordings of popular music. Allan F. Moore, *Rock: The Primary Text* (Aldershot: Ashgate, 2001), 121.

NOTES TO PAGES 68–74 | 207

21. Théberge, Devine, and Everrett, "Introduction: Living Stereo," 6. The authors here draw on Rick Altman's entreaty to guard against a naive mimeticism and regard the object of representation in media technology in more hermetic terms: not as the real but as existing forms of representation. Rick Altman, "Sound Space," in Altman, ed., *Sound Theory, Sound Practice*, 46–64, 46.

22. Haigh et al. include the possibility of registering shifts in location within the sonic stage as singers move about, but they stress the need to avoid what they call "excessive lateral image movement." Rather, the emphasis is placed on the "coherency of image" generated by the stereo pairs of microphones. Caroline Haigh, John Dunkerley, and Mark Rogers, *Classical Recording: A Practical Guide in the Decca Tradition* (London: Routledge, 2020), 369–73.

23. Moylan, *The Art of Recording*, 50–51.

24. Moylan, *The Art of Recording*, 49.

25. Haigh, Dunkerley, and Rogers, *Classical Recording*, 17.

26. Haigh, Dunkerley, and Rogers, 376–77.

27. Haigh, Dunkerley, and Rogers, 376.

28. Haigh, Dunkerley, and Rogers, 368, 351.

29. Haigh, Dunkerley, and Rogers, 370.

30. For more on the exit door effect, see Mark Kerins, *Beyond Dolby (Stereo): Cinema in the Digital Sound Age* (Bloomington: Indiana University Press, 2011), 72.

31. Emma Dillon, "Vocal Philologies: *Written on Skin* and the Troubadours," *Opera Quarterly* 33, nos. 3–4 (Summer–Autumn 2017): 207–48.

32. Thomas Y. Levin, "Rhetoric of the Temporal Index: Surveillant Narration and the Cinema of 'Real Time,'" in *CTRL [SPACE]: Rhetorics of Surveillance from Bentham to Big Brother*, ed. Thomas Y. Levin (Cambridge, MA: MIT Press, 2002), 578–93, 592.

33. Katie Mitchell, "Mit der Wucht des Thrillers gegen überkommene Bilder," in the program booklet accompanying the February 2020 Bayerische performance of *Judith*, 30–33, 32.

34. Rüdiger Sturm, "Thriller," *Crescendo*, February 14, 2020, https://crescendo .de/katie-mitchell-bayerische-staatsoper. Writing for *Opera Today*, Andrew Moravcsik notes, disapprovingly, the "made-for-TV" style of Gee's film. Andrew Moravcsik, "*Bluebeard's Castle*, Munich," *Opera Today*, March 7, 2020, http://www .operatoday.com/content/2020/03/bluebeards_cast.php. That the producers are unapologetic about the televisual model is signaled by the front cover of the program booklet accompanying the February 2020 Bayerische performance of *Judith*, which features no text and one image, a still from the UK television series *Prime Suspect* (1991–2006).

35. In a biographical-historical sense, the *Concerto for Orchestra* film becomes a form of prequel. As Wolfgang Rathert notes, the two works effectively bookend Bartók's career, the *Concerto* even quoting the "lake of tears" gesture from the opera. Wolfgang Rathert, "Die verborgenen Tränen des Béla Bartók," in the program booklet accompanying the February 2020 Bayerische performance of *Judith*, 50–61, 58.

36. One critic, echoing the online community of film continuity nerds, complained that some of the details of staging and film, such as the exact model of

the car, were mismatched. Wolf-Dieter Peter, "Filmnahe Verbrecherjagd—Bartóks 'Blaubart' und 'Konzert für Orchester' im Münchner Nationaltheater," February 2, 2020, https://www.nmz.de/online/filmnahe-verbrecherjagd-Bartóks-blaubart-und -konzert-fuer-orchester-im-muenchner-nationalthea.

37. Simon Stone, another director invested in naturalistic stage design and compartments in grids, takes this scrolling a step further in the premiere production of Saariaho's *Innocence* (Aix-en-Provence, 2021). Like the design for *Written on Skin*, its two stories juxtapose narratively noncontiguous spaces and time, but here the grid becomes a three-dimensional edifice in almost constant rotation.

38. Norman Schwarze, "Tatort München: Bayerische Staatsoper inszeniert mit *Judith* einen packenden Thriller," *Bachtrack*, February 3, 2020, https:// bachtrack.com/kritik-Bartók-judith-herzog-blaubarts-burg-mitchell-lyniv -stemme-lundgren-bayerische-staatsoper-februar-2020; Alexander Pschera, "Der Tod des alten, weißen Mannes," *Die Tagespost*, February 19, 2020, https://www .die-tagespost.de/gesellschaft/kultur/Der-Tod-des-alten-weissen-Mannes;art4881 ,205664.

39. Michel Foucault, *Discipline and Punish: The Birth of the Prison*, trans. Alan Sheridan (New York: Vintage, 1995), 173.

40. Casetti, *The Lumière Galaxy*, 163.

41. Cavell "The Fact of Television," 89.

42. Marcus Sanchez Svensson, Christian Heath, and Paul Luff, "Monitoring Practice: Event Detection and System Design," in *Intelligent Distributed Video Surveillance Systems*, ed. Sergio Velastin and Paolo Remagnino (London: Institution of Engineering and Technology, 2006), 31–54, 36.

43. Haigh, Dunkerley, and Rogers, *Classical Recording*, 372.

44. Anthony Tommasini, "Wearing a Wire at the Opera, Secretly, of Course," *New York Times*, June 30, 2013, https://www.nytimes.com/2013/06/30/arts/music/ wearing-a-wire-at-the-opera-secretly-of-course.html.

45. Wagner Society of New York, "Opera in HD: A Panel Discussion," pt. 2, March 27, 2012, https://youtu.be/I91pp-M6VTg.

46. Haigh, Dunkerley, and Rogers, *Classical Recording*, 295.

47. Tommasini, "Wearing a Wire at the Opera."

48. Jonathan Allen, "Mixing and Broadcasting from the Royal Opera House," *Sound on Sound*, February 2017, https://www.soundonsound.com/techniques/ immersive-audio-opera.

49. Haigh, Dunkerley, and Rogers, *Classical Recording*, 372.

50. Megan Steigerwald Ille, "The Operatic Ear: Mediating Aurality," *Sound Stage Screen* 1, no. 1 (Spring 2021): 119–43, 138–39.

51. This is not to say, of course, that these practices are immutable. Steigerwald Ille is right to stress the reciprocality of operatic production and listening. Steigerwald Ille, "The Operatic Ear: Mediating Aurality," 138. Part of the anxiety associated with microphones may be the perceived threat that the very model of operatic aurality is under threat.

52. For more on *The Conversation* and cinematic cinema's engagement with audio surveillance, see Miguel Mera, "Listening-Feeling-Becoming: Cinema Sur-

NOTES TO PAGES 81–91 | 209

veillance," in *The Oxford Handbook of Cinematic Listening*, ed. Carlo Cenciarelli (New York: Oxford University Press, 2021), 407–26.

53. Tommasini, "Wearing a Wire at the Opera."

54. Senici, "Porn Style," 73. To illustrate his point, Senici cites a much less adventurous video production of the same staging.

55. Opera North, *The Ring Cycle*, 2016, https://youtube.com/playlist?list =PLQg96imuuOC8owUuCZiSA-Ql9SdpQn6hv.

56. Kay Armatage, "Barbara Willis Sweete: Queen of HD Transmissions," in *Doing Women's Film History: Reframing Cinemas, Past and Future*, ed. Christine Gledhill and Julia Knight (Urbana: University of Illinois Press, 2015), 242–55, 248, 247.

57. Lev Manovich, *The Language of New Media* (Cambridge, MA: MIT Press, 2002), 269–73.

58. As Malte Hagener argues, the role of the split screen in public consciousness has been radically transformed by the global COVID-19 pandemic, which confronted us all with the audiovisual economy of virtual-meeting software. Malte Hagener, "Divided, Together, Apart: How Split Screen Became Our Everyday Reality," in *Pandemic Media: Preliminary Notes toward an Inventory*, ed. Philipp Dominik Keidl, Laliv Melamed, Vinzenz Hediger, and Antonio Somaini (Lüneberg: Meson, 2020), 33–40. I will have more to say about this in the book's conclusion.

59. Casetti, *The Lumière Galaxy*, 150–63, 168 (quote).

60. Casetti, *The Lumière Galaxy*, 174, 206.

61. "'Opera Cinema, the Modern *Gesamtkunstwerk?*,'" 352.

62. Wagner Society of New York, "Opera in HD," pt. 2.

63. Halvorson quoted in Mitch Jacobsen, *Mastering Multi-Camera Techniques: From Pre-production to Editing and Deliverables* (Burlington, VA: Foca, 2010), 254.

64. Carlo Cenciarelli, "At the Margins of the Televisual: Picture Frames, Loops and 'Cinematics' in the Paratexts of Opera Videos," *Cambridge Opera Journal* 25 (2013): 203–23, 223.

65. There is a parallel here, too, with paratexts in television, specifically the title sequences of television drama and comedy. If split screens have not typically featured in the main body of that programming, it has often formed a part of the (sometimes elaborate) introductory credits.

66. Mitchell quoted in Mario Frendo, "Opera's Second Life: Katie Mitchell's Contributions to Contemporary Opera-Making," *Contemporary Theatre Review* 30, no. 2 (2020): 211–25, 221.

67. Senici, "'In the Score.'"

68. Cavell, "The Fact of Television," 90.

CHAPTER THREE

1. Mary Ann Doane, "An Ontology of Everyday Distraction: The Freeway, the 193 Mall, and Television," in *Logics of Television: Essays in Cultural Criticism*, ed. Patricia Mellencamp (Bloomington: Indiana University Press, 1990), 193–221, 223.

2. Jane Feuer famously identified television's construction of liveness as rooted in ideology. Jane Feuer, "The Concept of Live Television: Ontology as Ideol-

ogy," in *Regarding Television: Critical Approaches—an Anthology*, ed. E. Ann Kaplan (Bethesda, MD: University Publications of America, 1983), 12–22.

3. Jacques Derrida and Bernard Stiegler, *Echographies of Television: Filmed Interviews*, trans. Jennifer Bajorek (Cambridge: Polity, 2002), 89. Speculating on the potential for video remediation to restore to art music a sense of event once the privilege of the concert hall, Lawrence Kramer invokes Derrida's characterization of the event as a singularity paradoxically poised between possibility and impossibility. Kramer, however, wants to associate this understanding of event with exceptional cases, and I hesitate to invoke this sense of singularity in the context of a well-established series, one that has had more than its share of banal moments. Lawrence Kramer, "Classical Music for the Postmodern Condition," in Richardson, Gorbman, and Vernallis, eds., *The Oxford Handbook of New Audiovisual Aesthetics*, 39–52, 51.

4. Metropolitan Opera, "The Metropolitan Opera Season, 2011–2012: At Any Moment, a Great Moment," September 8, 2011, https://youtu.be/fnAfc1_yAZo.

5. Peter Galison, *Einstein's Clocks, Poincaré's Maps: Empires of Time* (New York: Norton, 2004), 480.

6. Peter Galison, *Einstein's Clocks, Poincaré's Maps: Empires of Time* (New York: Norton, 2004), 480, 53. The debate between Bergson and Einstein, including a public exchange in 1922, pitted not just individual models of time but whole modes of inquiry against one another. For Bergson, science was inadequate to consider the metaphysics of time, while Einstein dismissed the foundation of Bergson's account with the observation: "The time of the philosophers does not exist." Henri Bergson, "Discussion avec Einstein," in *Mélanges*, ed. André Robinet (Paris: Presses universitaires de France, 1972), 1340–47, 1346.

7. In an article calling for greater British investment in cable and wireless communication, the telegraph engineer and historian Charles Bright highlights "the enormous value attached to any synchronous, unified system of intercommunication betwixt all branches of the Empire." Charles Bright, "The Empire's Telegraph and Trade," *Fortnightly Review*, March 1923, 457–74, 460.

8. Writing on the impact of the BBC's overseas broadcasting, Sir Evelyn Wrench declared: "Reading letters from overseas listeners leaves the impression that if the chief object of Empire Broadcasting, as at present conducted, is to link up lonely dwellers in remote parts of the Empire, it has succeeded." Evelyn Wrench, "A Vision of Empire Broadcasting," *World-Radio*, December 22, 1933, 815.

9. "Melba Sings by Wireless," *Daily Mail*, June 16, 1920.

10. Hugo Gernsback, "Grand Opera by Wireless," *Radio Amateur News* 1, no. 3 (September 1919): 106. On August 27, 1920, opera formed the program of the first radio broadcast in Argentina, a complete performance of *Parsifal* transmitted live from the roof of the Teatro Coliseo (though picked up only in Buenos Aires). The BBC's first outside broadcast was a British National Opera Company production of *The Magic Flute* from the Royal Opera House in January 1923.

11. As Simon Potter observes of British broadcasting, this reach could be mobilized to contrasting ends. If, from the late 1930s, the BBC was directly funded as an agent of "cultural diplomacy," its Empire Service tasked with promoting British interests overseas and cementing imperial bonds, the broadcaster had

already, from its formative years in the 1920s, assumed this burden without funding. "The BBC," Potter contends, "voluntarily participated in the overseas projection of Britishness as part of its public-service remit, in order to link the British nation at home with its diasporic branches outside the home islands." Simon Potter, *Broadcasting Empire: The BBC and the British World, 1922–1970* (New York: Oxford University Press, 2012), 7.

12. "Melba—Queen of Song," *Daily Mail*, June 15, 1920, 6. For more on this broadcast, see Kate Guthrie, "Marconi's Phoney Future," *Cambridge Opera Journal* 28, no. 2 (2016): 247–49.

13. For an interview with Gelb on the genesis of the initiative, see Peter Conrad, "Opera from New York in Your Home Town? Easy. Just Go to the Pictures," *The Observer*, April 22, 2007, https://www.theguardian.com/music/2007/apr/22/classicalmusicandopera.features1.

14. James Steichen, "The Metropolitan Opera Goes Public: Peter Gelb and the Institutional Dramaturgy of the Met: Live in HD," *Music and the Moving Image* 2, no. 2 (2009): 24–30, 28.

15. Steichen, "HD Opera," 446.

16. Michael Cooper, "The Met Opera's Credit Outlook Darkens After Modest Deficits," *New York Times*, November 20, 2019, https://www.nytimes.com/2019/11/20/arts/music/metropolitan-opera.html.

17. "10,000,000 Hear Opera over the Radio," *New York Times*, January 22, 1927, 1. No stranger to pioneering events in wireless opera, Chicago had hosted experimental broadcasts in 1919 (see pp. 93–94) and 1921. For more on these experiments, see Timothy D. Taylor, "The Role of Opera in the Rise of Radio in the United States," in Baade and Deaville, eds., *Music and the Broadcast Experience*, 69–87.

18. "10,000,000 Hear Opera over the Radio."

19. "Television Seen as New Hope for Radio Opera," *New York Times*, January 4, 1931, 178.

20. Orrin E. Dunlap Jr., "Listening-In," *New York Times*, March 22, 1931, 160.

21. "The Problem of Opera," in *The B.B.C. Year-Book, 1932* (London: British Broadcasting Corp., 1932), 133–34, 133.

22. Ernst Schoen, "Broadcast Opera in Germany," in *The B.B.C. Year-Book, 1934* (London: British Broadcasting Corp., 1934), 67–71, 70–71. Dismissed from his post at Radio Frankfurt and later detained on the charge of protecting Jewish and socialist colleagues, Schoen (1884–1960) left Germany and was appointed to the BBC in November 1933. For a report on his appointment, see "Ernst Schoen, Reich Playwright, Joins British Broadcasting Corporation," *Jewish Daily Bulletin*, November 19, 1933, 1, http://pdfs.jta.org/1933/1933-11-19_2696.pdf.

23. As Kevin Birth notes, clocks conflate two distinct functions: one is to indicate points in time, the other to measure durations. Birth furnishes the example of the conventions associated with the timing of sunrise and sunset. These are expressed as durations before or after midnight or midday (7:00 a.m., 6:00 p.m., 19:00), but midnight and midday do not actually fall at the midpoint between sunrise and sunset (as they did, e.g., in the Roman time system). In other words, identification of points in time (midnight, midday) coexists with and in this case

is actually subordinated to measures of duration. Kevin K. Birth, *Objects of Time: How Things Shape Temporality* (London: Palgrave Macmillan, 2012), 40.

24. Peter Kirwan, "Cheek by Jowl: Reframing Complicity in Web-Streams of *Measure for Measure*," in Aebischer, Greenhalgh, and Osborne, eds., *Shakespeare and the "Live" Theatre Broadcast Experience*, 161–74, 161–62.

25. Richard Bammer, "Live, in High-Def and Dolby, It's the Met Opera on the Big Screen," *The Reporter*, January 4, 2008, https://www.thereporter.com/2008/01/04/live-in-high-def-and-dolby-its-the-met-opera-on-the-big-screen.

26. Fathom Events, "Case Study: The Met: Live in HD," https://res.cloudinary.com/fathomevents/image/upload/v1566427381/corporateWebsite/Corporate%20-%20Distribution/Case%20Studies/PDF/The_Met_Live_in_HD.pdf (accessed June 21, 2023).

27. Bernadette Cochrane and Frances Bonner, "Screening from the Met, the NT, or the House: What Changes with the Live Relay," *Adaptation* 7, no. 2 (2014): 121–33, 122.

28. Ellis, *Visible Fictions*, 32.

29. "Television Seen as New Hope for Radio Opera," 178.

30. Orrin E. Dunlap Jr., "Scanning Tele-Opera," *New York Times*, November 14, 1937, 14.

31. The article reports that *Carmen* was seen by an audience of 67,000 across its network of thirty-one cinemas in twenty-seven cities. "Carmen No Box Office Sensation but Stirs Hope for Future," *Boxoffice*, December 20, 1952, 9.

32. Hy Hollinger, "Theatre-TV Pulls 'Em In," *Variety* 96, no. 10 (November 10, 1954): 20.

33. As Schulz et al. explain, the introduction of digital projectors during the first decade of the new millennium formed part of a wider digitization of production and distribution undertaken primarily as a means of lowering cost and improving efficiency. Anne Schulz, Amelie Eder, Victor Tiberius, Samantha Casas Solorio, Manuela Fabro, and Nataliia Brehmer, "The Digitalization of Motion Picture Production and Its Value Chain Implications," *Journalism and Media* 2, no. 3 (2021): 397–416.

34. Ellis, *Visible Fictions*, 33.

35. William Urricchio, "Storage, Simultaneity, and the Media Technologies of Modernity," in John Fullerton and Jan Olsson, eds., *Allegories of Communication: Intermedial Concerns from Cinema to the Digital* (Eastleigh: John Libbey, 2004), 123–38, 135.

36. Cowan cites in particular "city" films like Ruttmann's *Berlin: Die Sinfonie der Großstadt* (Berlin: Symphony of a great city; 1927) and Vertov's *Chelovek s kino-apparatom* (Man with a movie camera; 1929). See Michael Cowan, "The Realm of the Earth: Simultaneous Broadcasting and World Politics in Interwar Cinema," *Intermédialités*, no. 23 (September 2014), https://www.erudit.org/en/journals/im/2014-n23-im02092/1033343ar.

37. Birth, *Objects of Time*, 151.

38. Arjun Appadurai, *Modernity at Large: Cultural Dimensions of Globalization* (Minneapolis: University of Minnesota Press, 1996), 2–11.

39. Parks writes: "In cultural theory the satellite has been missing in action,

lying at the threshold of everyday visibility and critical attention, but moving persistently through orbit, structuring the global imaginary, the socioeconomic order, and the tissue of everyday experience across the planet. . . . Its uses structure and reflect global material conditions that fixate us, but these uses have themselves remained in their own orbit." Lisa Parks, *Cultures in Orbit: Satellites and the Televisual* (Durham, NC: Duke University Press, 2005), 7.

40. "Our World on Your Screen," n.d., Australian Telescope National Facility, press release, https://www.parkes.atnf.csiro.au/people/sar049/our_world/PDF/Our_World_on_Your_Screen_OCR.pdf (accessed June 21, 2023). Samuel Weber offers a rather less enthusiastic view. Televisual simultaneity, he observes, is predicated not just on the erasure of distance but on dispersal, across spaces of recording, transmission, and spectatorship, of the very act of seeing and hearing. It "overcomes spatial distance but only by *splitting the unity of place* and with it the unity of everything that defines its identity with respect to place: events, bodies, subjects." Samuel Weber, *Mass Mediauras: Form, Technics, Media* (Stanford, CA: Stanford University Press, 1996), 117.

41. "Meist Nettes," *Der Spiegel*, June 18, 1967, https://www.spiegel.de/kultur/meist-nettes-a-81d976d2-0002-0001-0000-000046251916.

42. Andrea Andermann, "A Timeless Contemporaneity," in the booklet accompanying *3 Live Films: Rigoletto in Mantua, La traviata in Paris, Tosca in Rome*, Blu-ray discs, Naxos NBD0052–54 (2016), 58–59. A coproduction of five broadcasters in Europe and the United States, *La traviata in Paris* was broadcast to 125 countries. All three Andermann productions were released in 2016 in a DVD box set (Naxos NBD0052–54).

43. Andermann, "A Timeless Contemporaneity," 58.

44. Max Jammer, *Concepts of Simultaneity from Antiquity to Einstein and Beyond* (Baltimore: Johns Hopkins University Press, 2006), 11.

45. Marcia Citron remarks on the "docu-soap" quality of the camerawork in Andermann's *Tosca*. Marcia Citron, "Visual Media," in *The Oxford Handbook of Opera*, ed. Helen M. Greenwald (New York: Oxford University Press, 2014), 921–40, 930.

46. Cachopo notes the "singularity of Andermann's idea." Cachopo, "The Aura of Opera Reproduced," 270.

47. Richard Hubbell, *Television: Programming and Production* (New York: Rinehart, 1950), 24.

48. Rudy Bretz, "TV as an Art Form," *Hollywood Quarterly* 5, no. 2 (1950): 153–63, 154.

49. Ellis, *Visible Fictions*, 33.

50. Mimi White, "The Attractions of Television: Reconsidering Liveness," in *MediaSpace: Place, Scale and Culture in a Media Age*, ed. Nick Couldry and Anna McCarthy (New York: Routledge, 2004), 75–92, 82.

51. *Digital Broadcast of Theatre: Learning from the Pilot Season* (NESTA, 2010), https://media.nesta.org.uk/documents/nt_live.pdf.

52. Hytner quoted in Margaret Jane Kidnie, "The Stratford Festival of Canada: Mental Tricks and Archival Documents in the Age of NTLive," in Aebischer, Greenhalgh, and Osborne, eds., *Shakespeare and the "Live" Theatre Broadcast Experience*, 133–46, 136.

53. Kidnie, "The Stratford Festival of Canada," 136.

54. Kidnie, "The Stratford Festival of Canada," 141.

55. Daniel J. Wakin, "Broadcast of 'Die Walküre' Performance at the Met Is Delayed," *ArtsBeat: New York Times Blog*, May 14, 2011, https://artsbeat.blogs.nytimes.com/2011/05/14/broadcast-of-die-walkure-performance-at-the-met-is-delayed.

56. *"Live in HD* FAQ," n.d., https://www.metopera.org/about/faq/live-in-hd-faq (accessed June 21, 2023).

57. Rebecca Schneider, *Performing Remains: Art and War in Times of Theatrical Reenactment* (New York: Routledge, 2011), 7.

58. Schneider grounds her understanding of *retroaction* in the temporal logic Derrida associates with the archive. For Derrida, the objects housed in the archive concern not the past but a future engagement with the past: they concern "what will have been." Jacques Derrida, "Archive Fever: A Freudian Impression," trans. Eric Prenowitz, *Diacritics* 25, no. 2 (Summer 1995): 9–63, 27. For Schneider, the role of the archive in performance is to generate "a future for pasts that have, much like a play-script in relation to production or dance steps sedimented in trained bodies, not yet taken place." Schneider, *Performing Remains*, 109. For more on the role of repetition in opera, see Risi, *Opera in Performance*, 157–59.

59. We might think of this as an analogue to another ubiquitous but largely unremarked form of simultaneity: the radio dial or television remote, which allows the device to tune in one frequency among many being broadcast at the same time. Although the plethora of signals and channels features in accounts of media saturation, their simultaneity does not. This too has repercussions for opera. For example, on Christmas Day, 1931, the date of the inaugural US national broadcast from the Metropolitan Opera, European listeners could choose from six relays of opera and operetta on shortwave radio: *Tannhäuser* from Dresden, *The Bajadere* from Vienna, *Il trovatore* from Berlin, *The Blue Mazurka* from Rome, acts 2–3 of *Cendrillon* from the UK, and act 3 of *Die Meistersinger* from Darmstadt.

CHAPTER FOUR

1. Robert T. Tally stresses the value of the convention as a foil to the frustration of being lost: "The map offers a fictional or figurative representation of the space in which we find ourselves, and the reassuring 'You are here' arrow or dot or other marker provides the point of reference from which we can both imagine and navigate the space." Robert T. Tally Jr., *Spatiality* (Abingdon: Routledge, 2013), 2.

2. Chris Berry, Soyoung Kim, and Lynn Spigel, eds., *Electronic Elsewheres: Media, Technology, and the Experience of Social Space* (Minneapolis: University of Minnesota Press, 2010).

3. Metropolitan Opera, "The Metropolitan Opera Reaches Groundbreaking Agreements," September 6, 2006, press release, http://www.operatoday.com/documents/Met_New_Media_release.pdf.

4. "Hundreds of Americans Hear Europe Broadcasting," *New York Times*, November 30, 1924, 15.

NOTES TO PAGES 111–115 | 215

5. By the early 1930s, experimentation was beginning to give way to regular programming. For example, on Christmas Day, 1931, the date of the inaugural US national broadcast from the Metropolitan Opera, European listeners could choose from any one of six relays of opera and operetta broadcast that evening: *Tannhäuser* from Dresden, *The Bajadere* from Vienna, *Il trovatore* from Berlin, *The Blue Mazurka* from Rome, acts 3–4 of *Cendrillon* from the BBC's studios, and act 3 of *Die Meistersinger von Nürnberg* from Darmstadt.

6. "Radio to 'Attend' Opera," *New York Times*, December 6, 1936, 6.

7. "Television Seen as New Hope for Radio Opera," 178.

8. Frank Warschauer, "Die Zukunft der Oper im Rundfunk," *Musikblätter des Anbruch* 11, no. 6 (June 1929): 274–76, reprinted as "The Future of Opera on the Radio," in *The Weimar Republic Sourcebook*, ed. Anton Kaes, Martin Jay, and Edward Dimendberg, trans. Don Reneau (Berkeley and Los Angeles: University of California Press, 1995), 1:607–9, 608.

9. Harry Stephen Keeler, *The Box from Japan* (New York: Wildside, 1932), 161.

10. Peter Lev, *Transforming the Screen, 1950–1959* (New York: Charles Scribner's Sons, 2003), 131–32.

11. "Carmen No Box Office Sensation," 9. See also Kira Kitsopanidou, "Electronic Delivery of Alternative Contents in Cinemas Before the Digital Era: The Case of Theater Television in the US Exhibition Market in the 1940s and 1950s," *Mise au point*, no. 4 (2012), https://journals.openedition.org/map/775?gathStatIcon =true&lang=en.

12. "Carmen No Box Office Sensation," 9. As a trade publication catering to exhibitors, *Boxoffice* highlights the search for content that would "bring in new patrons and bring back old ones." Ibid. See also "Sales Meet OK, Opera Only Fair via Theater TV," *Billboard*, December 20, 1952, 4.

13. "Metropolitan Openings Signed for Theatre TV," *Boxoffice*, January 30, 1954, 20. See also William J. Hoffmann Jr., "Nationwide Opening Night," *Opera News* 19, no. 2 (November 1, 1954): 12–13. Hoffmann quotes Nathan J. Halpern, the president of TNT, as characterizing the *Carmen* telecast as an "experiment" and promising a much-improved experience, thanks in part to months of preparation, the benefit of experience, and improvements in technology. See also Howard Taubman, "Nation Shares 'Met' Opening in Gala Theater-TV Parties," *New York Times*, November 9, 1954, 1.

14. "Metopera's Closed-Circuit Special Grossed $180,000," *Variety*, November≈17, 1954, 3.

15. Jack Singer, "Theater TV Breaks Barrier," *Billboard*, August 21, 1954, 1, 15, 15.

16. Hoffmann, "Nationwide Opening Night," 13.

17. Taubman, "Nation Shares 'Met' Opening," 1.

18. Rose Heylbut, "Telecasting the Metropolitan Opera," *Étude* 73 (January 1955): 26, 61, 61.

19. Flora Bella, "Superb camera work," comment on Kris Biffle Rudin, "Did I see?," Facebook, January 7, 2017, https://www.facebook.com/groups/ metliveinhdfans/permalink/1412533992092705.

20. "The Met Opera: Live in HD Opens Season," *The Pilot*, October 21, 2021,

https://www.thepilot.com/news/features/the-met-opera-live-in-hd-opens-season/
article_25dddc64-2157-11ec-9313-e3163da88ece.html.

21. "The Metropolitan Opera Reaches Groundbreaking Agreements."

22. "Metropolitan Opera Live in HD," *Rye Record*, October 27, 2014, https://
ryerecord.com/metropolitan-opera-live-in-hd.

23. David Salazar, "Met Opera 2021–22 Season: Here Is All the Information for
This Season's Live in HD Performances," *Operawire*, September 23, 2020, https://
operawire.com/met-opera-2021-22-season-here-is-all-the-information-for-this
-seasons-live-in-hd-performances.

24. Zachary Woolfe, "The Screen Can't Hear When You Yell 'Bravo,'" *New York
Times*, May 4, 2012, https://www.nytimes.com/2012/05/06/arts/music/met-operas
-live-in-hd-series-outside-of-new-york.html. See also Wagner Society of New York,
"Opera in HD," pt. 1, in which panelists repeatedly distinguish between the live
performance and "the HD."

25. "*Live in HD* FAQ."

26. Citron, "Visual Media," 924.

27. Margaret Morse observes that television's "interaction" with the viewers
is a legacy of the role of the host in radio. Margaret Morse, *Virtualities: Television,
Media Art, and Cyberculture* (Bloomington: Indiana University Press, 1998), 6.

28. As Morse writes of television's direct address: "A talking head with a direct
gaze regularly hails a virtual viewer it pretends to see." Morse, *Virtualities*, 20.

29. Jeremy G. Butler, *Television: Visual Storytelling and Screen Culture*, 5th ed.
(Abingdon: Routledge, 2018), 370.

30. Paddy Scannell, "Television and History," in *A Companion to Television*, ed.
Janet Wasko (Oxford: Blackwell, 2005), 51–66, 59.

31. Frances Babbage, "Adaptation and Storytelling in the Theatre," *Critical
Stages/Scènes critiques*, no. 12 (December 2015), https://www.critical-stages.org/
12/adaptation-and-storytelling-in-the-theatre.

32. "*Live in HD* FAQ."

33. Wagner Society of New York, "Opera in HD," pt. 2.

34. Wagner Society of New York, "Opera in HD," pt. 2. Large characterizes his
work in ways not unlike the "rhetoric of fidelity to the music" that Senici associates with stage directors in opera. Senici, "'In the Score,'" 216.

35. Armatage, "Barbara Willis Sweete," 250.

36. Tom Galley cited in "The Metropolitan Opera Reaches Groundbreaking
Agreements."

37. Kerins, *Beyond Dolby (Stereo)*, 40–44.

38. Subwoofer speakers, designed with cinematic "low-frequency effects" in
mind, are technically available for bass, although in practice the relatively modest
bass range of opera is well handled by the other speakers.

39. Luiz Gazzola, "The Exclusive *Opera Lively* Interview with Mark Schubin,
Media Engineer at the Met," June 29, 2013, https://operalively.com/forums/
content.php/848-The-Exclusive-Opera-Lively-Interview-with-Mark-Schubin-media
-engineer-at-the-Met. Schubin points out that the audio mix for DVD/Blu-ray releases of *Met: Live in HD* productions is different from the mix transmitted to
cinemas: the former assumes that the surround speakers will be behind the au-

ditor, whereas the latter allows for a configuration in which at least some of the wall-mounted surround speakers will be in front of the auditor's seating position.

40. Tommasini, "Wearing a Wire at the Opera."

41. Only recently has this privilege begun to be reflected in the attention devoted to televisual sound in scholarship. See Michele Hilmes, "Television Sound: Why the Silence?," *Music, Sound, and the Moving Image* 2, no. 2 (Autumn 2008): 153–61; James Deaville, ed., *Music in Television: Channels of Listening* (New York: Routledge, 2011); and Marida Rizzuti and Anna Scalfaro, eds., "L'ora della musica in tv: La divulgazione della musica in televisione dal 1954 a oggi," special issue, *Gli spazi della musica*, vol. 9 (2020).

42. Rick Altman, "Television/Sound," in *Studies in Entertainment: Critical Approaches to Mass Culture*, ed. Tania Modleski (Bloomington: Indiana University Press, 1986), 39–54, 42.

43. "The properly televisual," Michelle Chion writes, "is the image as something extra." Michelle Chion, *Audio-Vision*, ed. and trans. Claudia Gorbman (New York: Columbia University Press, 1994), 159. Chion defines sound in television primarily as spoken voice. The overlaps between radio and television are less obvious in the case of music, for which television speakers have not historically been well equipped.

44. See Svein Høier, "The Relevance of Point of Audience in Television Sound: Rethinking a Problematic Term," in "Rethinking Theories of Television Sound," ed. Carolyn Birdsall and Anthony Enns, special issue, *Journal of Sonic Studies* 3, no. 1 (October 2012), https://www.researchcatalogue.net/view/252390/252391.

45. Typical is this comment in a review of an SACD release: "Subtle use of the surrounds pervades the multichannel mixes—sometimes almost not there until you switch off the surrounds entirely—but in every case the surround version provided a more natural and enveloping acoustic." John Sunier, review of SACD MO41, *The Artistry of Teresa Perez, Cello*, Enjoy the Music, December 2001, http://www.enjoythemusic.com/audiophileaudition/1201/sacdreviews.htm. An even shorter-lived rival format, DVD-Audio, offered similar options.

46. Dwarfed in scale by cinema audio systems, home theater is not directly comparable, although it is possible that a multichannel home system designed primarily for music (as opposed to movies) may offer sonic advantages over cinema installations, customized as they are for the delivery of sound effects and dialogue. For more on home theater, see Kevin Donnelly, *The Spectre of Sound* (London: Bloomsbury, 2005); and Barbara Klinger, *Beyond the Multiplex: Cinema, New Technologies, and the Home* (Berkeley and Los Angeles: University of California Press, 2006).

47. Richard King, *Recording Orchestra and Other Classical Music Ensembles* (London: Routledge, 2017), 163.

48. Some anomalies remain. As the Met engineer-in-charge Mark Schubin explains, the distance of the microphone from the singer and the distance of the movie-theater spectator from speakers can both introduce audio delays. But the audience perception of this delay, he adds, is not the same in a wide shot (where we might expect delayed audio) as it is in a close-up, where a tighter sync is expected: "We get the occasional complaint that lip sync has changed during

218 | NOTES TO PAGES 124–128

the transmission of a show. That hasn't happened; there's really just been the introduction of an acoustic perception issue." Mark Schubin, interviewed in Gary Eskow, "New York's Met in HD," *Mix*, April 1, 2008, https://www.mixonline.com/sfp/new-yorks-met-hd-369201.

49. As examples of this cautious mobilization of the surround field, Kerins cites *Armageddon* (1998) and *Signs* (2002). Kerins, *Beyond Dolby (Stereo)*, 165–69.

50. Kerins, *Beyond Dolby (Stereo)*, 166; Tony Grajeda, "The 'Sweet Spot': The Technology of Stereo and the Field of Auditorship," in Théberge, Devine, and Everett, eds., *Living Stereo*, 37–64, 40. Gunning coined the phrase *cinema of attractions* to connote early cinema's appeal to the spectacle and wonder of the moving image. Tom Gunning, "The Cinema of Attractions: The Early Film, Its Spectator and the Avant-Garde," in *Early Cinema: Space, Frame, Narrative*, ed. Thomas Elsaesser (London: BFI, 1990), 56–62.

CHAPTER FIVE

1. Hoffmann, "Nationwide Opening Night," 13.

2. Lawrence Johnson, "HD at the Opera," *Musical America Worldwide*, 2009, https://www.musicalamerica.com/features/?fid=153&fyear=2009.

3. For more on this question of scale, see Mary Ann Doane, *Bigger Than Life: The Close-Up and Scale in the Cinema* (Durham, NC: Duke University Press, 2021). Doane observes that the question of scale has been strangely neglected in scholarship on screen media.

4. Scale of display is not the only distinguishing feature. The relatively low display resolution of television did not, historically, favor the representation of detail, a discrepancy now largely evened out thanks to new display technologies in television and home video and the digital convergence of display technologies.

5. The example Haswell offers is Jonas Kaufmann's performance of "Recondita armonia" in the Royal Opera House's *Tosca* (2011). "'Opera Cinema, the Modern *Gesamtkunstwerk*?,'" 352.

6. "Whereas the cinema close-up accentuates the difference between screen-figure and any attainable human figure by drastically increasing its size, the broadcast TV close-up produces a face that approximates to normal size." Ellis, *Visible Fictions*, 131.

7. Martine Beugnet and Annie van den Oever, "Gulliver Goes to the Movies: Screen Size, Scale, and Experiential Impact—a Dialogue," in *Screens: From Materiality to Spectatorship—a Historical and Theoretical Reassessment*, ed. Dominique Chateau and José Moure (Amsterdam: Amsterdam University Press, 2016), 247–57, 256. See also Erkki Huhtamo, "Gulliver in Figurine Land," trans. Linda Pollack, *Mediamatik* 4, no. 3 (1990): 101–5.

8. This can be one and the same venue, such as, e.g., the *Opera at the Ballpark* series, which features live transmissions from the San Francisco Opera to the big screen at Oracle Park, home of the San Francisco Giants.

9. "The viewer," Wells writes, "experiences herself as an audience in multiple registers, responding to a confluence of performance elements that ren-

der the operatic experience, as well as the specific work, both close to and strangely alien from other operatic experiences or expectations." Wells, "'Secret Mechanism,'" 198.

10. Tom Gunning, "Renewing Old Technologies: Astonishment, Second Nature, and the Uncanny in Technology from the Previous Turn-of-the-Century," in *Rethinking Media Change: The Aesthetics of Transition*, ed. David Thorburn, Henry Jenkins, and Brad Seawell (Cambridge, MA: MIT Press, 2003), 39–60.

11. John Wyver, "Who Needs Opera Glasses? The Met's Screen Revolution," *The Guardian*, March 27, 2008, https://www.theguardian.com/music/musicblog/2008/mar/27/whoneedsoperaglassestheme. Wyver went on to direct cinecasts for the Royal Shakespeare Company and has written extensively on his experiences as a multicamera director.

12. Tim Ashley, "A Bit of New York Beamed Live into South London," *The Guardian*, March 26, 2007, https://www.theguardian.com/music/musicblog/2007/mar/26/abitofnewyorkbeamedlive.

13. Conrad, "Opera from New York."

14. Conrad, *Television*, 14.

15. Anthony Tommasini, "You Go to the Movie Theater, and an Opera Breaks Out," *New York Times*, January 3, 2008, https://www.nytimes.com/2008/01/03/arts/music/03hans.html.

16. Conrad, "Opera from New York."

17. John Wyver "'All the Trimmings?': The Transfer of Theatre to Television in Adaptations of Shakespeare Stagings," *Adaptation* 7, no. 2 (August 2014): 104–20, 107; Will, "Zooming in, Gazing Back," 36.

18. W. Anthony Sheppard, "Review of the Metropolitan Opera's New HD Movie Theater Broadcasts," *American Music* 25, no. 3 (Fall 2007) 383–87, 386.

19. *Live at the Met: From Stage to Screen* (director, Susan Froemke, 2015).

20. Tom Gunning, "'Nothing Will Have Taken Place Except Place': The Unsettling Nature of Camera Movement," in *Screen Space Reconfigured*, ed. Susanne Ø. Saether and Synne T. Bull (Amsterdam: Amsterdam University Press, 2020), 263–82, 266. "Camera movement often seems to make us approach deeper into the world of the film, to merge into it. We become in some sense immersed." Ibid.

21. Pascale Aebischer, "South Bank Shakespeare Goes Global: Broadcasting from Shakespeare's Globe and the National Theatre," in Aebischer, Greenhalgh, and Osborne, eds., *Shakespeare and the "Live" Theatre Broadcast Experience*, 113–32, 122. Gunning points out that camera movement is surprisingly underresearched, given its historical prominence in cinematic practice. Gunning, "'Nothing Will Have Taken Place Except Place,'" 266.

22. Sheppard, "Review of the Metropolitan Opera's New HD Movie Theater Broadcasts," 386.

23. Sam O'Connell, "Making Culture Popular: Opera and the Media Industries," in Fryer, ed., *Opera in the Media Age*, 32–42, 36.

24. Peter Gelb, "Theatrical Nuance on a Grand Scale," *New York Times*, March 25, 2011, https://www.nytimes.com/2011/03/27/arts/music/metropolitan-opera-hones-dramatic-values-for-stage-and-screen.html. It was indeed Dessay's last performance of that role.

220 | NOTES TO PAGES 136–141

25. *Live at the Met: From Stage to Screen.*

26. For more on stage performers' experience of being filmed (in this case in spoken theater), see Beth Sharrock, "A View from the Stage: Interviews with Performers," in Aebischer, Greenhalgh, and Osborne, eds., *Shakespeare and the "Live" Theatre Broadcast Experience*, 95–102.

27. "'Opera Cinema, the Modern *Gesamtkunstwerk?*,'" 346–47. Gelb too concedes in his interview that makeup, lighting, and costume may be adjusted for the cinecasts.

CHAPTER SIX

1. Halpern quoted in Heylbut, "Telecasting the Metropolitan Opera," 26.

2. Daniel J. Wakin, "The Met Will Lower Ticket Prices," *New York Times*, February 26, 2013, https://www.nytimes.com/2013/02/27/arts/music/metropolitan -opera-to-reduce-ticket-prices-next-season.html.

3. Anthony Evans, "Live in HD: Verdi's La traviata from the Met," Planethugill .com, March 13, 2017, https://www.planethugill.com/2017/03/live-in-hd-verdis-la -traviata-from-met.html.

4. Steichen, "HD Opera," 447.

5. Palazzetti, "Backstage Live."

6. Typical is the exchange between the host, Eric Owens, and the bass Rene Pape after act 1 of *Parsifal* (2013). Owens: "Bravo! I am such a fan. It's a wonderful thing, what you do. You just sang more in the first act than you do in most complete operas. Can you explain what it feels like after a monumental amount of singing?" Pape: "First, you are really happy when you finish the first act, of course. But, you know, the music takes you somewhere in another dimension."

7. Mihir Bose, "But Can Medallists Write?," *British Journalism Review* 23, no. 4 (December 2012): 8–11.

8. Cachopo, "The Aura of Opera Reproduced," 274.

9. Esse, "Don't Look Now," 81.

10. "Stan," "Close-Ups Do No Favours in Met Live Otello," *Seen and Heard International*, October 27, 2012, https://seenandheard-international.com/2012/ 11/close-ups-do-no-favours-in-met-live-otello.

11. "Metopera's Closed-Circuit Special Grossed $180,000," 3.

12. Zachary Woolfe, "I'm Ready for My Close-Up, Mr. Puccini," *New York Times*, April 27, 2012, https://www.nytimes.com/2012/04/29/arts/music/the-mets-hd -broadcasts-are-changing-opera.html.

13. Doane, *Bigger Than Life*, 151.

14. "Many details won't be caught by even the most powerful opera glasses," writes Michael Cooper, "but now that the Met simulcasts its performances to cinemas around the world through its Live in HD series, every opera must be ready for its close-up." Michael Cooper, "See How the Met Built 'Tosca,' Its Biggest Production of the Season," *New York Times*, December 28, 2017, https://www .nytimes.com/2017/12/28/arts/music/tosca-metropolitan-opera.html.

15. Herbert Blau, *The Audience* (Baltimore: Johns Hopkins University Press, 1990), 10.

16. See the discussion of these historical concerns in my "Digital Diva," 96–97. I address the more recent embrace of screen media in theater and performance studies in "The Deadness of Live Opera."

17. Senici, "Porn Style," 78.

18. Wyver, "Who Needs Opera Glasses?"

19. Anita Sanseverino, "I usually do not see opera in HD," comment on George Walker, "I love Puccini and this opera," Facebook, November 9, 2019, https://www.facebook.com/groups/metliveinhdfans/posts/2827123197300437/?comment_id=2827612263918197. Comments in this thread prompted a group administrator to remind members that Met camera operators were members of the group.

20. Penny Schmitt, "I want to see all the stage," Facebook, November 23, 2019, https://www.facebook.com/groups/metliveinhdfans/permalink/2860177447328345.

21. Christophe Huss, "Metropolitan Opera: La damnation de Lepage: Un échec affligeant," *Le devoir*, November 24, 2008, https://www.ledevoir.com/culture/musique/218268/metropolitan-opera-la-damnation-de-lepage-un-echec-affligeant.

22. Of course, these negative comparisons with the theater might be redundant if, as Alex Ross provocatively suggests, the productions are no longer intended for those in the auditorium but in fact designed for the camera. This would extend the argument that the cinecast captures an especially heightened performance to imply that the whole production is determined by the needs of the cinecast, in which case the here of the virtual spectator does not so much exceed that of the opera house as displace it altogether. Alex Ross, "Diminuendo: A Downturn for Opera in New York City," *New Yorker*, March 12, 2012, https://www.newyorker.com/magazine/2012/03/12/diminuendo-2. Gelb, as we have seen, acknowledges the peculiar nature of the cinecast performance, but he refutes the claim that the productions are, in effect, camera ready. "Only after productions have opened," he wrote in the *New York Times*, "do we consider relatively minor adjustments to lighting, makeup, and costumes for our Live in HD presentations." Gelb, "Theatrical Nuance on a Grand Scale."

23. Will, "Zooming in, Gazing Back," 57.

24. "'Opera Cinema, the Modern *Gesamtkunstwerk?*,'" 345–46, 346 (first quote), 353 (second quote).

25. Lawrence Kramer, *Opera and Modern Culture: Wagner and Strauss* (Berkeley and Los Angeles: University of California Press, 2007).

26. Linda Breuning, "When we see opera in theater," comment on Bruce Hoffman, "Can anyone shed some light?," Facebook, October 11, 2014, https://www.facebook.com/groups/metliveinhdfans/posts/868952876450822/?comment_id=870380449641398.

27. David Salazar, "Opera Meets Film: The Lost Art of Filming Live Opera in HD," *Operawire*, April 11, 2019, https://operawire.com/opera-meets-film-the-lost-art-of-filming-live-opera-in-hd.

28. Christophe Huss, "Le Met au cinéma: Gary et le travelling de 'Kapo,'" *Le devoir*, February 4, 2019, https://www.ledevoir.com/culture/musique/547031/le-metropolitan-opera-au-cinema-gary-et-le-travelling-de-kapo.

29. Gaudréault and Marion, *The End of Cinema?*, 91.

30. Will, "Zooming in, Gazing Back," 42.

31. Ann M. Martinez, "Shakespeare at a Theatre Near You: Student Engagement in Northeast Ohio," in Aebischer, Greenhalgh, and Osborne, eds., *Shakespeare and the "Live" Theatre Broadcast Experience*, 199–206, 201.

32. Erin Sullivan, "'The forms of things unknown': Shakespeare and the Rise of the Live Broadcast," *Shakespeare Bulletin* 35, no. 4 (Winter 2017): 627–62, 645.

33. Sullivan, "'The forms of things unknown,'" 649.

34. Kramer, *Opera and Modern Culture*, 174.

35. Armatage, "Barbara Willis Sweete," 251.

36. Admittedly, each singer assumes slightly different locations and adopts her own gestures and poses, but there is enough in common between the two performances to be able to detect distinct directorial strategies.

37. John Belton, "The Bionic Eye: Zoom Aesthetics," *Cinéaste* 11, no. 1 (Winter 1980–81): 20–27, 21.

38. Gunning, "'Nothing Will Have Taken Place Except Place,'" 277.

39. Barker, *Live to Your Local Cinema*, 12.

40. Tommasini, "Wearing a Wire at the Opera."

41. Eskow, "New York's Met in HD."

42. Høier, "The Relevance of Point of Audience in Television Sound."

43. Saks defends the practice of up-conversion, citing positive feedback even from audio professionals. Eskow, "New York's Met in HD."

44. Tommasini, "Wearing a Wire at the Opera." Saks questions an audience's ability to detect, sonically, when body microphones are in use but adds that he would prefer not to use them: "For one thing, I don't get calls from people wanting to know why we do this sort of thing."

45. The dissatisfaction of critics who articulate reservations about audio in the cinecasts—that the balance is wrong (Ashley) or the sound muddy (Huss)—may or may not be provoked by the effects of audio processing, but this is certainly not the cause they identify, assuming they are even aware of the practice. "The sound quality," wrote Tim Ashley of *The Barber of Seville* (2007), "proved to be the principal drawback." Ashley, "A Bit of New York Beamed Live into South London." "After ten years," wrote Christophe Huss of *Elektra* (2016), "the Met Live in HD product needs to be seriously rethought and renewed . . . above all, in the sound quality." Huss, "Trop de compromis," *Le devoir*, May 2, 2016, https://www.ledevoir.com/culture/musique/469698/le-metropolitan-opera-au-cinema-trop-de-compromis.

46. Eskow, "New York's Met in HD." Saks adds that, although a multichannel recording is made of each of these performances, it is stored and reserved for the postproduction of DVDs and for archival purposes.

47. Trippett, "Facing Digital Realities," 54.

48. Lisa Coulthard, "Affect, Intensities, and Empathy: Sound and Contemporary Screen Violence," in *The Routledge Companion to Screen Music and Sound*, ed. Miguel Mera, Ronald Sadoff, and Ben Winters (New York: Routledge, 2017), 50–60, 54. Mark Kerins adds that the term is "grossly overused" in media scholarship. Kerins, *Beyond Dolby (Stereo)*, 130. An anonymous article defines *immersive sound* as follows: "The term used to describe sound that emanates from sources

beyond the horizontal plane by means of enhanced spatial properties such as additional height and overhead speakers and localized apparent sound sources within the auditorium." "The Spectrum of Immersive Sound: New Technologies Create Enhanced Audio Experience," *Film Journal International*, August 18, 2014, http://fj.webedia.us/content/spectrum-immersive-sound-new-technologies-create-enhanced-audio-experience. See also Bill Cribbs and Larry McCrigler, "The Spectrum of Immersive Sound," *Film Journal International* 117, no. 9 (September 2014): 62–65, 65.

49. Claudia Gorbman and John Richardson, "Introduction," in Richardson, Gorbman, and Vernallis, eds., *The Oxford Handbook of New Audiovisual Aesthetics*, 3–38, 4.

50. As Allen points out, the height channels in Dolby Atmos are integrated in part by sonic objects defined during the mixing process. Embedded in the three-dimensional sound field, these objects are encoded with data that allow them to be panned across the channels in ways that adapt to the speaker configuration of the playback environment. Allen, "Mixing and Broadcasting from the Royal Opera House."

51. Allen, "Mixing and Broadcasting from the Royal Opera House."

52. Allen, "Mixing and Broadcasting from the Royal Opera House."

53. "The Metropolitan Opera Reaches Groundbreaking Agreements."

54. John Emmett, "Multichannel Audio for Television," *EBU Technical Review*, October 2002, https://tech.ebu.ch/docs/techreview/trev_292-emmett.pdf; Paul Grainge, *Brand Hollywood: Selling Entertainment in a Global Media Age* (New York: Routledge, 2008), 94–95.

55. Agnieszka Roginska and Paul Geluso, eds., *Immersive Sound: The Art and Science of Binaural and Multi-Channel Audio* (New York: Routledge, 2018), xii.

56. Niels Christian Nilsson, Rolf Nordahl, and Stefania Serafin, "Immersion Revisited: A Review of Existing Definitions of Immersion and Their Relation to Different Theories of Presence," *Human Technology* 12, no. 2 (November 2016): 108–34, 109. As Nilsson et al. point out, Marvin Minsky coined the term *telepresence* to connote the impression in teleoperation systems of being there. See Minsky, "Telepresence." Nilsson et al. arguably contribute to the confusion here when they propose a definition of *virtual reality* that embraces "any form of mediated reality" and adopt the term *virtual environment* for the interactive systems typically defined as virtual reality. Nilsson, Nordahl, and Serafin, "Immersion Revisited," 109.

57. Doane, *Bigger Than Life*, 202–3.

58. I will have more to say about this in the book's conclusion.

59. Wagner Society of New York, "Opera in HD," pt. 2.

60. Allen, "Mixing and Broadcasting from the Royal Opera House."

61. Allen's assessment of the vagaries of cinema sound support his belief in the potential of systems like Dolby Atmos to mitigate this local factor by encoding the audio mix with metadata that allow a playback rendering device to map the sounds in real time according to the speaker placement of a given auditorium. This too has generated anxiety among professionals about ceding final control of the playback mix to a renderer. See Benjamin Wright, "Atmos Now: Dolby Labora-

tories, Mixing Ideology and Hollywood Sound Production," in Théberge, Devine, and Everrett, eds., *Living Stereo*, 227–46, 236.

62. On one memorable occasion, on learning that I had research interests in cinecasts, a cinema manager consulted with me during the transmission and adjusted the balance to my liking.

63. Alexandra Coughlan, "Why Arias in the Multiplex Fall Flat," *The Independent*, December 4, 2012, https://www.independent.co.uk/arts-entertainment/classical/features/why-arias-in-the-multiplex-fall-flat-8376326.html.

64. Tyroneslothrop, "Opera in the Cinema House," Talkclassical.com, December 5, 2012, https://www.talkclassical.com/22723-opera-cinema-house.html; Jessoperasopranogirl, "Met in HD vs. live in-theater performance," Reddit, April 21, 2015, https://www.reddit.com/r/opera/comments/33erpo/met_in_hd_vs_live _intheater_performance/?utm_source=share&utm_medium=web2x&context=3; Eloise Lee, "Does anyone else think that the HD transmissions sound muted?," Facebook, March 6, 2016, https://www.facebook.com/groups/metliveinhdfans/permalink/1146036362075804.

65. Timothy Shary, *Generation Multiplex: The Image of Youth in Contemporary American Cinema* (Austin: University of Texas Press, 2002). For a more recent account of the global prominence of the multiplex, see Stuart Hanson, *Screening the World: Global Development of the Multiplex Cinema* (London: Palgrave Macmillan, 2019). For a lament on the decline of traditional picture palaces, see Richard Gray, *Cinemas in Britain: One Hundred Years of Cinema Architecture* (London: Lund Humphreys, 1996).

66. Laurie E. Osborne, "Epilogue: Revisiting Liveness," in Aebischer, Greenhalgh, and Osborne, eds., *Shakespeare and the "Live" Theatre Broadcast Experience*, 215–26, 222.

67. Perhaps because it dates from an early phase of the emergence of the multiplex, Marc Augé's *Non-Places: Introduction to an Anthropology of Supermodernity*, trans. John Howe (London: Verso, 1995), 79 (originally published as *Non-lieux: Introduction à une anthropologie de la surmodernité* [Paris: Editions du Seuil, 1992]), makes no mention of it; more recent accounts of the nonplace have repeatedly added the multiplex to Augé's list. See, e.g., Phil Hubbard, Rob Kitchin, and Gill Valentine, eds., *Key Thinkers on Space and Place* (Cambridge: Polity, 2004), 8; and David Held and Anthony McGrew, eds., *Globalization Theory: Approaches and Controversies* (Cambridge: Polity, 2007), 154.

68. Grainge, *Brand Hollywood*, 156, 163.

69. On live cinema, see Sarah Atkinson and Helen W. Kennedy, eds., *Live Cinema: Cultures, Economies, Aesthetics* (London: Bloomsbury, 2019).

70. Thomas Elsaesser, *Film History as Media Archaeology: Tracking Digital Cinema* (Amsterdam: Amsterdam University Press, 2016), 246–47.

71. Sheppard, "Review of the Metropolitan Opera's New HD Movie Theater Broadcasts," 385.

72. Gaudréault and Marion, *The End of Cinema?*, 85, 139, 86.

73. Barker, *Live to Your Local Cinema*, 55–57.

74. Mike Weed, "The Pub as a Virtual Football Fandom Venue: An Alternative to 'Being There'?," *Soccer and Society* 8, nos. 2–3 (2007): 399–414, 410.

75. Barker, *Live to Your Local Cinema*, 56–57.

76. Tim Greiving, "Opera for the Masses Reps Cash Cow for the Met," *Variety*, August 25, 2015, https://variety.com/2015/music/features/met-brings-highbrow-opera-to-the-masses-1201577973.

CHAPTER SEVEN

1. Joanne Tompkins, "The 'Place' and Practice of Site-Specific Theatre and Performance," in *Performing Site-Specific Theatre: Politics, Place, Practice*, ed. Anna Birch and Joanne Tompkins (London: Palgrave Macmillan, 2012). Some of the key titles in the field include Nick Kaye, *Site-Specific Art: Performance, Place and Documentation* (London: Routledge, 2002); Cathy Turner, "Palimpsest or Potential Space? Finding a Vocabulary for Site-Specific Performance," *New Theatre Quarterly* 20, no. 4 (2004): 373–90; Judith Rugg, *Exploring Site-Specific Art: Issues of Space and Internationalism* (London: I. B. Tauris, 2010); Mike Pearson, *Site-Specific Performance* (London: Palgrave Macmillan, 2010); and Miwon Kwon, *One Place after Another: Site-Specific Art and Locational Identity* (Cambridge, MA: MIT Press, 2002).

2. Tompkins, "'Place' and Practice," 5, 15.

3. Andy Field, "'Site-Specific Theatre'? Please Be More Specific," *The Guardian*, February 6, 2008, http://www.theguardian.com/stage/theatreblog/2008/feb/06/sitespecifictheatrepleasebe.

4. Gay McAuley, "Site-Specific Performance: Place, Memory and the Creative Agency of the Spectator," *Arts: The Journal of the Sydney University Arts Association* 27 (2005): 27–51, 35.

5. Henri Lefebvre, *The Production of Space*, trans. Donald Nicholson-Smith (Oxford: Wiley-Blackwell, 1991).

6. Mike Pearson and Michael Shanks, *Theatre/Archeology* (London: Routledge, 2001), 23.

7. See Arnold Aronson, *The History and Theory of Environmental Scenography* (Ann Arbor, MI: UMI Research Press, 1981); and Richard Schechner, *Environmental Theater* (New York: Hawthorn, 1973).

8. *Locative performance* is a term widely used in the context of digital performance. See, e.g., Martin Rieser, *The Mobile Audience: Media Art and Mobile Technologies* (Amsterdam: Rodopi, 2011).

9. See, e.g., Áine Sheil and Craig Vear, "Digital Opera, New Means and Meanings: An Introduction in Two Voices," in "Digital Opera, New Means and New Meanings," ed. Áine Sheil and Craig Vear, special issue, *International Journal of Performance Art and Digital Media* 8 (2012): 3–9.

10. "The Industry's Cultural Equity and Inclusion Statement," The Industry, n.d., https://theindustryla.org/about/our-values (accessed June 21, 2023).

11. "About On Site Opera," On Site Opera, n.d., https://osopera.org/about (accessed June 21, 2023).

12. On the *Peter Grimes* production, see Danielle Ward-Griffin, "Virtually There: Site-Specific Performance on Screen," *Opera Quarterly* 30, no. 4 (Autumn 2014): 362–68.

13. David Patrick Stearns, "Rameau's *Pygmalion* Waxes Operatic at Madame Tussauds," Operavore, June 18, 2014, https://www.wqxr.org/story/review-rameaus-pygmalion-waxes-operatic-madame-tussauds.

14. Monica C. Chieffo, "'Uber Opera': The Politics of Site-Specific Mobile Opera in Los Angeles," in *Experiencing Music and Visual Cultures: Threshold, Intermediality, Synchresis*, ed. Antonio Cascelli and Denis Condon (London: Routledge, 2021), 107–19.

15. Two of the productions were released on DVD: *La traviata im Hauptbahnhof* (Schweizer Fernsehen, 2008, 7640117266161); and *La bohème im Hochhaus* (Schweizer Fernsehen, 2009, 7640117266185). Immanuel Schipper's characterization of the train station in *La traviata im Hauptbahnhof* as a "substitute opera stage" is fair up to a point, but his observation that the production endeavored to "keep the scene free from the mixing of art and everyday life" overlooks a number of key scenes in which spectators take up observing positions in and around the everyday locales (cafés, waiting areas) that are the production's set. Imanuel Schipper, "City as Performance," *TDR: The Drama Review* 58, no. 3 (2014): 18–26. For more on the train station project, see my "Digital Diva." Writing on *La bohème im Hochhaus,* Clemens Risi notes the allusions to a flash mob in act 3. For Risi, the deliberately layered combination and "collision" of normally distinct modes of spectatorship and participation is the most intriguing quality of the production. Risi, *Opera in Performance*, 157.

16. Andrea Andermann, "Electronic Tosca," in the booklet accompanying *3 Live Films*, 14.

17. *Making of Rigoletto aus Mantua*, ORF 2, telecast September 4, 2010.

18. Andrea Malvano, "'La via della musica': Rischi e trasformazioni del live film opera nelle produzioni Rai di Andrea Andermann," in Rizzuti and Scalfaro, eds., "L'ora della musica in tv," 85–103, 93. Malvano adds that the opera itself, with its individual rather than collective focus, might encourage a certain stillness.

19. Alan Riding, "A 'Traviata' Roams Paris, Partaking of Its Rhythms," *New York Times*, June 6, 2000, https://www.nytimes.com/2000/06/06/arts/a-traviata-roams-paris-partaking-of-its-rhythms.html. In the lavish booklet accompanying the DVD release of the *Via della musica* productions, a special featurette outlines the role of the steadicam, including a quote from its inventor, Garrett Brown (who participated in the production), and Andermann's observation that the production was effectively a "score for soloists, orchestra and . . . steadicam." Andermann also quoted in ibid., 90.

20. Malvano, "'La via della musica,'" 94.

21. Typical is a press release from the UK theater company HOME that recounts how an office building was "brought to life in 2012 with the Library Theatre Company's acclaimed production of Jackie Kay's *Manchester Lines*." "We Launch Our Site-Specific Theatre Season for 14/15," https://homemcr.org/article/launch-site-specific-theatre-season-1415.

22. For a succinct overview of the architecture of the Palazzo Ducale and its use in performance, see Paola Besutti, "Spaces for Music in Late Renaissance Mantua," in *The Cambridge Companion to Monteverdi*, ed. John Whenham and Richard Wistreich (Cambridge: Cambridge University Press, 2007), 76–94.

23. Close camerawork of this kind is a feature of Bellocchio's film direction.

In *I pugni in tasca* (Fists in the pocket, 1965), extreme close-ups convey a sense of formal loss of control, mirroring the frenzied protagonist's state of mind, and, in *Vincere* (2009), the immediacy of the camera forensically registers the affective fragility of Ida Dalser, Mussolini's abandoned first wife. The decisive difference is the medium: on video the quality of the image cannot but summon a different kind of immediacy, that of news gathering and reality TV. Patroni Griffi's film work anticipates the mobile camera of *La traviata in Paris*. In *Addio, fratello crudele* (Farewell, cruel brother, 1971), a collaboration with Storaro on a film with a Renaissance Mantua setting, cameras harnessed to the actors track their movement in an anticipation of the effect of the selfie stick.

24. Brigitte Peucker, *The Material Image: Art and the Real in Film* (Stanford, CA: Stanford University Press, 2007).

25. Anne Ozorio, "Unique *Rigoletto* Live from Mantua," September 8, 2010, http://www.operatoday.com/content/2010/09/rigoletto_live_.php.

26. Stefano L'Occaso, "The Stronghold of Sparafucile," in the booklet accompanying *3 Live Films*, 145.

27. Malvano, "'La via della musica,'" 99.

28. Mike Clark, "Rigoletto in Mantua," *Sound & Lite* 86 (November–December 2010): 76–80, 77.

29. John Culshaw, *Ring Resounding: The Recording of Der Ring des Nibelungen* (1967; London: Pimlico, 2012), 24.

30. Marcia Citron notes the suddenly dry quality of the vocal sound in *Tosca* when the scene shifts outdoors to the ramparts of the Castel Sant'Angelo. These kinds of contrasts are far less evident in *Rigoletto in Mantua*, perhaps thanks in part to the more enclosed outdoor locations featured there and to the sound recording and mixing technology available eighteen years later. Citron, "Visual Media," 931–32.

31. Lefebvre in fact took housing projects like these as paradigmatic of the contemporary organization of urban space. More specifically, he took the "daily life of the tenant of a government-subsidized high-rise housing project" as the embodiment of contemporary "spatial practice." Lefebvre, *The Production of Space*, 38.

32. One of the questions posed by the working group on site-specific performance in Performance Studies International, the professional body in the field of performance studies, was: "What are the emerging ethics and methodologies for engaging communities?"

33. "Das vom Volksmund zum Ghetto von Bern degradierte Quartier wird zur Bühne für die Hochkultur." "Making of *La bohème*," included on *La bohème im Hochhaus* (DVD, Schweizer Fernsehen 7640117266185, 2009).

34. "Making of *La bohème*."

35. Renat Künzi, "'La bohème' bringt Wohnblock B zum Klingen," Swissinfo .ch, https://www.swissinfo.ch/ger/kultur/-la-bohème--bringt-wohnblock-b-zum -klingen/140652.

36. Cited in "Bern empfing uns mit offenen Armen," *Berner Zeitung*, August 26, 2009, https://www.bernerzeitung.ch/bern-empfing-uns-mit-offenen-armen -792609430421.

37. Giacosa and Ilica may have stopped short of the more political dimensions of the *scapigliatura* tradition, the northern Italian response to bohemianism, but the opera holds on, at least in places, to that tradition's mocking spirit.

38. Ellen Lockhart observes: "[The Puccini] repertory is held to require considerable *loyalty* in staging: it offers a visual medium that adheres to scenic indications and eschews directorial intervention." Ellen Lockhart, "Photo-Opera: *La fanciulla del West* and the Staging Souvenir," *Cambridge Opera Journal* 23 (2011): 145–66, 148. And, in a review of another *Bohème* production on video (one directed by Stefan Herheim in Oslo in 2012), Arman Schwartz argues that Puccini is a "composer whose operas often seem—unlike those of, say, Mozart or Verdi—ineradicably, embarrassingly dependent their original *mise-en-scène*." Arman Schwartz, "The Eye of a Poet," *Opera Quarterly* 29, no. 2 (Spring 2013): 162–67, 163.

39. Künzi, "'La bohème' bringt Wohnblock B zum Klingen." That all six productions feature much-performed Italian repertoire suggests a harnessing of familiarity and popularity (at least in operatic terms) as a means of bridging the perceived high-low divide of opera and television. Beck insists: "People who are not used to the necessary high level of concentration need to be kept engaged, i.e., in front of the screen." Ibid. Andermann introduces a national dimension, stressing the capacity of his project to affirm to a global audience the value of Italian culture. Andermann, "Electronic Tosca," 14.

40. Max Nyffeler, "Tod im Busbahnhof: Zur Live-Übertragung von Puccinis 'Bohème' aus Bern," *Neue Musikzeitung*, October 1, 2009, https://www.nmz.de/online/tod-im-busbahnhof-zur-live-uebertragung-von-puccinis-boheme-aus-einem-berner-hochhaus.

41. "Per sogni e per chimere e per castelli in aria l'anima ho milionaria."

42. Nina Sun Eidsheim, *Sensing Sound: Singing and Listening as Vibrational Practice* (Durham, NC: Duke University Press, 2015).

43. Chion, *Audio-Vision*, 109–14.

44. Mark Kerins traces the emergence of this fragmented sound editing to the development of audio technology in cinema. The transition from Dolby stereo to surround sound, he contends, challenged the stable, centered point of audition and its goal of generating continuity across a fragmented visual track. Instead, the sound now follows and precisely situates the visual track, in effect creating a "dual fragmentation" that undermines the continuity of the soundtrack in its own terms but heightens spatial coherence in audiovisual terms by repeatedly resituating sound to conform with image. Kerins, *Beyond Dolby (Stereo)*, 108–9.

45. Shuhei Hosokawa, "The Walkman Effect," *Popular Music* 4 (1984): 162–78, 177; Michael Bull, *Sound Moves: iPod Culture and Urban Experience* (Aldershot: Ashgate, 2007).

46. CROWNVIC1, "La bohème—Live behind the Scenes," October 1, 2009, https://youtu.be/ZpKoyafKIk4?t=194.

47. On the soundscapes in *La fanciulla del West*, see Emanuele Senici, *Landscape and Gender in Italian Opera: The Alpine Virgin from Bellini to Puccini* (Cambridge: Cambridge University Press, 2005); Arman Schwartz, "Puccini, in the Dis-

tance," *Cambridge Opera Journal* 23, no. 3 (November 2011): 167–89; and Richard Leppert, *Aesthetic Technologies of Modernity, Subjectivity, and Nature: Opera, Orchestra, Phonograph, Film* (Oakland: University of California Press, 2015), 21–55.

48. Mike Pearson, "Special Worlds, Secret Maps: A Poetics of Performance," in *Staging Wales: Welsh Theatre, 1979–1997*, ed. Anna Marie Taylor (Cardiff: University of Wales Press, 1997), 95–96.

49. Turner, "Palimpsest or Potential Space," 374.

50. Jean Baudrillard, "Aesthetic Illusion and Virtual Reality," in *Art and Artefact*, ed. Nicholas Zurbrugg (London: Sage, 1997), 19–27, 19.

51. Cachopo, "The Aura of Opera Reproduced," 269–70. The quote from Andermann can be found in "Electronic Tosca," 14.

52. Alessandra Campana, "Acoustic Signatures: Alban Bassuet," *Opera Quarterly* 27, no. 4 (Autumn 2011): 481–82.

53. Eidsheim, *Sensing Sound*, 69.

54. Barbara Klinger cites data from the Consumer Electronics Association showing that, by 2004, 30 percent of homes in the United States were equipped with home-theater systems. Klinger, *Beyond the Multiplex*, 22.

55. Rarely discussed bar the occasional line in a review, the surround-sound tracks on opera DVDs occupy an oddly peripheral role. It may be that DVDs have often been played on computers/laptops rather than on home-theater systems. Or perhaps the households equipped with home-theater systems are not those that tend to watch opera on DVD. By now featured on a back catalog that numbers in the thousands, these tracks must represent some of the most redundant resourcing and labor in all of media technology.

56. The DVD releases of the earlier Andermann productions also feature surround-sound tracks, but these have clearly been up-converted from stereo recordings. In *Tosca*, e.g., the center channel, confined to occasional sound effects (footsteps, turning locks), is largely silent, while the conventional mix in *La traviata* (essentially stereo panned across front and center speakers with ambient sound in the rear) contrasts markedly with the mobile camerawork.

CONCLUSION

1. Helen Shaw and Mark Harris, "The *Hamilton* Movie Swings Open the Doors of Broadway," Vulture.com, July 2, 2020, https://www.vulture.com/2020/07/hamilton-movie-review-swing-open-the-doors-of-broadway.html.

2. Jackson McHenry, "Who Tells Your Story on Camera? How *Hamilton* Was Edited into a Movie," Vulture.com, July 10, 2020, https://www.vulture.com/article/how-hamilton-was-edited-into-a-movie.html.

3. The commentary on *Hamilton* has little to say, either, about the remediation of spoken theater, despite the apparent success of the cinecasts.

4. *Variety* reported that, in the week of its release (in July 2020) on *Disney+*, *Hamilton* achieved a 37 percent audience share of streaming titles, trebling its nearest rival. Kevin Tran, "'Hamilton' Far Bigger Than Anything on Netflix in July, Audience

Data Reveals," *Variety*, August 10, 2020, https://variety.com/vip/disney-hamilton-audience-nearly-3x-bigger-than-any-netflix-program-in-july-1234729439.

5. Joshua Barone, "Think Outside the Opera House, and Inside the Parking Garage," *New York Times*, October 21, 2020, https://www.nytimes.com/2020/10/21/arts/music/twilight-gods-detroit-opera.html.

6. "Falstaff: The (Other) Finale," Bayerische Staatsoper, December 2020, https://www.staatsoper.de/editorial/detail/falstaff-the-other-finale.

7. Steven Connor, *Dumbstruck: A Cultural History of Ventriloquism* (New York: Oxford University Press, 2000).

8. Steven Connor, "Panophonia" (paper presented at the Pompidou Centre, Paris, February 22, 2012), 8, http://www.stevenconnor.com/panophonia/panophonia.pdf.

9. Morris, "Digital Diva," 96.

10. Ed Harsh, moderator, "New Technologies and Their Impact: Panel Discussion," Opera America Annual Conference, May 20, 2020, https://youtu.be/LMSFedTxQKk. The recommendation was made by the panelist Joe Kluger.

11. Doug McLennan, "New Technologies and Their Impact: Lead Presentation," Opera America Annual Conference, May 18, 2020, https://youtu.be/vHvy3ouUn4s.

12. Nicholas Payne, "Survival of the Fittest," *Opera*, January 2021, 49–52, 52.

13. Forner wonders whether there are now reasons to be less skeptical than Cachopo had been when he considered the potential of opera-film hybrids in 2014. See Jane Forner, "*Svadba on the Beach*: Opera for the Streaming Age," *Opera Quarterly* (in press); and João Pedro Cachopo, "Opera's Screen Metamorphosis: The Survival of a Genre or a Matter of Translation?," *Opera Quarterly* 30, no. 4 (2014): 315–29.

14. Jeremy Tambling, "Introduction: Opera in the Distraction Culture," in Tambling, ed., *A Night in at the Opera*, 1–24, 12–17.

Bibliography

Abbate, Carolyn, and Roger Parker. *A History of Opera: The Last Four Hundred Years*. New York: Penguin Group, 2015.

Aebischer, Pascale. *Shakespeare, Spectatorship and the Technologies of Performance*. Cambridge: Cambridge University Press, 2020.

Albera, François, and Maria Tortajada. "Introduction to an Epistemology of Viewing and Listening Dispositives." In *Cinema beyond Film*, ed. François Albera and Maria Tortajada, 9–22. Amsterdam: Amsterdam University Press, 2010.

Allen, Jonathan. "Mixing and Broadcasting from the Royal Opera House." Sound on Sound, February 2017. https://www.soundonsound.com/techniques/immersive-audio-opera.

Altman, Rick. "Television/Sound." In *Studies in Entertainment: Critical Approaches to Mass Culture*, ed. Tania Modleski, 39–54. Bloomington: Indiana University Press, 1986.

———. "Sound Space." In *Sound Theory, Sound Practice*, ed. Rick Altman, 46–64. New York and London: Routledge, 1992.

Andermann, Andrea. "A Timeless Contemporaneity." In the booklet accompanying *3 Live Films: Rigoletto in Mantua, La traviata in Paris, Tosca in Rome*, Blu-ray discs, Naxos NBD0052–54 (2016), 58–59.

Anker, François van den. "Gary Halvorson: De Man Achter Live in HD." Place de l'Opéra, May 26, 2020. https://www.operamagazine.nl/achtergrond/52214/gary-halvorson-de-man-achter-live-in-hd.

Appadurai, Arjun. *Modernity at Large: Cultural Dimensions of Globalization*. Minneapolis: University of Minnesota Press, 1996.

Armatage, Kay. "Barbara Willis Sweete: Queen of HD Transmissions." In *Doing Women's Film History: Reframing Cinemas, Past and Future*, ed. Christine Gledhill and Julia Knight, 242–55. Urbana: University of Illinois Press, 2015.

Aronson, Arnold. *The History and Theory of Environmental Scenography*. Ann Arbor, MI: UMI Research Press, 1981.

Ashley, Tim. "A Bit of New York Beamed Live into South London." *The Guardian*, March 26, 2007. https://www.theguardian.com/music/musicblog/2007/mar/26/abitofnewyorkbeamedlive.

Atkinson, Sarah, and Helen W. Kennedy, eds. *Live Cinema: Cultures, Economies, Aesthetics*. London: Bloomsbury, 2019.

Attard, Joseph. *Opera Cinema: A New Cultural Experience*. New York: Bloomsbury, 2022.

Attard, Joseph, and Christopher Morris, eds. "Opera at the Multiplex," special issue, *Opera Quarterly* 34, no. 4 (Autumn 2018): 261–65.

Augé, Marc. *Non-Places: Introduction to an Anthropology of Supermodernity*. Translated by John Howe. London: Verso, 1995.

Auslander, Philip. *Liveness: Performance in a Mediatized Culture*. 1999. 2nd ed. London: Routledge, 2008.

Baade, Christina L., and James Deaville, eds. *Music and the Broadcast Experience: Performance, Production, and Audiences*. Oxford: Oxford University Press, 2016.

Babbage, Frances. "Adaptation and Storytelling in the Theatre." *Critical Stages/ Scènes critiques*, no. 12 (December 2015). https://www.critical-stages.org/12/adaptation-and-storytelling-in-the-theatre.

Bammer, Richard. "Live, in High-Def and Dolby, It's the Met Opera on the Big Screen." *The Reporter*, January 4, 2008. https://www.thereporter.com/2008/01/04/live-in-high-def-and-dolby-its-the-met-opera-on-the-big-screen.

Barker, Martin. *Live to Your Local Cinema: The Remarkable Rise of Livecasting*. London: Palgrave Macmillan, 2013.

Barnes, Jennifer. *Television Opera: The Fall of Opera Commissioned for Television*. London: Boydell, 2003.

Barone, Joshua. "Think Outside the Opera House, and Inside the Parking Garage." *New York Times*, October 21, 2020. https://www.nytimes.com/2020/10/21/arts/music/twilight-gods-detroit-opera.html.

———. "When Opera Livestreams Became Live Performances." *New York Times*, October 28, 2021. https://www.nytimes.com/2021/09/03/arts/music/opera-livestreams.html.

Baudrillard, Jean. "Aesthetic Illusion and Virtual Reality." In *Art and Artefact*, ed. Nicholas Zurbrugg, 19–27. London: Sage, 1997.

Baudry, Jean-Louis. "Ideological Effects of the Basic Cinematographic Apparatus." Translated by Alan Williams. *Film Quarterly* 28, no. 2 (Winter 1974–75): 39–47.

Bayreuther Festspiele. "Tannhäuser im Roadmovie." August 14, 2019. https://youtu.be/CI2GMG3teqk.

Belton, John. "The Bionic Eye: Zoom Aesthetics." *Cinéaste* 11, no. 1 (Winter 1980–81): 20–27.

Bergson, Henri. "Discussion avec Einstein." In *Mélanges*, ed. André Robinet, 1340–47. Paris: Presses universitaires de France, 1972.

"Bern empfing uns mit offenen Armen." *Berner Zeitung*, August 26, 2009. https://www.bernerzeitung.ch/bern-empfing-uns-mit-offenen-armen-792609430421.

Berry, Chris, Soyoung Kim, and Lynn Spigel, eds. *Electronic Elsewheres: Media, Technology, and the Experience of Social Space*. Minneapolis: University of Minnesota Press, 2010.

Berry, Mark. "Opera and the Politics of Postdramatic Theatre: Frank Castorf's Bayreuth *Ring*." *Cambridge Opera Journal* 33, nos. 1–2 (March 2021): 24–49.

Besutti, Paola. "Spaces for Music in Late Renaissance Mantua." In *The Cambridge Companion to Monteverdi*, ed. John Whenham and Richard Wistreich, 76–94. Cambridge: Cambridge University Press, 2007.

Beugnet, Martine, and Annie van den Oever. "Gulliver Goes to the Movies: Screen Size, Scale, and Experiential Impact—a Dialogue." In *Screens: From Materiality to Spectatorship—a Historical and Theoretical Reassessment*, ed. Dominique Chateau and José Moure, 247–57. Amsterdam: Amsterdam University Press, 2016.

Billington, Michael. "Let's Stop Pretending That Theatre Can't Be Captured on Screen." *The Guardian*, June 18, 2014. https://www.theguardian.com/stage/2014/jun/18/ghosts-digital-theatre-richard-eyre-almeida.

Billington, Michael, and Tim Ashley. "After Dido." *The Guardian*, April 17, 2009. https://www.theguardian.com/stage/2009/apr/17/theatre-review-after-dido -young-vic.

Birth, Kevin K. *Objects of Time: How Things Shape Temporality*. London: Palgrave Macmillan, 2012.

Blau, Herbert. *The Audience*. Baltimore: Johns Hopkins University Press, 1990.

Boenisch, Peter M. "Frank Castorf and the Berlin Volksbühne, *The Humiliated and Insulted* (2001)." In *Mapping Intermediality in Performance*, ed. Sarah Bay-Cheng, Chiel Kattenbelt, Andy Lavender, and Robin Nelson, 198–203. Amsterdam: Amsterdam University Press, 2010.

———. "Towards a Theatre of Encounter and Experience: Reflexive Dramaturgies and Classic Texts." *Contemporary Theatre Review* 20, no. 2 (2010): 162–72.

Bolter, Jay David, and Richard Grusin. *Remediation: Understanding New Media*. Cambridge, MA: MIT Press, 1999.

Bose, Mihir. "But Can Medallists Write?" *British Journalism Review* 23, no. 4 (December 2012): 8–11.

Bretz, Rudy. "TV as an Art Form." *Hollywood Quarterly* 5, no. 2 (1950): 153–63.

Bright, Charles. "The Empire's Telegraph and Trade." *Fortnightly Review*, March 1923, 457–74.

Buhrmann, Dirk. "Interview: Myriam Hoyer." July 4, 2016. https://www.sky.at/musik-kultur/live-von-den-bayreuther-festspielen/interview-myriam-hoyer -104263. (Accessed May 4, 2022; link no longer active.)

Bull, Michael. *Sound Moves: iPod Culture and Urban Experience*. Aldershot: Ashgate, 2007.

Butler, Jeremy G. *Television: Visual Storytelling and Screen Culture*. 5th ed. Abingdon: Routledge, 2018.

Cachopo, João Pedro. "Opera's Screen Metamorphosis: The Survival of a Genre or a Matter of Translation?" *Opera Quarterly* 30, no. 4 (2014): 315–29.

———. "The Aura of Opera Reproduced: Fantasies and Traps in the Age of the Cinecast." *Opera Quarterly* 34, no. 4 (Autumn 2018): 266–83.

Campana, Alessandra. "Acoustic Signatures: Alban Bassuet." *Opera Quarterly* 27, no. 4 (Autumn 2011): 481–82.

"Carmen No Box Office Sensation but Stirs Hope for Future." *Boxoffice*, December 20, 1952, 9.

Casetti, Francesco. *The Lumière Galaxy: Seven Key Words for the Cinema to Come*. New York: Columbia University Press, 2015.

Cavell, Stanley. "The Fact of Television." *Daedalus* 111, no. 4 (Fall 1982): 75–96.

Cenciarelli, Carlo. "At the Margins of the Televisual: Picture Frames, Loops and

'Cinematics' in the Paratexts of Opera Videos." *Cambridge Opera Journal* 25 (2013): 203–23.

Chieffo, Monica C. "'Uber Opera': The Politics of Site-Specific Mobile Opera in Los Angeles." In *Experiencing Music and Visual Cultures: Threshold, Intermediality, Synchresis*, ed. Antonio Cascelli and Denis Condon, 107–19. New York: Routledge, 2021.

Chion, Michelle. *Audio-Vision*. Edited and translated by Claudia Gorbman. New York: Columbia University Press, 1994.

Chotzinoff, Samuel. "Opera on Radio." In *Music in Radio Broadcasting*, ed. Gilbert Chase, 1–17. New York: McGraw-Hill, 1946.

Citron, Marcia. *Opera on Screen*. New Haven, CT: Yale University Press, 2000.

———. *When Opera Meets Film*. Cambridge: Cambridge University Press, 2010.

———. "Visual Media." In *The Oxford Handbook of Opera*, ed. Helen M. Greenwald, 921–40. New York: Oxford University Press, 2014.

———. "Opera-Film as Television: Remediation in Tony Britten's *Falstaff*." *Journal of the American Musicological Society* 70, no. 2 (Summer 2017): 475–522.

Clark, Mike. "Rigoletto in Mantua." *Sound & Lite* 86 (November–December 2010): 76–80.

Clements, Andrew. "*Written on Skin*—Review." *The Guardian*, July 8, 2012. https://www.theguardian.com/music/2012/jul/08/written-on-skin-review.

Cochrane, Bernadette, and Frances Bonner. "Screening from the Met, the NT, or the House: What Changes with the Live Relay." *Adaptation* 7, no. 2 (2014): 121–33.

Comolli, Jean-Louis. "Notes sur le nouveau spectateur." *Cahiers du cinéma*, no. 177 (April 1966): 66–67.

Connor, Steven. *Dumbstruck: A Cultural History of Ventriloquism*. New York: Oxford University Press, 2000.

———. "Panophonia." Paper presented at the Pompidou Centre, Paris, February 22, 2012. http://www.stevenconnor.com/panophonia/panophonia.pdf.

———. "Sounding Out Film." In *The Oxford Handbook of New Audiovisual Aesthetics*, ed. John Richardson, Claudia Gorbman, and Carol Vernallis, 107–20. Oxford: Oxford University Press, 2013.

Conrad, Peter. *Television: The Medium and Its Manners*. Abingdon: Routledge, 1982.

———. "Opera from New York in Your Home Town? Easy. Just Go to the Pictures." *The Observer*, April 22, 2007. https://www.theguardian.com/music/2007/apr/22/classicalmusicandopera.features1.

Cooper, Michael. "See How the Met Built 'Tosca,' Its Biggest Production of the Season." *New York Times*, December 28, 2017. https://www.nytimes.com/2017/12/28/arts/music/tosca-metropolitan-opera.html.

———. "The Met Opera's Credit Outlook Darkens After Modest Deficits." *New York Times*, November 20, 2019. https://www.nytimes.com/2019/11/20/arts/music/metropolitan-opera.html.

Coughlan, Alexandra. "Why Arias in the Multiplex Fall Flat." *The Independent*, December 4, 2012. https://www.independent.co.uk/arts-entertainment/classical/features/why-arias-in-the-multiplex-fall-flat-8376326.html.

Coulthard, Lisa. "Affect, Intensities, and Empathy: Sound and Contemporary Screen Violence." In *The Routledge Companion to Screen Music and Sound*, ed. Miguel Mera, Ronald Sadoff, and Ben Winters, 50–60. New York: Routledge, 2017.

Cowan, Michael. "The Realm of the Earth: Simultaneous Broadcasting and World Politics in Interwar Cinema." *Intermédialités*, no. 23 (Spring 2014). https://www.erudit.org/en/journals/im/2014-n23-im02092/1033343ar.

Cribbs, Bill, and Larry McCrigler. "The Spectrum of Immersive Sound." *Film Journal International* 117, no. 9 (September 2014): 62–65.

Culshaw, John. *Ring Resounding: The Recording of Der Ring des Nibelungen*. 1967. Reprint, London: Pimlico, 2012.

D'Agostino, Peter, and David Tafler, eds. *Transmission: Toward a Post-television Culture*. Thousand Oaks, CA: Sage, 1994.

Davies, Owen. "Written on Skin." Plays to See: International Theatre Reviews, January 14, 2017. https://playstosee.com/written-on-skin.

Davis, Desmond. *The Grammar of Television Production*. London: Barrie & Rockliff, 1960.

Deaville, James, ed. *Music in Television: Channels of Listening*. New York: Routledge, 2011.

Derrida, Jacques. *Speech and Phenomena and Other Essays on Husserl's Theory of Signs*. Translated and edited by David B. Allison. Evanston, IL: Northwestern University Press, 1973.

———. *The Truth in Painting*. Translated by Geoffrey Bennington and Ian McLeod. Chicago: University of Chicago Press, 1987.

———. "Archive Fever: A Freudian Impression." Translated by Eric Prenowitz. *Diacritics* 25, no. 2 (Summer 1995): 9–63.

Derrida, Jacques, and Bernard Stiegler. *Echographies of Television: Filmed Interviews*. Translated by Jennifer Bajorek. Cambridge: Polity, 2002.

Diederichsen, Diedrich. "Theater ist kein Medium—aber was bewirkt es, wenn der Mann mit der Videokamera auf der Bühne arbeitet?" *Dramaturg: Zeitschrift der Dramaturgischen Gesellschaft* 1 (2004): 3–7.

Dillon, Emma. "Vocal Philologies: *Written on Skin* and the Troubadours." *Opera Quarterly* 33, nos. 3–4 (Summer–Autumn 2017): 207–48.

Doane, Mary Ann. "An Ontology of Everyday Distraction: The Freeway, the 193 Mall, and Television." In *Logics of Television: Essays in Cultural Criticism*, ed. Patricia Mellencamp, 193–221. Bloomington: Indiana University Press, 1990.

———. *Bigger Than Life: The Close-Up and Scale in the Cinema*. Durham, NC: Duke University Press, 2021.

Donnelly, Kevin. *The Spectre of Sound*. London: Bloomsbury, 2005.

Duncan, Michelle. "The Operatic Scandal of the Singing Body: Voice, Presence, Performativity." *Cambridge Opera Journal* 16, no. 3 (2004): 283–306.

Dunlap, Orrin E., Jr. "Listening-In." *New York Times*, March 22, 1931, 160.

———. "Scanning Tele-Opera." *New York Times*, November 14, 1937, 14.

Eidsheim, Nina Sun. *Sensing Sound: Singing and Listening as Vibrational Practice*. Durham, NC: Duke University Press, 2015.

Elcott, Noam. *Artificial Darkness: An Obscure History of Modern Art and Media.* Chicago: University of Chicago Press, 2016.

Ellis, John. *Visible Fictions: Cinema, Television, Video.* London: Routledge & Kegan Paul, 1982.

Ellis Haworth, Ruth. "One Giant Leap for Opera Video." The Rehearsal Studio, March 22, 2008. http://therehearsalstudio.blogspot.com/2008/03/one-giant-leap-for-opera-video.html.

———. "The Met's HD Transmission Fails Tristan und Isolde." Yappa Ding, March 24, 2008. http://yappadingding.blogspot.com/2008/03/mets-hd-transmission-fails-tristan-und.html.

———. "Is Barbara Willis Sweete Destroying the Met HD Program?" Yappa Ding, January 18, 2009. http://yappadingding.blogspot.com/2009/01/is-barbara-willis-sweete-destroying-met.html.

Elsaesser, Thomas. *Film History as Media Archaeology: Tracking Digital Cinema.* Amsterdam: Amsterdam University Press, 2016.

Emmett, John. "Multichannel Audio for Television." *EBU Technical Review*, October 2002. https://tech.ebu.ch/docs/techreview/trev_292-emmett.pdf.

Ender, Daniel. "Die Ölkrise des multimedialen Theaters." *Der Standard*, July 29, 2013. https://www.derstandard.at/story/1373513958167/die-oelkrise-des-multimedialen-theaters.

Englhart, Andreas. *Das Theater der Gegenwart.* Berlin: C. H. Beck, 2013.

Eskow, Gary. "New York's Met in HD." *Mix*, April 1, 2008. https://www.mixonline.com/sfp/new-yorks-met-hd-369201.

Esse, Melina. "Don't Look Now: Opera, Liveness, and the Televisual." *Opera Quarterly* 26, no. 1 (Winter 2010): 81–95.

Evans, Anthony. "Live in HD: Verdi's *La traviata* from the Met." Planethugill.com, March 13, 2017. https://www.planethugill.com/2017/03/live-in-hd-verdis-la-traviata-from-met.html.

"Falstaff: The (Other) Finale." Bayerische Staatsoper, December 2020. https://www.staatsoper.de/editorial/detail/falstaff-the-other-finale.

Feuer, Jane. "The Concept of Live Television: Ontology as Ideology." In *Regarding Television: Critical Approaches—an Anthology*, ed. E. Ann Kaplan, 12–21. Bethesda, MD: University Publications of America, 1983.

Field, Andy. "'Site-Specific Theatre'? Please Be More Specific." *The Guardian*, February 6, 2008. http://www.theguardian.com/stage/theatreblog/2008/feb/06/sitespecifictheatrepleasebe.

Fischer-Lichte, Erika. *Routledge Introduction to Theatre and Performance Studies.* Edited by Minou Arjomand and Ramona Mosse. Translated by Minou Arjomand. London: Routledge, 2014.

Forner, Jane. "*Svadba on the Beach*: Opera for the Streaming Age." *Opera Quarterly* (in press).

Foucault, Michel. *Discipline and Punish: The Birth of the Prison.* Translated by Alan Sheridan. New York: Vintage, 1995.

Frendo, Mario. "Opera's Second Life: Katie Mitchell's Contributions to Contemporary Opera-Making." *Contemporary Theatre Review* 30, no. 2 (2020): 211–25.

BIBLIOGRAPHY | 237

Friedberg, Anne. *The Virtual Window: From Alberti to Microsoft*. Cambridge, MA: MIT Press, 2009.

Fry, Tony. "Introduction." In *R U A TV? Heidegger and the Televisual*, ed. Tony Fry, 11–23. Sydney: Power, 1993.

Fryer, Paul, ed. *Opera in the Media Age: Essays on Art, Technology and Popular Culture*. Jefferson, NC: McFarland, 2014.

Galison, Peter. *Einstein's Clocks, Poincaré's Maps: Empires of Time*. New York: Norton, 2004.

Gardner, Lyn. "Waves Sets a High-Water Mark for Multimedia Theater." *The Guardian*, December 4, 2006. https://www.theguardian.com/stage/theatreblog/2006/dec/04/wavessetsahighwatermarkfo.

Gaudréault, André, and Philippe Marion. *The End of Cinema? A Medium in Crisis in the Digital Age*. Translated by Timothy Barnard. New York: Columbia University Press, 2015.

Gelb, Peter. "Theatrical Nuance on a Grand Scale." *New York Times*, March 25, 2011. https://www.nytimes.com/2011/03/27/arts/music/metropolitan-opera-hones-dramatic-values-for-stage-and-screen.html.

Gernsback, Hugo. "Grand Opera by Wireless." *Radio Amateur News* 1, no. 3 (September 1919): 106.

Giesekam, Greg. *Staging the Screen: The Use of Film and Video in Theatre*. London: Palgrave Macmillan, 2007.

Gilman, Sander, and Jeongwon Joe, eds. *Wagner and Cinema*. Bloomington: Indiana University Press, 2010.

Goddard, Peter. "A Reaction to Opera's Video Projection Fetish." *Toronto Star*, February 14, 2008. https://www.thestar.com/discard/2008/02/14/a_reaction_to_operas_video_projection_fetish.html.

Gorbman, Claudia, and John Richardson. "Introduction." In *The Oxford Handbook of New Audiovisual Aesthetics*, ed. Claudia Gorbman, John Richardson, and Carol Vernallis, 3–38. New York: Oxford University Press, 2013.

Graf, Herbert. "Opera in Television." In *Music in Radio Broadcasting*, ed. Gilbert Chase, 138–40. New York: McGraw-Hill, 1946.

Grainge, Paul. *Brand Hollywood: Selling Entertainment in a Global Media Age*. New York: Routledge, 2008.

Grajeda, Tony. "The 'Sweet Spot': The Technology of Stereo and the Field of Auditorship." In *Living Stereo: Histories and Cultures of Multichannel Sound*, ed. Paul Théberge, Kyle Devine, and Tom Everrett, 37–64. London: Bloomsbury, 2015.

Gray, Richard. *Cinemas in Britain: One Hundred Years of Cinema Architecture*. London: Lund Humphreys, 1996.

Greiving, Tim. "Opera for the Masses Reps Cash Cow for the Met." *Variety*, August 25, 2015. https://variety.com/2015/music/features/met-brings-highbrow-opera-to-the-masses-1201577973.

Groupe Lou Sin d'intervention idéologique. "À armes égales: Analyse d'une émission télévisée." *Cahiers du cinéma*, nos. 236–37 (March–April 1972): 4–29.

Grover-Friedlander, Michal. *Vocal Apparitions: The Attraction of Cinema to Opera*. Princeton, NJ: Princeton University Press, 2005.

Groves, Nancy. "Arts Head: David Sabel, Head of Digital, National Theatre." *The Guardian*, April 10, 2012. https://www.theguardian.com/culture-professionals-network/culture-professionals-blog/2012/apr/10/david-sabel-digital-national-theatre.

Gumbrecht, Hans-Ulrich. *The Production of Presence: What Meaning Cannot Convey*. Stanford, CA: Stanford University Press, 2004.

Gunning, Tom. "The Cinema of Attractions: The Early Film, Its Spectator and the Avant-Garde." In *Early Cinema: Space, Frame, Narrative*, ed. Thomas Elsaesser, 56–62. London: BFI, 1990.

———. "Renewing Old Technologies: Astonishment, Second Nature, and the Uncanny in Technology from the Previous Turn-of-the-Century." In *Rethinking Media Change: The Aesthetics of Transition*, ed. David Thorburn, Henry Jenkins, and Brad Seawell, 39–60. Cambridge, MA: MIT Press, 2003.

———. "'Nothing Will Have Taken Place Except Place': The Unsettling Nature of Camera Movement." In *Screen Space Reconfigured*, ed. Susanne Ø. Saether and Synne T. Bull, 263–82. Amsterdam: Amsterdam University Press, 2020.

Guthrie, Kate. "Marconi's Phoney Future." *Cambridge Opera Journal* 28, no. 2 (2016): 247–49.

Hagener, Malte. "Divided, Together, Apart: How Split Screen Became Our Everyday Reality." In *Pandemic Media: Preliminary Notes toward an Inventory*, ed. Philipp Dominik Keidl, Laliv Melamed, Vinzenz Hediger, and Antonio Somaini, 33–40. Lüneberg: Meson, 2020.

Hagmann, Peter. "Auf der Spur des Öls." *Neue Zürcher Zeitung*, July 29, 2013. https://www.nzz.ch/feuilleton/auf-der-spur-des-oels-1.18124338.

Haigh, Caroline, John Dunkerley, and Mark Rogers. *Classical Recording: A Practical Guide in the Decca Tradition*. London: Routledge, 2020.

Hanson, Stuart. *Screening the World: Global Development of the Multiplex Cinema*. London: Palgrave Macmillan, 2019.

Harsh, Ed, moderator. "New Technologies and Their Impact: Panel Discussion." Opera America Annual Conference, May 20, 2020. https://youtu.be/LMSFedTxQKk.

Havelková, Tereza. *Opera as Hypermedium: Meaning-Making, Immediacy, and the Politics of Perception*. New York: Oxford University Press, 2021.

Henson, Karen, ed. *Technology and the Diva: Sopranos, Opera, and Media from Romanticism to the Digital Age*. Cambridge: Cambridge University Press, 2016.

Heylbut, Rose. "Telecasting the Metropolitan Opera." *Étude* 73 (January 1955): 26.

Hilmes, Michele. "Television Sound: Why the Silence?" *Music, Sound, and the Moving Image* 2, no. 2 (Autumn 2008): 153–61.

Hoffmann, William J., Jr. "Nationwide Opening Night." *Opera News* 19, no. 2 (November 1, 1954): 12–13.

Høier, Svein. "The Relevance of Point of Audience in Television Sound: Rethinking a Problematic Term." In "Rethinking Theories of Television Sound," ed. Carolyn Birdsall and Anthony Enns, special issue, *Journal of Sonic Studies*, vol. 3, no. 1 (October 2012). https://www.researchcatalogue.net/view/252390/252391.

Hollinger, Hy. "Theatre-TV Pulls 'Em In." *Variety* 96, no. 10 (November 10, 1954): 20.

BIBLIOGRAPHY | 239

Hosokawa, Shuhei. "The Walkman Effect." *Popular Music* 4 (1984): 162–78.

Hubbell, Richard. *Television: Programming and Production*. New York: Rinehart, 1950.

Hugill, Robert. "Written on Skin at Covent Garden." Planethugill.com, March 17, 2013. https://www.planethugill.com/2013/03/written-on-skin-at-covent-garden.html.

Huhtamo, Erkki. "Gulliver in Figurine Land." Translated by Linda Pollack. *Mediamatik* 4, no. 3 (1990): 101–5.

"Hundreds of Americans Hear Europe Broadcasting." *New York Times*, November 30, 1924. 15.

Hunter, Brandon. *Playing Real: Mimesis, Media, and Mischief*. Evanston, IL: Northwestern University Press, 2021.

Huss, Christophe. "Metropolitan Opera: La damnation de Lepage: Un échec affligeant." *Le devoir*, November 24, 2008. https://www.ledevoir.com/culture/musique/218268/metropolitan-opera-la-damnation-de-lepage-un-echec-affligeant.

———. "Trop de compromis." *Le devoir*, May 2, 2016. https://www.ledevoir.com/culture/musique/469698/le-metropolitan-opera-au-cinema-trop-de-compromis.

———. "Le Met au cinéma: Gary et le travelling de 'Kapo.'" *Le devoir*, February 4, 2019. https://www.ledevoir.com/culture/musique/547031/le-metropolitan-opera-au-cinema-gary-et-le-travelling-de-kapo.

Jacobsen, Mitch. *Mastering Multi-Camera Techniques: From Pre-production to Editing and Deliverables*. Burlington, VA: Focal, 2010.

Jammer, Max. *Concepts of Simultaneity from Antiquity to Einstein and Beyond*. Baltimore: Johns Hopkins University Press, 2006.

Joe, Jeongwon. "The Cinematic Body in the Operatic Theater: Philip Glass's *La belle et la bête*." In *Between Opera and Cinema*, ed. Jeongwon Joe and Rose Theresa, 59–74. New York: Routledge, 2002.

———. *Opera as Soundtrack*. Farnham: Ashgate, 2013.

Johnson, Lawrence. "HD at the Opera." *Musical America Worldwide*, 2009. https://www.musicalamerica.com/features/?fid=153&fyear=2009.

Kaye, Nick. *Site-Specific Art: Performance, Place and Documentation*. London: Routledge, 2002.

Keeler, Harry Stephen. *The Box from Japan*. New York: Wildside, 1932.

Kerins, Mark. *Beyond Dolby (Stereo): Cinema in the Digital Sound Age*. Bloomington: Indiana University Press, 2011.

Kettle, Martin. Review of *Die Walküre*, Bayreuth Festival, *The Guardian*, July 28, 2013. https://www.theguardian.com/music/2013/jul/28/das-rheingold-die-walkure-review.

Kidnie, Margaret Jane. "The Stratford Festival of Canada: Mental Tricks and Archival Documents in the Age of *NT Live*." In *Shakespeare and the "Live" Theatre Broadcast Experience*, ed. Pascale Aebischer, Susanne Greenhalgh, and Laurie Osborne, 133–46. London: Bloomsbury, 2018.

King, Richard. *Recording Orchestra and Other Classical Music Ensembles*. London: Routledge, 2017.

Kirwan, Peter. "Cheek by Jowl: Reframing Complicity in Web-Streams of *Measure for Measure*." In *Shakespeare and the "Live" Theatre Broadcast Experience*, ed. Pascale Aebischer, Susanne Greenhalgh, and Laurie Osborne, 161–74. London: Bloomsbury, 2018.

Kitsopanidou, Kira. "Electronic Delivery of Alternative Contents in Cinemas Before the Digital Era: The Case of Theater Television in the US Exhibition Market in the 1940s and 1950s." *Mise au point*, no. 4 (2012). https://journals.openedition.org/map/775?gathStatIcon=true&lang=en.

Klinger, Barbara. *Beyond the Multiplex: Cinema, New Technologies, and the Home.* Berkeley and Los Angeles: University of California Press, 2006.

Kramer, Lawrence. *Opera and Modern Culture: Wagner and Strauss.* Berkeley and Los Angeles: University of California Press, 2007.

———. "'The Threshold of the Visible World': Wagner, Bill Viola, and *Tristan*." In *Wagner and Cinema*, ed. Sander L. Gilman and Jeongwon Joe, 381–407. Bloomington: Indiana University Press, 2010.

———. "Classical Music for the Postmodern Condition." In *The Oxford Handbook of New Audiovisual Aesthetics*, ed. John Richardson, Claudia Gorbman, and Carol Vernallis, 39–52. Oxford, New York: Oxford University Press, 2013.

Kreuzer, Gundula. *Curtain, Gong, Steam: Wagnerian Technologies of Nineteenth-Century Opera.* Berkeley and Los Angeles: University of California Press, 2018.

———. "Flat Bayreuth: A Genealogy of Opera as Screened." In *Screen Genealogies: From Optical Device to Environmental Medium*, ed. Craig Buckley, Rüdiger Campe, and Francesco Casetti, 237–68. Amsterdam: Amsterdam University Press, 2019.

Kuhn, Bernhard. "Live at the Cinema: The Metropolitan Opera's Cinecast of *La traviata*." In *Verdi on Screen*, ed. Delphine Vincent, 210–25. Lausanne: L'age d'homme, 2016.

Künzi, Renat. "'La bohème' bringt Wohnblock B zum Klingen." Swissinfo.ch. https://www.swissinfo.ch/ger/kultur/-la-bohème--bringt-wohnblock-b-zum-klingen/140652.

Kwon, Miwon. *One Place after Another: Site-Specific Art and Locational Identity.* Cambridge, MA: MIT Press, 2002.

Lefebvre, Henri. *The Production of Space.* Translated by Donald Nicholson-Smith. Oxford: Wiley-Blackwell, 1991.

Lehmann, Hans-Thies. *Postdramatic Theatre.* Translated by Karen Jürs-Munby. London: Routledge, 2006.

Leppert, Richard. *Aesthetic Technologies of Modernity, Subjectivity, and Nature: Opera, Orchestra, Phonograph, Film.* Oakland: University of California Press, 2015.

Lev, Peter. *Transforming the Screen, 1950–1959.* New York: Charles Scribner's Sons, 2003.

Levin, David J. *Unsettling Opera: Staging Mozart, Verdi, Wagner, and Zemlinsky.* Chicago: University of Chicago Press, 2007.

Levin, Thomas Y. "Rhetoric of the Temporal Index: Surveillant Narration and the Cinema of 'Real Time.'" In *CTRL [SPACE]: Rhetorics of Surveillance from*

Bentham to Big Brother, ed. Thomas Y. Levin, 578–93. Cambridge, MA: MIT Press, 2002.

L'Occaso, Stefano. "The Stronghold of Sparafucile." In the booklet accompanying *3 Live Films: Rigoletto in Mantua, La traviata in Paris, Tosca in Rome*. Blu-ray discs, Naxos NBD0052–54 (2016).

Lockhart, Ellen. "Photo-Opera: *La fanciulla del West* and the Staging Souvenir." *Cambridge Opera Journal* 23 (2011): 145–66.

Lombard, Matthew, and Theresa Ditton. "At the Heart of It All: The Concept of Presence." *Journal of Computer-Mediated Communication*, vol. 13, no. 3 (September 1997). https://academic.oup.com/jcmc/article/3/2/JCMC321/4080403.

Maddocks, Fiona. "Lucia di Lammermoor Review—Flawed but Full of Provocative Thought." *The Guardian*, April 10, 2016. https://www.theguardian.com/music/2016/apr/10/lucia-di-lammermoor-review-royal-opera-katie-mitchell-diana-damrau.

Malvano, Andrea. "'La via della musica': Rischi e trasformazioni del live film opera nelle produzioni Rai di Andrea Andermann." In "L'ora della musica in tv: La divulgazione della musica in televisione dal 1954 a oggi," ed. Marida Rizzuti and Anna Scalfaro, special issue, *Gli spazi della musica* 9 (2020): 85–103.

Manovich, Lev. *The Language of New Media*. Boston: MIT Press, 2002.

Martinez, Ann M. "Shakespeare at a Theatre Near You: Student Engagement in Northeast Ohio." In *Shakespeare and the "Live" Theatre Broadcast Experience*, ed. Pascale Aebischer, Susanne Greenhalgh, and Laurie Osborne, 199–206. London: Bloomsbury, 2018.

McAuley, Gay. "Site-Specific Performance: Place, Memory and the Creative Agency of the Spectator." *Arts: The Journal of the Sydney University Arts Association* 27 (2005): 27–51.

McHenry, Jackson. "Who Tells Your Story on Camera? How *Hamilton* Was Edited into a Movie." Vulture.com, July 10, 2020. https://www.vulture.com/article/how-hamilton-was-edited-into-a-movie.html.

McLennan, Doug. "New Technologies and Their Impact: Lead Presentation." Opera America Annual Conference, May 18, 2020. https://youtu.be/vHvy3ouUn4s.

"Meist Nettes." *Der Spiegel*, June 18, 1967. https://www.spiegel.de/kultur/meist-nettes-a-81d976d2-0002-0001-0000-000046251916.

Mera, Miguel. "Listening-Feeling-Becoming: Cinema Surveillance." In *The Oxford Handbook of Cinematic Listening*, ed. Carlo Cenciarelli, 407–26. New York: Oxford University Press, 2021.

"The Met Opera: Live in HD Opens Season." *The Pilot*, October 21, 2021. https://www.thepilot.com/news/features/the-met-opera-live-in-hd-opens-season/article_25dddc64-2157-11ec-9313-e3163da88ece.html.

"Metopera's Closed-Circuit Special Grossed $180,000." *Variety*, November 17, 1954, 3.

"Metropolitan Openings Signed for Theatre TV." *Boxoffice*, January 30, 1954, 20.

"Metropolitan Opera Live in HD." *Rye Record*, October 27, 2014. https://ryerecord.com/metropolitan-opera-live-in-hd.

"The Metropolitan Opera Reaches Groundbreaking Agreements." Metropolitan Opera, September 6, 2006. Press release. http://www.operatoday.com/documents/Met_New_Media_release.pdf.

Minsky, Marvin. "Telepresence." *Omni*, June 1980, 45–51.

Mitchell, Katie. "Mit der Wucht des Thrillers gegen überkommene Bilder." In the program booklet accompanying the February 2020 Bayerische performance of *Judith*, 30–33.

Mitoma, Judy, ed. *Envisioning Dance on Film and Video*. New York: Routledge, 2002.

Moravcsik, Andrew. "*Bluebeard's Castle*, Munich." *Opera Today*, March 7, 2020. http://www.operatoday.com/content/2020/03/bluebeards_cast.php.

Morris, Christopher. "Digital Diva: Opera on Video." *Opera Quarterly* 26, no. 1 (Winter 2010): 96–119.

———. "The Mute Stones Sing: *Rigoletto* Live from Mantua." *TDR: The Drama Review* 59, no. 4 (2015): 51–66.

———. "The Deadness of Live Opera." In *Performing Arts in Transition: Moving between Media*, ed. Susanne Foellmer, Maria Katharina Schmidt, and Cornelia Schmitz, 126–39. Abingdon: Routledge, 2018.

Morse, Margaret. *Virtualities: Television, Media Art, and Cyberculture*. Bloomington: Indiana University Press, 1998.

Moylan, William. *The Art of Recording*. New York: Springer, 1992.

Nilsson, Niels Christian, Rolf Nordahl, and Stefania Serafin. "Immersion Revisited: A Review of Existing Definitions of Immersion and Their Relation to Different Theories of Presence." *Human Technology* 12, no. 2 (November 2016): 108–34.

Nyffeler, Max. "Tod im Busbahnhof: Zur Live-Übertragung von Puccinis 'Bohème' aus Bern." *Neue Musikzeitung*, October 1, 2009. https://www.nmz.de/online/tod-im-busbahnhof-zur-live-uebertragung-von-puccinis-boheme-aus-einem-berner-hochhaus.

Oberender, Thomas. "Das Drama des Sehens: Live-Video auf der Bühne oder die Politik des Blicks." *Dramaturg* 1 (2004): 15–21.

O'Connell, Sam. "Making Culture Popular: Opera and the Media Industries." In *Opera in the Media Age: Essays on Art, Technology and Popular Culture*, ed. Paul Fryer, 32–42. Jefferson, NC: McFarland, 2014.

O'Connor, John. "TV: 'Gioconda' Week Begins on Channel 13." *New York Times*, April 14, 1980, C18. https://www.nytimes.com/1980/04/14/archives/tv-gioconda-week-begins-on-channel-13.html.

Osborne, Laurie E. "Epilogue: Revisiting Liveness." In *Shakespeare and the "Live" Theatre Broadcast Experience*, ed. Pascale Aebischer, Susanne Greenhalgh, and Laurie Osborne, 215–26. London: Bloomsbury, 2018.

O'Shaughnessy, Luke. "Audience Development: Introducing the Opera Europa Streaming Platform." Presentation at the European Theatre Convention, October 27, 2017. https://youtu.be/5gNESI3CL2g.

Ozorio, Anne. "Unique Rigoletto live from Mantua." *Opera Today*, September 8, 2010. http://www.operatoday.com/content/2010/09/rigoletto_live_.php.

Palazzetti, Nicolò. "Backstage Live: Opera and the Obscene in the Visual Age." In "Re-Envisaging Music: Listening in the Visual Age," ed. Antonio Cascelli and

Christopher Morris, special issue, *Chigiana: Journal of Musicological Studies*, ser. 3, 3 (2021): 43–60.

Parks, Lisa. *Cultures in Orbit: Satellites and the Televisual*. Durham, NC: Duke University Press, 2005.

Payne, Nicholas. "Survival of the Fittest." *Opera*, January 2021, 49–52.

Pearson, Mike. "Special Worlds, Secret Maps: A Poetics of Performance." In *Staging Wales: Welsh Theatre, 1979–1997*, ed. Anna Marie Taylor, 95–96. Cardiff: University of Wales Press, 1997.

———. *Site-Specific Performance*. London: Palgrave Macmillan, 2010.

Pearson, Mike, and Michael Shanks. *Theatre/Archeology*. London: Routledge, 2001.

Pérez, Héctor J., ed. *Opera and Video: Technology and Spectatorship*. Bern: Peter Lang, 2012.

Peter, Wolf-Dieter. "Filmnahe Verbrecherjagd—Bartóks 'Blaubart' und 'Konzert für Orchester' im Münchner Nationaltheater." NMZ, February 2, 2020. https://www.nmz.de/online/filmnahe-verbrecherjagd-Bartóks-blaubart-und-konzert-fuer-orchester-im-muenchner-nationalthea.

Peucker, Brigitte. *The Material Image: Art and the Real in Film*. Stanford, CA: Stanford University Press, 2007.

Porter, Andrew. Review of *Das Rheingold*. *Gramophone* 36, no. 430 (March 1959): 472–73.

Potter, Simon J. *Broadcasting Empire: The BBC and the British World, 1922–1970*. New York: Oxford University Press, 2012.

Pschera, Alexander. "Der Tod des alten, weißen Mannes." *Die Tagespost*, February 19, 2020. https://www.die-tagespost.de/gesellschaft/kultur/Der-Tod-des-alten-weissen-Mannes;art4881,205664.

"Radio to 'Attend' Opera." *New York Times*, December 6, 1936, 6.

Rathert, Wolfgang. "Die verborgenen Tränen des Béla Bartók." In the program booklet accompanying the February 2020 Bayerische performance of *Judith*, 50–61.

Ridout, Nicholas. "Opera and the Technologies of Theatrical Reproduction." In *The Cambridge Companion to Opera Studies*, ed. Nicholas Till, 159–78. Cambridge: Cambridge University Press, 2012.

Rieser, Martin. *The Mobile Audience: Media Art and Mobile Technologies*. Amsterdam: Rodopi, 2011.

Risi, Clemens. *Opera in Performance: Analyzing the Performative Dimension of Opera Productions*. Abingdon: Routledge, 2021.

Rizzuti, Marida, and Anna Scalfaro, eds. "L'ora della musica in tv: La divulgazione della musica in televisione dal 1954 a oggi." Special issue, *Gli spazi della musica*, vol. 9 (2020).

Roginska, Agnieszka, and Paul Geluso, eds. *Immersive Sound: The Art and Science of Binaural and Multi-Channel Audio*. New York: Routledge, 2018.

Ross, Alex. "Diminuendo: A Downturn for Opera in New York City." *New Yorker*, March 12, 2012. https://www.newyorker.com/magazine/2012/03/12/diminuendo-2.

Rugg, Judith. *Exploring Site-Specific Art: Issues of Space and Internationalism*. London: I. B. Tauris, 2010.

Salazar, David. "Opera Meets Film: The Lost Art of Filming Live Opera in HD." Operawire, April 11, 2019. https://operawire.com/opera-meets-film-the-lost-art-of-filming-live-opera-in-hd.

———. "Met Opera 2021–22 Season: Here Is All The Information for This Season's Live in HD Performances." Operawire, September 23, 2020. https://operawire.com/met-opera-2021-22-season-here-is-all-the-information-for-this-seasons-live-in-hd-performances.

"Sales Meet OK, Opera Only Fair via Theater TV." *Billboard*, December 20, 1952, 4.

Scannell, Paddy. "Television and History." In *A Companion to Television*, ed. Janet Wasko, 51–66. Oxford: Blackwell, 2005.

Schechner, Richard. *Environmental Theater*. New York: Hawthorn, 1973.

Schipper, Imanuel. "City as Performance." *TDR: The Drama Review* 58, no. 3 (2014): 18–26.

Schneider, Rebecca. *Performing Remains: Art and War in Times of Theatrical Reenactment*. New York: Routledge, 2011.

Schoen, Ernst. "Broadcast Opera in Germany." In *The B.B.C. Year-Book, 1934*, 67–71. London: British Broadcasting Corp., 1934.

Schulz, Anne, Amelie Eder, Victor Tiberius, Samantha Casas Solorio, Manuela Fabro, and Nataliia Brehmer. "The Digitalization of Motion Picture Production and Its Value Chain Implications." *Journalism and Media* 2, no. 3 (2021): 397–416.

Schwartz, Arman. "Puccini, in the Distance." *Cambridge Opera Journal* 23, no. 3 (November 2011): 167–89.

———. "Stefan Herheim's *La bohème* on DVD: A Review Portfolio." *Opera Quarterly* 29, no. 2 (Spring 2013): 162–67.

———. "Opera and Objecthood: Sedimentation, Spectatorship, and *Einstein on the Beach*." *Opera Quarterly* 35, nos. 1–2 (Winter–Spring 2019): 40–62.

Schwartz, Lloyd. "Opera on Television." *The Atlantic*, January 1983, 84–90.

Schwarze, Norman. "Tatort München: Bayerische Staatsoper inszeniert mit *Judith* einen packenden Thriller." Bachtrack, February 3, 2020. https://bachtrack.com/kritik-Bartók-judith-herzog-blaubarts-burg-mitchell-lyniv-stemme-lundgren-bayerische-staatsoper-februar-2020.

Senici, Emanuele. *Landscape and Gender in Italian Opera: The Alpine Virgin from Bellini to Puccini*. Cambridge: Cambridge University Press, 2005.

———. "Porn Style? Space and Time in Live Opera Videos." *Opera Quarterly* 26, no. 1 (Winter 2010): 63–80.

———. "Opera on Italian Television: The First Thirty Years, 1954–1984." In *Opera and Video: Technology and Spectatorship*, ed. Héctor J. Pérez, 45–70. Bern: Peter Lang, 2012.

———. "'In the Score': Music and Media in the Discourse of Operatic *Mise-en-Scène*." *Opera Quarterly* 35, no. 3 (Summer 2019): 207–23.

Seymour, Claire. "*Written on Skin*: Royal Opera House." *Opera Today*, January 15, 2017. http://www.operatoday.com/content/2017/01/written_on_skin.php.

Shary, Timothy. *Generation Multiplex: The Image of Youth in Contemporary American Cinema*. Austin: University of Texas Press, 2002.

Shaw, Helen, and Mark Harris. "The *Hamilton* Movie Swings Open the Doors of Broadway." Vulture.com, July 2, 2020. https://www.vulture.com/2020/07/hamilton-movie-review-swing-open-the-doors-of-broadway.html.

Sheil, Áine, and Craig Vear, eds. "Digital Opera, New Means and Meanings." Special issue, *International Journal of Performance Art and Digital Media*, vol. 8 (2012).

———. "The Opera Director's Voice: DVD 'Extras' and the Question of Authority." In *Opera and Video: Technology and Spectatorship*, ed. Héctor J. Pérez, 129–52. Bern: Peter Lang, 2012.

Sheppard, W. Anthony. "Review of the Metropolitan Opera's New HD Movie Theater Broadcasts." *American Music* 25, no. 3 (Fall 2007): 383–87.

Simon, Jesse. "Countdown to Ecstasy." Mundoclasico.com, February 23, 2018. https://www.mundoclasico.com/articulo/30583/Countdown-to-Ecstasy.

Singer, Jack. "Theater TV Breaks Barrier." *Billboard*, August 21, 1954, 1, 15.

Sirmons, Julia. "'Guarda un po': Seductive Visuality in Remediated Opera." *Opera Quarterly* 35, no. 4 (Autumn 2019): 297–322.

Speckenbach, Jan. "Der Einbruch der Fernsehntechnologie." In *Einbruch der Realität: Politik und Verbrechen*, ed. Carl Hegemann, 80–84. Berlin: Alexander Verlag/Volksbühne am Rosa-Luxemburg-Platz, 2002.

"Stan." "Close-Ups Do No Favours in Met Live Otello." *Seen and Heard International*, October 27, 2012. https://seenandheard-international.com/2012/11/close-ups-do-no-favours-in-met-live-otello.

Stearns, David Patrick. "Rameau's *Pygmalion* Waxes Operatic at Madame Tussauds." Operavore, June 18, 2014. https://www.wqxr.org/story/review-rameaus-pygmalion-waxes-operatic-madame-tussauds.

Steichen, James. "The Metropolitan Opera Goes Public: Peter Gelb and the Institutional Dramaturgy of the Met: Live in HD." *Music and the Moving Image* 2, no. 2 (2009): 24–30.

———. "HD Opera: A Love/Hate Story." *Opera Quarterly* 27. no. 4 (Winter 2012): 443–59.

Steigerwald Ille, Megan. "The Operatic Ear: Mediating Aurality." *Sound Stage Screen* 1, no. 1 (Spring 2021): 119–43.

Strangelove, Michael. *Post-TV: Piracy, Cord-Cutting, and the Future of Television*. Toronto: University of Toronto, 2015.

Sturm, Rüdiger. "Thriller." *Crescendo*, February 14, 2020. https://crescendo.de/katie-mitchell-bayerische-staatsoper.

Sullivan, Erin. "'The forms of things unknown': Shakespeare and the Rise of the Live Broadcast." *Shakespeare Bulletin* 35, no. 4 (Winter 2017): 627–62.

Sunier, John. Review of SACD *The Artistry of Teresa Perez, Cello*, Enjoy the Music, December 2001. http://www.enjoythemusic.com/audiophileaudition/1201/sacdreviews.htm.

Svensson, Marcus Sanchez, Christian Heath, and Paul Luff. "Monitoring Practice: Event Detection and System Design." In *Intelligent Distributed Video Surveil-*

lance Systems, ed. Sergio Velastin and Paolo Remagnino, 31–54. London: Institution of Engineering and Technology, 2006.

Tambling, Jeremy, ed. *A Night in at the Opera: Media Representations of Opera*. London: John Libby, 1994.

Tanner, Michael. "Tame and Drowning in Detail: Royal Opera's *Lucia di Lammermoor* Reviewed." *The Spectator*, April 16, 2016. https://www.spectator.com.au/2016/04/tame-and-drowning-in-detail-royal-operas-lucia-di-lammermoor-reviewed.

Taubman, Howard. "Nation Shares 'Met' Opening in Gala Theater-TV Parties." *New York Times*, November 9, 1954, 1.

Taylor, Paul. "The Waves, National Theatre Cottesloe, London." *The Independent*, November 20, 2006. https://www.independent.co.uk/arts-entertainment/theatre-dance/reviews/the-waves-national-theatre-cottesloe-london-424996.html.

"Television Seen as New Hope for Radio Opera." *New York Times*, January 4, 1931, 178.

Theresa, Rose, and Jeongwon Joe, eds. *Between Opera and Cinema*. London: Routledge, 2002.

Theurich, Werner. "Wie man aus Trash Gold macht." *Der Spiegel*, July 26, 2013. https://www.spiegel.de/kultur/gesellschaft/bayreuther-festspiele-premiere-rheingold-castorf-a-913318.html.

Tommasini, Anthony. "You Go to the Movie Theater, and an Opera Breaks Out." *New York Times*, January 3, 2008. https://www.nytimes.com/2008/01/03/arts/music/03hans.html.

———. "Wearing a Wire at the Opera, Secretly, of Course." *New York Times*, June 30, 2013. https://www.nytimes.com/2013/06/30/arts/music/wearing-a-wire-at-the-opera-secretly-of-course.html.

———. "The Real Rhinemaidens of Route 66." *New York Times*, July 28, 2013. https://www.nytimes.com/2013/07/29/arts/music/wagners-ring-opens-at-bayreuth-with-reality-cam-touch.html.

Tompkins, Joanne. "The 'Place' and Practice of Site-Specific Theatre and Performance." In *Performing Site-Specific Theatre: Politics, Place, Practice*, ed. Anna Birch and Joanne Tompkins, 1–20. London: Palgrave Macmillan, 2012.

Tran, Kevin. "'Hamilton' Far Bigger Than Anything on Netflix in July, Audience Data Reveals." *Variety*, August 10, 2020. https://variety.com/vip/disney-hamilton-audience-nearly-3x-bigger-than-any-netflix-program-in-july-1234729439.

Trippett, David. "Facing Digital Realities: Where Media Do Not Mix." *Cambridge Opera Journal* 26, no. 1 (2014): 41–64.

Trueman, Matt. "The Surprise Success of NT Live." *The Guardian*, June 9, 2013. https://www.theguardian.com/stage/2013/jun/09/nt-live-success.

Turner, Cathy. "Palimpsest or Potential Space: Finding a Vocabulary for Site-Specific Performance." *New Theatre Quarterly* 20, no. 4 (November 2004): 373–90.

Urricchio, William. "Storage, Simultaneity, and the Media Technologies of Modernity." In *Allegories of Communication: Intermedial Concerns from Cinema to the Digital*, ed. John Fullerton and Jan Olsson, 123–38. Rome: John Libbey/CIC, 2004.

VanCour, Shawn. "Spectacular Sound: Classical Music Programming and the Problem of 'Visual Interest' in Early US Television." In Baade and Deaville, eds., *Music and the Broadcast Experience: Performance, Production, and Audiences*, 91–108.

Vincent, Caitlin. *Digital Scenography in Opera in the Twenty-First Century*. New York: Routledge, 2021.

Vincent, Delphine. "'Temps spatialisé': Opera Relays and the Sense of Temporality." In *Opera and Video: Technology and Spectatorship*, ed. Héctor J. Pérez, 71–90. Bern: Peter Lang, 2012.

———, ed. *Verdi on Screen*. Lausanne: L'age d'homme, 2015.

Wakin, Daniel J. "Broadcast of 'Die Walküre' Performance at the Met Is Delayed." *ArtsBeat: New York Times Blog*, May 14, 2011. https://artsbeat.blogs.nytimes.com/2011/05/14/broadcast-of-die-walkure-performance-at-the-met-is-delayed.

———. "The Met Will Lower Ticket Prices." *New York Times*, February 26, 2013. https://www.nytimes.com/2013/02/27/arts/music/metropolitan-opera-to-reduce-ticket-prices-next-season.html.

Waleson, Heidi. "'Written on Skin' Review." *Wall Street Journal*, August 12, 2015. https://www.wsj.com/articles/written-on-skin-review-1439417190.

Ward-Griffin, Danielle. "Virtually There: Site-Specific Performance on Screen." *Opera Quarterly* 30, no. 4 (Autumn 2014): 362–68.

———. "As Seen on TV: Putting the NBC Opera on Stage." *Journal of the American Musicological Society* 71, no. 3 (2018): 595–654.

———. "Realism Redux: Staging *Billy Budd* in the Age of Television." *Music and Letters* 100, no. 3 (August 2019): 447–80.

Warschauer, Frank. "Die Zukunft der Oper im Rundfunk." *Musikblätter des Anbruch* 11, no. 6 (June 1929): 274–76. Reprinted as "The Future of Opera on the Radio," in *The Weimar Republic Sourcebook*, ed. Anton Kaes, Martin Jay, and Edward Dimendberg, trans. Don Reneau (Berkeley and Los Angeles: University of California Press, 1995), 1:607–9.

Weber, Samuel. *Mass Mediauras: Form, Technics, Media*. Stanford, CA: Stanford University Press, 1996.

Weed, Mike. "The Pub as a Virtual Football Fandom Venue: An Alternative to 'Being There'?" *Soccer and Society* 8, nos. 2–3 (2007): 399–414.

Wells, Brianna. "'Secret Mechanism': *Les contes d'Hoffmann* and the Intermedial Uncanny in the Metropolitan Opera's Live in HD Series." *19th-Century Music* 36, no. 2 (Fall 2012): 191–203.

White, Mimi. "The Attractions of Television: Reconsidering Liveness." In *MediaSpace: Place, Scale and Culture in a Media Age*, ed. Nick Couldry and Anna McCarthy, 75–92. New York: Routledge, 2004.

Wiens, Birgit E. "Introduction." In *Contemporary Scenography: Practices and Aesthetics in German Theater, Arts and Design*, ed. Birgit E. Wiens, 1–30. London: Methuen, 2019.

Wierzbicki, James. "Rapt/Wrapped Listening: The Aesthetics of 'Surround Sound.'" *Sound Stage Screen* 1, no. 2 (Fall 2021): 101–24.

Will, Richard. "Zooming in, Gazing Back: *Don Giovanni* on Television." *Opera Quarterly* 27, no. 1 (Spring 2011): 32–65.

———. *Don Giovanni Captured: Performance, Media, Myth.* Chicago: University of Chicago Press, 2022.

Woolfe, Zachary. "I'm Ready for My Close-Up, Mr. Puccini." *New York Times*, April 27, 2012. https://www.nytimes.com/2012/04/29/arts/music/the-mets-hd-broadcasts-are-changing-opera.html.

———. "The Screen Can't Hear When You Yell 'Bravo.'" *New York Times*, May 4, 2012. https://www.nytimes.com/2012/05/06/arts/music/met-operas-live-in-hd-series-outside-of-new-york.html.

Wrench, Evelyn. "A Vision of Empire Broadcasting." *World-Radio*, December 22, 1933, 815.

Wright, Benjamin. "Atmos Now: Dolby Laboratories, Mixing Ideology and Hollywood Sound Production." In *Living Stereo: Histories and Cultures of Multichannel Sound*, ed. Paul Théberge, Kyle Devine, and Tom Everrett, 227–46. London: Bloomsbury, 2015.

Wright, Kenneth A. "Television and Opera." *Tempo* 45 (Autumn 1957): 8–14.

Wurtzler, Steve. "She Sang Live, but the Microphone Was Turned Off: The Live, the Recorded, and the Subject of Representation." In *Sound Theory, Sound Practice*, ed. Rick Altman, 87–103. New York: Routledge, 1992.

Wyver, John. "Who Needs Opera Glasses? The Met's Screen Revolution." *The Guardian*, March 27, 2008.

———. "'All the Trimmings?': The Transfer of Theatre to Television in Adaptations of Shakespeare Stagings." *Adaptation* 7, no. 2 (August 2014): 104–20.

———. *Screening the Royal Shakespeare Company: A Critical History.* London and New York: Bloomsbury/The Arden Shakespeare, 2019.

Žižek, Slavoj. "David Lynch; or, The Feminine Depression." In *The Metastases of Enjoyment: Six Essays on Women and Causality*, 113–36. London: Verso, 1994.

———. *The Abyss of Freedom.* Ann Arbor: University of Michigan Press, 1997.

———. *The Parallax View.* Cambridge, MA: MIT Press, 2006.

Videography

La bohème im Hochhaus. Directed by Anja Horst. 2009. DVD Schweizer Fernsehen 7640117266185, 2009.

Judith. Directed by Katie Mitchell. Live stream, Staatsoper.tv, 2020.

Lucia di Lammermoor. Directed by Mary Zimmerman. 2009. Met Opera on Demand. https://www.metopera.org/season/on-demand/opera/?upc=811357012314.

Das Rheingold. Directed by Frank Castorf. 2016 (original production 2013). Deutsche Grammophon Stage+, 2022. https://www.stage-plus.com/video/vod_concert_APNM8GRFDPHMASJKBSP3ADO.

Samson et Dalila. Directed by Darko Tresnjak. 2018. Met Opera on Demand. https://www.metopera.org/season/on-demand/opera/?upc=810004200609.

Tannhäuser. Directed by Tobias Kratzer. 2019. Blu-ray Deutsche Grammophon 0735760, 2020.

3 Live Films: Rigoletto in Mantua, La traviata in Paris, Tosca in Rome. Blu-ray discs, Naxos NBD0052–54, 2016.

Tosca. Directed by Christophe Honoré. 2019. On-demand stream, Arte Concert, 2019.

La traviata. Directed by Willy Decker. 2006. Blu-ray Deutsche Grammophon 0734525.

La traviata. Directed by Willy Decker. 2012. Met Opera on Demand. https://www.metopera.org/season/on-demand/opera/?upc=811357015179.

Tristan und Isolde. Directed by Dmitri Tcherniakov. 2018. Live stream, Staatsoper Unter den Linden.

Written on Skin. Directed by Katie Mitchell. Blu-ray Opus Arte OABD7136D, 2013

Index

Page numbers in *italics* refer to figures.

Abbate, Carolyn, 206n17
Adams, John. See *Nixon in China*
Adams, Robin, *182*
Aebischer, Pascale, 134
Aix-en-Provence, 38, 58, 62–64, 73, 162
Akhnaten (Glass), 142
Akzeybek, Tansel, *43*
Allen, Jonathan, 80, 81, 118, 151, 152, 153
ambient sound, 80, 121, 122, 150, 154, 172, 184. *See also* surround sound
Andermann, Andrea, 103–4, 164–66, 171–72, 182
Appadurai, Arjun, 101
apparatus. *See* television
Armatage, Kay, 83, 87, 120, 146
Arte (broadcaster), *41*, 62–67, 73, 172
Ashley, Tim, 60, 129
aspect ratio, 34, 49, 62–63, 73, 85–86
Attard, Joseph, 199n39
Augé, Marc, 155
Auslander, Philip, 108

Babbage, Frances, 119
Barker, Martin, 11, 149, 157
Barnes, Jennifer, 197n31
Barone, Joshua, 53
Bartók, Béla, 74, 87, 207n35
Baudrillard, Jean, 180, 182
Bayreuth: Festival, 25, 28, 29–32, 35, 38; Festspielhaus, 48–51, 102

BBC (broadcaster), 12, 62, 83, 94, 101, 111
Beck, Thomas, 165, 174
Bellocchio, Marco, 166, *168*, *169*, *170*
Belton, John, 147
Benjamin, George, 60. See also *Written on Skin*
Berg, Alban. See *Wozzeck*
Bergson, Henri, 93
Berlioz, Hector. See *La damnation de Faust*
Berry, Mark, 30
Beyer, Michael, 36, 49
Béziat, Philippe, 38, 39, 40, 53, 83
Birth, Kevin K., 100, 101
Bizet, Georges. See *Carmen*
Blau, Herbert, 141
Blue, Angel, 38–40, 74
Bluebeard's Castle (Bartók). See *Judith*
body microphone. *See* radio microphone
Boenisch, Peter M., 29, 31, *43*, 53, 64
Bolter, Jay David, 6, 7, 11, 13, 20, 54, 58
Bonner, Frances, 98
Boog, Maya, *181*
boom shot, 133, 145, 147–49
Bose, Mihir, 139
Braun, Manuel, 25, 35, 46, 60
Bretz, Rudy, 104
broadcast: broadcasters, 12, 92, 102, 190; outside, 8, 38, 40; radio, 17,

broadcast (*continued*)
  93–96, 111, 117–18, 122, 150;
  sports, 110, 139–40, 150. *See also*
  cinecast; television
Bull, Michael, 177
Butler, Jeremy G., 118

Cachopo, João Pedro, 140, 182
Callas, Maria, 39, *41*
Campana, Alessandra, 183
Carmen (Bizet), 99, 113, 114, 117, 143
Casetti, Francesco, 14, 26, 78, 84, 191
Castorf, Frank, 27–34, 42–44, 49, 51–53
Cavell, Stanley, 9, 57, 58, 64, 78, 82, 87
CCTV. *See* closed-circuit television
Cenciarelli, Carlo, 85
Chion, Michel, 122, 176
Chotzinoff, Samuel, 17
cinecast, 15–16, 20–21, 92–97, 116–18,
  120–22; audio, 149–54; globaliza-
  tion, 97–98; grammar, 128–29,
  140–42, 145–49; location, 154–58;
  marketing, 110–11; presentation,
  135–38; terminology, 116. *See also*
  Met: Live in HD, The; movie theater
Citron, Marcia, 116, 117
Clements, Andrew, 60
closed-circuit television (CCTV), 72–73,
  81–82, 178–79. *See also* surveillance
close-up, 77–79, 118–20, 126–29,
  131–32, 140–44; reaction to,
  142–43. *See also* scale
Cochrane, Bernadette, 98
Comolli, Jean-Louis, 14
Connor, Steven, 16, 18, 188–89
Conrad, Peter, 1, 3–5, 7, 9, 130, 142
Coulthard, Lisa, 150, 151
Cowan, Michael, 100
Crimp, Martin, 59. *See also Written
  on Skin*
Culshaw, John, 17, 68, 172

Das Rheingold (Wagner), 29, 31–35, 40,
  42, 43, *44*, 52. See also *Der Ring des
  Nibelungen*
Davidsen, Lise, 37

Davies, Peter Maxwell, 186
Davis, Desmond, 9, 54, 190
Decker, Willy, 107, 108
Denić, Aleksandar, 49
Derrida, Jacques, 35, 91
Der Ring des Nibelungen (Wagner),
  29–30, 32, 35, 40, 43, 45, 48–49, 52
Dessay, Natalie, 117, 136, 146
Diederichsen, Diedrich, 25
Die Walküre (Wagner), *51*, 83. See also
  Der Ring des Nibelungen
digital video disc (DVD), 12–13, 62–63,
  65–67, 173–74, 178–79; audio,
  122–23, 181–84; paratexts, 85–86
Dillon, Emma, 71
display (Casetti), 14, 84–85, 191
Doane, Mary Ann, 91, 128, 129, 141,
  152
dolly shot, 52, 134, 135, 144, 146–47
Domingo, Plácido, 167, *168, 169, 170*
Donizetti, Gaetano. See *Lucia di
  Lammermoor*
Duncan, Michelle, 195n8
Dunlap, Orrin E., Jr., 96, 99
DVD. *See* digital video disc

Eggenberger, Christian, 165, 175, 179
Eidsheim, Nina Sun, 176, 183
Einbruch der Realität (Volksbühne), 28
Ellis, John, 9, 98, 100, 104, 127, 128,
  129
Elsaesser, Thomas, 156
encore, 104–8, 154
Englhart, Andreas, 28
Esse, Melina, 140
event, 9, 19, 55, 59, 61, 118–19,
  156–58; evental, 16, 40, 63, 91–92,
  128, 135; "eventness," 35, 43, 97,
  110; live, 92–96, 101–8, 113–15,
  116–17; television, 57, 102–6,
  165–66. *See also* simultaneity

Falstaff (Verdi), 187–90
Feuer, Jane, 108
Field, Andy, 161
Fischer-Lichte, Erika, 6

Fleming, Renée, 117, 140
Forner, Jane, 190
Foucault, Michel, 77–78
Fowler, Benjamin, 205n9
frame: image, 35, 62–64, 85–86,
133–34, 146–47; proscenium, 48–
51; in stage design, 59–60, 66–67

Galison, Peter, 92–93
Gardner, Lyn, 25
Gaudréault, André, 10, 144, 156
Gee, Grant, 74, 77, 78, 82
Gelb, Peter, 80, 94, 111, 115, 125,
136–37, 139, 157
ghost (Pearson), 38, 179–80
Giesekam, Greg, 26
Girard, François, 146
Glass, Philip, 201n11. See also
Akhnaten
Goddard, Peter, 25
Götterdämmerung, 29, 186. See also
Der Ring des Nibelungen
Gould, Stephen, 37, *46*, *47*, *48*
Gounod. See *Roméo et Juliette*
Graf, Herbert, 17
Graham, Susan, 117, 136, 138, 139
Grainge, Paul, 152, 155
Grajeda, Tony, 124
Grusin, Richard, 6, 7, 11, 13, 20, 54, 58
gulliverization (Huhtamo), 129
Gumbrecht, Hans-Ulrich, 6
Gunning, Tom, 124, 129, 133, 149

Hagener, Malte, 209n58
Hagmann, Peter, 29
Haigh, Caroline, 68–71, 79–81, 123
Halvorson, Gary, 8, 10, 118, 129,
131–35, 143–44, 147
Hamilton (Miranda), 185–86
Hampson, Thomas, 138
Haswell, Jonathan, 10, 85, 118, 126
Havelková, Tereza, 26, 54
HD. *See* high definition
Herzog, Werner, 176
Heylbut, Rose, 115
high definition (HD), 115–16

Hoffmann, E. T. A., 174
Hoffmann, William J., Jr., 215n13
Honoré, Christophe, 38–40, *41*, 61
Horst, Anja, *173*, 178–79, *181*, 182
Hosokawa, Shuhei, 177
Hoyer, Myriam, 30–32, 34–35, 48–51,
52–53
Hubbell, Richard, 104
Huhtamo, Erkki, 129
Huss, Christophe, 142, 143–44
Hytner, Nicholas, 10, 105

immediacy, 21, 115–16, 145, 147, 158;
and image, 38, 50, 63–64, 129–30;
and sound, 176–77; of television,
104, 121
immersion, 15, 21, 110, 119, 133, 163;
sonic, 121–23, 150–53, 176–77
indexicality, 68, 73, 152, 171
intimacy: of close-up, 132, 135, 141,
145; sonic, 81, 123–24; televisual,
32, 115, 118, 125, 127–28, 137

Jacob, Ellis, 111
Jammer, Max, 103
Joe, Jeongwon, 201n11
Judith, 74–75, *76*, 77, 79–82, 87

Kail, Thomas, 185
Kampe, Anja, *47*
Keeler, Harry Stephen, 112–13
Kerins, Mark, 124, 154, 222n48
Kettle, Martin, 29
Kidnie, Margaret Jane, 106
King, Richard, 123
Kirwan, Peter, 97
Koch, Wolfgang, 188
Koležnik, Mateja, 188
Konradi, Katharina, *48*
Kramer, Lawrence, 143, 145, 201n11,
203n38, 210n3
Kratzer, Tobias, 25, 35–37, 46–48
Kreuzer, Gundula, 49, 204n43

La bohème. See *La bohème im
Hochhaus*

La bohème im Hochhaus (Puccini), 164, 172–76, 178–79, *181*, 182–84
La damnation de Faust (Berlioz), 120
Large, Brian, 11–12, 119–20, 130–31, 134–35, 182–83
La traviata (Verdi), 21, 103–4, 106, 108, 138, 164–67, 171–72
lavalier microphone. *See* radio microphone
Lefebvre, Henri, 162
Lehmann, Hans-Thies, 60, 88
Leonard, Isabel, 104–5
Lepage, Robert, 106
Leppert, Richard, 229n47
Levin, David J., 26
Levin, Thomas Y., 72–73
Liebau, Eva, *182*
live cinema (Mitchell), 61–62, 74, 156. *See also* cinecast
liveness, 91–98, 110–12, 117–18, 149–50, 165–66; marketing, 92; simulated, 62, 105; televisual, 100–107. *See also* simultaneity
Lohengrin (Wagner), 102
Lucia di Lammermoor (Donizetti), 60, 62, 111, 136, 145–49, *148*
Lundgren, John, *76*

Malfitano, Catherine, 38–39, *41*
Malvano, Andrea, 166, 171
Manovich, Lev, 84, 85
Marion, Philippe, 10, 144, 156
Mariotti, Michele, 187
Martinez, Ann M., 144, 145
matte (video production), 34–35, 49–51. *See also* frame
Mattila, Karita, 139
McAuley, Gay, 161, 162, 172
McLennan, Douglas, 189
mediality, 7, 38, 67, 87, 171
Mehta, Bejun, *66*, *73*
Mehta, Zubin, 171
Met: Live in HD, The, 20–21, 99–100, 104–8, 109–24, 125–42, 143–58; criticism of, 138–40, 142; market-

ing, 92, 110–11; origins, 94–95, 115–16; presentation style, 104–5, 117–18
Metropolitan Opera, 16, 21, 92, 93, 94–95, 109, 110–11, 114, 115, 117–18, 125
microcommunity (Elam), 156
mid-shot, 65, 70, 85, 120, 126, 134, 135
Minsky, Marvin, 6
Miranda, Lin-Manuel, 185
mise en abyme, 35, 38, 179
mise-en-scène, 34, 59–60, 74–75
Mitchell, Katie, 57–60, 61–62, *63*, *64*, 65–67, 73–75, *76*
"mixing for picture," 70–71, 123
monitor (screen), 27–28, 71–72, 77–79, 81–83. *See also* surveillance
montage: spatial, 51–52, 65, 82, 84; temporal, 52, 67, 71, 85–86
Moran, Jonah, 185
Mortimer, Vicki, 59, 61–62, 69
movie theater, 15–16, 97–98, 105–8, 113–17, 121–28, 140–42; amenities, 154–58; digitization, 99–100; sound systems, 150–53
Moylan, William, 68, 69
multicamera production: camera placement, 11, 19, 144–49; conventions, 7–14, 20–22, 26–27, 30–39, 52–55, 72–74, 77–79; directors, 9–10, 82–88. *See also* television
multiplex, 155–56, 190

NBC (broadcaster), 12, 17, 94
Netrebko, Anna, 147, *148*
Nixon in China (Adams), 130–31
NT Live (National Theatre), 10, 105, 118, 133, 134, 144–45, 149

Oberender, Thomas, 28, 32
OperaVision (streaming platform), 1–4, 5–6, 12, 14
Osborne, Laurie E., 155

O'Shaughnessy, Luke, 4
Owens, Eric, 80, 117

Palazzetti, Nicolò, 138
parallax, 27, 29, 31, 43, 45, 54, 134, 146, 147
parergon (Derrida), 35
Parker, Roger, 206n17
Parks, Lisa, 101, 102
Parsifal (Wagner), 136, 146
Payne, Nicholas, 190
PBS (broadcaster), 1–5, 7
Pearson, Mike, 161–62, 179
Personenregie, 77, 107
perspective audio, 70, 124, 172, 176
Peucker, Brigitte, 169
Pirgu, Saimir, *181*
Porter, Andrew, 17
postdramatic theater (Lehmann), 60
presence: definition, 6; in movie theater, 156–58; presencing, 21, 40, 110; virtual, 63–64, 112–13, 137–38, 140–42, 146–53. *See also* immediacy; immersion; intimacy
Puccini, Giacomo. See *La bohème im Hochhaus*; *Tosca*
Purves, Christopher, 73

radio microphone, 69, 70, 79–80, 123, 172
RAI (broadcaster), 12, 171
reality TV, 36–37, 135–36, 165–66, 178–79
remediation (Bolter and Grusin), 6–7, 9–11, 13–16, 20–22, 26–27, 177; hypermediacy, 6–7, 54, 58, 124; transparent immediacy, 9, 121, 145
repetition, 104–8; repetition machine (Derrida), 91–92, 106–7, 108. *See also* encore
Rigoletto in Mantua (Verdi), 164, 166–71, 177–78, 183–84
Roméo et Juliette (Gounod), 106
Ross, Alex, 221n22

Royal Opera House, 62–67, 70–71, 136, 138, 151

SACD (Super Audio CD), 122
Saint-Saëns, Camille. See *Samson et Dalila*
Saks, Jay David, 80, 81, 121, 149, 150
Salazar, David, 143
Samson et Dalila (Saint-Saëns), 132–33
satellite transmission, 30, 101–2, 128, 158; and cinecasts, 21, 92, 115, 116, 153. *See also* liveness; simultaneity
scale: and image, 14–15, 21, 58, 65–66, 113, 125–30, 141; and sound, 70–71
Schneider, Rebecca, 107
Schoen, Ernst, 96
Schwartz, Arman, 206n14, 228n38
Schwartz, Lloyd, 16, 17
screenscape (Casetti), 26, 78
scrim, 45–46
Sellars, Peter, 130–31, 134–35
Senici, Emanuele, 17, 83, 86–87, 126, 142, 204n44, 216n34
Shanks, Mike, 161–62
Sheppard, W. Anthony, 124, 130, 134, 135
Siegfried (Wagner), 34–35. See also *Der Ring des Nibelungen*
simultaneity: across distance, 21, 91–98, 100–108, 155, 156; on stage, 59–61, 64–65, 81–83. *See also* liveness
Singer, Aubrey, 101–2
site-specific performance, 21, 81, 161–65, 171–72, 174, 179, 182–83
speakers: home-theater, 122–23, 183–84; movie-theater, 105–6, 151–54. *See also* surround sound
Speckenbach, Jan, 28–29, 31, 32
split screen, 58, 82–84, 86, 117, 187
sports broadcasting, 128–29, 133–34, 139–40, 157–58

256 | INDEX

Staatsoper.tv (Bayerische Staatsoper), 74–79, 187–88, 190–91
steadicam, 166
Stearns, David Patrick, 164
Steichen, James, 95, 138
Steigerwald Ille, Megan, 81
Stemme, Nina, *76*
Stokowski, Leopold, 96, 98
Storaro, Vittorio, 165–67, 170
storytelling, 86, 118–19, 143
streaming, 5–6, 26–27, 77–78, 186–87, 190–91
Studer, Sandra, 179
Sullivan, Erin, 144, 145, 149
Super Audio CD (SACD), 122
surround sound, 15, 70, 121–23, 150–52, 154. *See also* ambient sound
surveillance, 11, 20, 26, 28, 57, 72–74, 77–82, 147, 178, 191
"sweetening" of audio, 150
synchronization: and editing, 120, 123–24, 176; synchronization machine (Stiegler), 91–92, 106; and time zones, 93–94, 95, 100–101, 107–8, 123–24, 171–72. *See also* liveness; simultaneity

tableau vivant, 134, 167, 169–70
Tambling, Jeremy, 190
Tannhäuser (Wagner), 25, 35–37, 46–48, 49–50
Taubman, Howard, 125
Taylor, Paul, 62
Tcherniakov, Dmitri, 45–46
tele-agora (Gaudréault and Marion), 157
television, 96, 101–4, 116–17, 127–28, 164–82; televisual, 9–10, 12–13, 27, 30–39, 105–6, 117–20, 128. *See also* multicamera production; satellite transmission; sports broadcasting
Theater Network Television (TNT), 99, 100, 113–15, 125, 128, 137, 140
Tommasini, Anthony, 29, 80, 130, 150
Tompkins, Joanne, 161
Tosca (Puccini), 38–40, *41*, 53, 61, 103, 139, 164–67, 171

Tresnjak, Darko, 132
Trippett, David, 150
Tristan und Isolde (Wagner), 45–46, *47*, 54, 83, 117, 129, 142
trompe l'oeil, 167, 169–70
Turner, Cathy, 179

Urricchio, William, 100

Verdi, Giuseppe. See *Falstaff*; *La traviata*; *Rigoletto in Mantua*
vocalic uncanny (Connor), 188

Wagner, Richard. See *Das Rheingold*; *Der Ring des Nibelungen*; *Die Walküre*; *Götterdämmerung*; *Lohengrin*; *Parsifal*; *Siegfried*; *Tannhäuser*; *Tristan und Isolde*
Ward-Griffin, Danielle, 196n13, 198n36, 225n12
Warschauer, Frank, 112
Weber, Samuel, 213n40
Weed, Mike, 157
Wells, Brianna, 128
White, Mimi, 105
wide shot, 36–38, 52–53, 64–67, 69–71, 126–27
Wiens, Birgit E., 28
Will, Richard, 130, 142, 144, 147, 206n18
Williams, Margaret, 62, 72, 86
Willis Sweete, Barbara, 83, 87, 120, 129–30, 142, 145–49
Woolfe, Zachary, 140, 141
Wozzeck (Berg), 96, 98, 117
Wright, Kenneth A., 11, 197n29
Written on Skin (Benjamin/Crimp), 58–69, 70–74
Wurtzler, Steve, 7
Wyver, John, 10, 129–30, 142

YouTube, 11, 30, 126, 177, 190

Zimmerman, Mary, 145, *148*
Žižek, Slavoj, 43, 45
zoom shot, 27, 31, 61, 77, 127, 131–34, 146–49